ADVANCED PRAISE

Yinglan gets into the minds of venture capitalists to show us how they think. There is much in common between VCs from the West and those from the East, but also much that is importantly different.

Tarun Khanna
Jorge Paulo Lemann Professor at the Harvard Business School
Author, Billions of Entrepreneurs: How China and India are Reshaping Their Futures and Yours

Friendly, thorough, and helpful. Yinglan has shown how VCs can help an entrepreneur's business and how to attract their attention.

Dan Schwartz
Former Chairman, Asian Venture Capital Journal
Author, The Future of Finance: How Private Equity and Venture Capital Will Shape the Global Economy

The Way of the VC is a must-read book for entrepreneurs and venture capital professionals. Yinglan achieved a harmonious balance between the theory–the Commandments–and the practice–first-hand accounts by VCs. The delightful stories clearly and effectively illustrate important lessons for all players in this industry.

Soo Book Koh
Founder and Managing Partner, iGlobe Partners

I have taught private equity courses for MBA's and executives for 15 years, and I have seldom run across such insight. Based on painstaking research, Yinglan Tan has demystified the venture capital investment process. If you want to know how venture capitalists think, what they are looking for, and how to choose one, read this book. Venture investors looking to grow in Asia will find penetrating observations and valuable advice. I highly recommend this book to anyone interested in building high-growth companies.

Philip Anderson
INSEAD Alumni Fund Chaired Professor of Entrepreneurship, and
Academic Director, The Abu Dhabi Centre, INSEAD

This book is a practical guide to the interplay between VCs and entrepreneurs that often contributes to the meteoric rise or utter failure of a startup venture. As entrepreneurship and venture capital are slowly transitioning from ad hoc activities into professions, the common principals applied by experienced professionals are emerging as foundations. Yinglan Tan's book provides a solid account of these emerging foundations.

Noubar Afeyan
Managing Partner and CEO, Flagship Ventures

The Way of the VC

HAVING TOP VENTURE CAPITALISTS ON YOUR BOARD

The Way of the VC

HAVING TOP VENTURE CAPITALISTS ON YOUR BOARD

Yinglan Tan

WILEY

John Wiley & Sons (Asia) Pte. Ltd.

Other Wiley Editorial Offices

John Wiley & Sons, 111 River Street, Hoboken, NJ 07030, USA

John Wiley & Sons, The Atrium, Southern Gate, Chichester, West Sussex, P019
    8SQ, United Kingdom

John Wiley & Sons (Canada) Ltd., 5353 Dundas Street West, Suite 400, Toronto,
    Ontario, M9B 6HB, Canada

John Wiley & Sons Australia Ltd, 42 McDougall Street, Milton, Queensland 4064,
    Australia

Wiley-VCH, Boschstrasse 12, D-69469 Weinheim, Germany

Library of Congress Cataloging-in-Publication Data

ISBN 978-0-470-82499-3

Typeset in 11/13pt New-BaskervilleRoman by Thomson Digital
Printed in Singapore by Toppan Security Printing Pte. Ltd.
10 9 8 7 6 5 4 3 2 1

Contents

Acknowledgments

This book leaves me heavily indebted to a remarkable group of people: CJ Hwu, Fiona Wong, Janis Soo, and Hilary Powers (who has the Midas touch with words), my trusty editors, who saw a book where none existed and rolled up their sleeves to make it happen. I am forever theirs. Professor Philip Anderson, my mentor and long-time friend, seeded the idea of the book and more important shepherded me into the world of entrepreneurship and venture capital. My advisers at Harvard, Professor Richard Zeckhauser and Professor Josh Lerner, who were always there with kind, generous, and insightful support—Richard for getting me hooked on behavioral economics, and Josh for his many gems of insights on venture capital. They deserve the credit for much of what is right about the book, but can't be blamed for its shortcomings.

I wish to thank my lovely precious beautiful wife, Belle, for her dedication and support in making sure I finally finished this work. She continues to stick by me through thick and thin, even though I give her countless reasons to give up on me. My daughter, Beth, for being the joy in my life. The many entrepreneurs, venture capitalists, and other business associates who have given me much more than I can ever return. My dear family, especially my mother and father, who invested in the unenviable venture of bringing me into the world and raising me. My students, Cai Lin, Kei, Daryl, Ashley, and Rashu, who worked tirelessly translating my incoherent gibberish into English.

I thank you one and all from the bottom of my heart.

Foreword

Virtually every high-growth business needs capital. Investors allocate assets to earn substantial returns. One would imagine that these two facts would bring venture capitalists and entrepreneurs together.

But in fact a significant gap separates the two groups. Entrepreneurs live in great uncertainty and assume significant risk in pursuing their business. Venture capitalists are a special breed of investor; they seek to help entrepreneurs triumph, but they have fiduciary responsibilities to their own investors (whether pension funds, sovereign wealth funds, endowments, or families), that limit their ability to absorb all the risk in new ventures. While venture capital has become a well-developed industry in the United States, in many other parts of the world, this gap has slowed the adoption of venture capital.

But in the past few years, the venture capital industry has been globalizing at a dramatic pace. Funds are increasingly being raised internationally and invested globally. More and more venture capital firms have established multinational operations. There is an increasing appreciation by entrepreneurs worldwide of the benefits that venture capitalists can bring. Company managers are increasingly setting ambitious goals and looking to venture capitalists to provide the capital, advice, and strategic partnerships they need to bring their plans to fruition.

Another important trend has been the professionalization of the venture capital industry itself. Venture capital organizations have matured. Their investment policies, procedures, and systems have been refined over decades of experience, and are becoming formalized and structured. As a result of these two trends, it is no surprise that many nations are making greater efforts to encourage venture capital activity with an eye to boosting innovation and entrepreneurship, and to counteract the recessionary impact of the global economic crisis.

With the emergence of venture capital investment as a professional practice, understanding the way in which this industry works is becoming critically important for practitioners and would-be practitioners, whether they are (or aspire to be) working for entrepreneurial ventures, venture firms, or large institutional capital pools. I applaud Yinglan Tan, who has distilled many interesting war stories and experiences of venture capitalists into a useful and effective framework in *The Way of the VC*.

Enjoy the reading, and good luck in your venturing endeavors!

Professor Josh Lerner
Jacob H. Schiff Professor of Investment Banking
Harvard Business School

Introduction

You've a brilliant idea and are thinking of building a prototype to test the market reaction. However, you lack the crucial seed funds for product development. Now it's time to locate some investors and find out what they can do for you, and you start to meet with a number of venture capital firms to present your business idea. Welcome to the world of venture capital: a world of heroes and sages.

Heroes have a powerful grip on people's collective imagination. For instance, the *gungfu* warriors of ancient China, defying all odds to succeed, are immortalized in sword-fighting novels and idolized by millions. The hero of such a tale is always guided by a wise and inscrutable mentor who points him in the right direction and teaches him the critical strokes. Entrepreneurs are the modern-day heroes, and standing beside each hero is a mentor, the venture capitalist.

Pioneer venture capitalists—VCs—like Arthur Rock, Tom Perkins, and Eugene Kleiner are legendary for the mentoring roles they play, growing companies like Google and Genentech. Alongside the innovators who dream up the ideas, VCs contribute the tactical brainpower that fuels Silicon Valley, Route 128, and other creative hubs. Their success in catalyzing innovation has been mirrored in technology hotbeds around the world, including Israel, China, and Singapore.[1] The next generation of star venture capitalists, Tim Draper, Lip Bu Tan, Dixon Doll, and Bing Gordon, are continuing in the footsteps of the pioneers.

The striking thing about the partnership between the venture capitalist and entrepreneur is that the journey is a marathon and not a sprint, a testing long-distance run fraught with pitfalls and challenges. Entrepreneurs often have to put their heads down and keep pushing, thinking hopefully ahead to the triumph of a successful finish (usually in the form of an IPO or a trade sale) but keeping their eyes on the work at hand. Companies take time to build and founders work for the day they will cross that finish line. Star VCs significantly increase the probability of a winning finish.

The role of the venture capitalist is to partner the entrepreneur in the journey—despite frequent misconceptions that make it seem more hostile. The start-up ecosystem has been termed a zoo (or in certain geographies, a jungle) where vulture capitalists pounce on innocent entrepreneurs as their hapless prey. By and large, however, a star VC can provide the missing expertise a start-up needs for winning the marathon. The best VCs don't just hand over cash; they help the companies in their portfolio plans and pace themselves like marathon runners, and they also help the companies make sound decisions and build teamwork, and they tap their own networks to strengthen each entrepreneur's team.

Why This Book?

Books on venture capital crowd the shelves. Unfortunately for the would-be entrepreneur, the academic books have generally failed to capture the true reality, while those that captured the life stories of successful entrepreneurs haven't adequately distilled the full essence of venture capital. This book focuses directly on the key concepts and winning techniques used in venture capital, translating what really goes on in a venture capitalist's mind into structured processes that you can use to promote your own ideas.

It was not that long ago that it might have been possible to cover the whole topic of venture capital in one white paper. Now, it is not possible to provide comprehensive coverage even in a book. The industry has flourished, as variations of the initial venture capital funds now operate in most developing and developed economies. To make the topic manageable, this book has a strong focus on U.S. and Asian business. That may still seem broad, but I've found a surprisingly high degree of agreement among interviewees on the key characteristics that VCs across this area were looking for in an ideal venture, their thought processes, and the venture assistance they provided. Despite vast differences in background, stage of investment, and geography, a consensus quickly emerged. The book is organized around the journey that the VC embarks upon with the entrepreneur, with each chapter encapsulating the winning moves for both parties at that specific stage of the journey.

It is through this process of high-stakes investing under uncertainty that unbelievable fortunes are made in the clubby world of big-bucks venture capital. *The Way of the VC: Having Top Venture Capitalists on Your Board* takes readers into this private world of extreme investing. For those who want to invest like the best, *The Way of the VC* distills winning moves from real-life venture capital experiences, revealing the unique strategies, the sectors VCs are tracking, and the screens and criteria they use. It discusses some of the best and worst investments, the pitfalls that await both sides in a deal, and the ways individuals can use the lessons they've learned.

The VC and the Chef

Venture capitalists are like skilled chefs. Their dishes—the successful companies in their portfolios—are most valuable when the firms remain small and retain their own distinct style. When a chef tries to mass-produce a menu item, the dish loses value—scaling a batch beyond its ideal size degrades its quality. Likewise, when partners of VC firms take on too many deals and overstretch themselves with too many companies to look after, they can no longer add sufficient value to each portfolio company.

The team in a restaurant closely mirrors that of a venture capitalist firm. The "analysts" of the kitchen, if you will, are the people who work the longest hours and do the tedious grunt work that no one else wants to do. They are young, durable, numerous, and disposable. The "associate" of the kitchen is the chef de partie, who also does a lot of work but has the commis chefs to boss around. In place of a vice president, there is the junior sous chef. Junior partner parallels the sous chef, and the top of the food chain stands the managing director—the much-feared yet highly revered executive chef. It is the challenge of the managing director to orchestrate the team to cook a winning dish time after time.

Some chefs are very rigid in their style, requiring that a specific list of ingredients be delivered to them before they can begin cooking. This rigidity is acceptable as long as the restaurant does not have an unexpectedly long line of would-be customers or if the people in line are not too hungry and can wait for the required ingredients to arrive. However, if the restaurant has hungry customers now and lacks the cash to buy more groceries until after they're fed, the chef needs to be flexible and work with the supplies on hand. Other chefs, the more flexible and entrepreneurial ones, will not wait for someone else to deliver a bag of groceries to them; they will instead immediately begin to search the pantry, refrigerator, and vegetable garden for what's available. They then use the items at hand to create a feast.

The best chefs have return customers. Serial entrepreneur Jim Clark called on Kleiner Perkins to build his second billion-dollar company (Netscape) and his third (Web MD). The true acid test of a venture capitalist firm is whether entrepreneurs return to work with it in their subsequent companies.

The best chefs neither undercook nor overcook their dishes; each guest receives the meal at the proper time. VCs who are prone to taking companies public prematurely in an effort to gain a reputation ultimately ruin their own brand. Similarly, the best VCs do not delay exiting. The best VCs time their exit perfectly.

Most cooks prepare dishes based on what they feel most customers will feel like ordering. Similarly, most VCs choose companies in an environment characterized by great uncertainty of outcomes, fast-changing market conditions, and an abundance of highly subjective information on potential investments—a process akin to a Keynesian beauty contest. VCs typically pick winners based on what they think other VCs are going to pick to win in the next round, and not on how good they assess the company to be. Behavioral economists call this *herd behavior*—a term that describes how individuals in a group tend to act together without planned direction in ways that are sometimes irrational and driven by emotions—greed in the bubbles, fear in the crashes. The timeless art that my colleagues and I found in the top VCs we interviewed is made up of winning techniques, disciplined thinking, and analysis designed to overcome the instincts and emotions that can misguide even VCs.

Voices of Experience

There are 10,000 VC firms—and only a couple of hundred are any good. This book is about how the one percent think differently: What got them there? How do they add value to entrepreneurs? What are their thoughts about failure and how does that separate them from the rest of the world?

The Way of the VC shows you what premier VC firms such as Kleiner Perkins, Draper Fisher Jurvetson, and Flagship Ventures look for in winning ventures and how they offer venture assistance, and how every entrepreneur can benefit from learning leading-edge techniques. *The Way of the VC* offers you:

- The enabler of entrepreneurial initiatives to improve performance, because A teams make initiatives successful and lesser teams don't
- A "silver bullet" technique for near-perfect communication with VCs
- A guide to coaching start-ups effectively
- The ultimate entrepreneurial development manual
- Insight and advice acquired by interviewing dozens of top-tier venture capitalists
- An easy read

Having gone through the long process of researching, writing, checking, revising, and editing *The Way of the VC*, I have learned that the start-up marathon, even with a star VC alongside, is not simple. Happily, my task did not require me to become an expert on either side of the relationship; I only had to interview experts, top entrepreneurs, and VCs and invite them to share their insights, anecdotes, and advice—a far more manageable goal. *The Way of the VC* illustrates the trials and tribulations that an entrepreneur has to go through in working with the star venture capitalist to finish the start-up race.

How can the star VC prepare, mentor, and change an entrepreneur's life? This is not a book on current best practices; rather, it separates the truth from the myth, drawing from the journeys of entrepreneurs who have worked with star venture capitalists. The book also has hiring implications. Suppose you are an entrepreneur looking to hire a VP of sales: What kind of experience do you need to find? What are star VCs looking for in your team? Would the candidate be able to withstand the trials and tribulations of the long journey?

For more tools, tips, and tricks, further resources are available at www.WayOfTheVC.com.

Interviewee Credentials

All interviewees are Venture Capitalists unless noted otherwise:

- Mr. Robert Ackerman, Managing Director and Co-founder, Allegis Capital
- Dr. Noubar Afeyan, Managing Partner and CEO, Flagship Ventures
- Mr. Tovio Annus, Co-founder, Ambient Sound Investments and Co-founder, Skype
- Mr. Sujit Banerjee, Partner, BlueRun Ventures
- Dr. Orna Berry, Venture Partner, Gemini Israel Funds Ltd.
- Mr. Zacchaeus Boon, Partner, McLean Watson Venture Capital
- Mr. Kelvin Chan, Senior Vice President, Partners Group Asia Pacific Ltd. (Limited Partner)
- Mr. K. Bobby Chao, Founding Managing Partner, DFJ DragonFund China
- Mr. York Chen, President and Managing General Partner, iD TechVentures
- Dr. Jeffrey Chi, Vice Chairman, Vickers Capital Group
- Mr. Dixon Doll, Co-founder and General Partner, Doll Capital Management
- Mr. Timothy C. Draper, Founder and Managing Director, Draper Fisher Jurvetson
- Mr. Barry Drayson, Chief Executive Officer, NanoComposites Inc.
- Mr. Norman Fogelsong, General Partner, Institutional Venture Partners
- Mr. Hian Goh and Ms. Maria Brown, Co-founders and Managing Directors, Asian Food Channel (Entrepreneurs)
- Mr. Bing Gordon, Partner, Kleiner Perkins Caufield & Byers
- Ms. Patricia Hedley, Senior Vice President, General Atlantic
- Mr. Pierre Hennes, Co-founder and Partner, Upstream Ventures
- Ms. Soo Boon Koh, Founder and Managing Partner, iGlobe Partners
- Dr. Josh Lerner, Jacob H. Schiff Professor of Investment Banking, Harvard Business School (Academic Expert)
- Mr. Damien Lim, General Partner, BioVeda Capital
- Mr. Scott Maxwell, Senior Managing Director, OpenView Venture Partners

- Mr. Hodong (Ho) Nam, General Partner and Co-founder, Altos Ventures
- Mr. Yoram Oron, Founder and Managing Partner, Vertex Venture Capital
- Mr. Joe Rouse, Former General Partner, Pioneer Capital Partners
- Mr. Kim Seng Tan, General Partner, 3V SourceOne Capital
- Mr. Lip Bu Tan, Chairman and Founder, Walden International
- Mr. Andy Tang, Managing Director, DFJ DragonFund China
- Dr. Eric Tao, Vice President, Keystone Ventures (former Kleiner Perkins Caufield & Byers)
- Mr. Hans Tung, Partner, Qiming Venture Partners
- Mr. David Weiden, General Partner, Khosla Ventures
- Mr. Lin Hong Wong, Managing Director, Wingz Capital Pte. Ltd. and Former Managing Director for Business Development, Temasek Capital
- Mr. Ken Xu, General Partner, Gobi Partners Inc.

Endnote

1. Bob Zider, "How Venture Capital Works," (December 1998); retrieved from http://web.mit.edu/peso/Pes1/HBS,%20Zider%20-%20How%20VC%20works.pdf, 18 June 2009.

1

The Call to Adventure

The first pitch an entrepreneur presents to a VC sets the tone of the future partnership. Such contacts are first and foremost light and subtle—however, they offer a good opportunity to watch out for those nearly imperceptible tell-tale signs. Both sides then size each other up and assess whether they want to continue with the engagement. Figure 1.1 sketches the interplay.

The Rules of the Game

Venture capital is the process of professional investment alongside management in young, rapidly growing companies, typically in early stages of company development, in return for equity securities in the start-up. The mandate of venture capitalists (called VCs; the abbreviation works for both the field and the people who practice in it) is to generate high rates of return over long periods of time, offering institutional investors and high-net-worth individuals high returns and strong diversification benefits from very low correlations with other asset classes. The major negatives of investing in VC are long time frames, lack of liquidity, higher risks (with the expectation of higher rewards), and high management fees. For start-up companies, venture capital is an important source of equity, but more important, venture capital fund managers play a significant role via active participation—providing related expertise to fuel the development of young and growing firms as well as funds for them to draw on. There is growing evidence that vibrant venture capital markets spur innovation and economic growth.

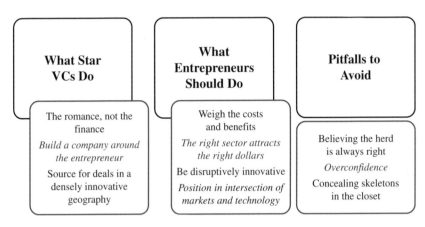

Figure 1.1 The Choice: To VC or Not VC?

Bridging the Gap

Many start-up firms require substantial capital, and their founders generally lack sufficient funds to go it alone. And today's start-ups—with their significant intangible assets and uncertain prospects—are unlikely to receive bank loans or other debt financing, and they typically struggle to attract normal equity financing. Venture capital aims to fill this gap in the supply of finance.

Venture capital is commonly seen as a subset of private equity: focused on equity or equity-linked investments in privately held, high-growth companies in their seed, start-up, and early expansion phases of development. Table 1.1 presents an overview of the field.

Who Is a Venture Capitalist?

The popular image of a venture capitalist is that of a wealthy financier who funds start-up companies. If an entrepreneur who develops a change-the-world invention needs capital and can't get it from a bank or from friends, fools, and family members, venture capitalists stand ready to step in and save the day.

In practice, a venture capitalist may look at several hundred investment opportunities before making a choice, investing in only a few selected companies with favorable investment opportunities. Far from simply looking for homes for money, venture capitalists foster growth in companies through their involvement in the management,

Table 1.1   Institutional Venture Capital at a Glance

Principle		Example
Definition[1]	Institutional venture capital comes from professionally managed funds that have $25 million to $1 billion to invest in emerging growth companies.	Intel Capital China Technology Fund II is a US$500 million fund that aims to invest in wireless broadband, media, telecommunications, and green technology in Xinhua.
		The Kleiner Perkins Caufield & Byers (KPCB) iFund™ is a US$100 million investment initiative that aims to fund innovators who are creating evolutionary applications atop the iPhone/iPod platform.
Ideal client	High-growth companies that are capable of reaching at least $25 million in sales.	E-bay: Subsequent to its IPO in September 1998, the company posted net revenue of US$12.9 million in the third quarter of 1998[2]
		Amazon: The company reported net revenue of US$27.9 million in the second quarter 1997, immediately after its IPO which raised US$54 million[3]
Best use	Varied—from financing product development to expansion of a proven and profitable product or service.	Expansion: Bessemer Venture Partners, DCM, Emergence Capital Partners, and Softbank Capital jointly contributed US$20 million to Goodmail Systems' third round of funding. The purpose of this fund is to expand Goodmail's client base to include banks, as well as retailers currently restricting themselves to paper mail despite the proliferation of e-mail.[4]
		Development: U.S. Venture Partners, Benchmark Capital

(continued)

Table 1.1   Continued

Principle		Example
		and several other prominent angels together raised US$6.5 million for Nanosolar. The fund was used to develop its technology in providing affordable solar panels and establish key supplier, manufacturer, and distribution partnership.[5]
Cost and funds typically available	Expensive. Institutional venture capitalists demand significant equity in a business. The earlier the investment stage, the more equity is required to convince an institutional venture capitalist to invest. The range of funds typically available is US$500,000 to US$10 million.	Sequoia Capital was among YouTube's first funders, providing US$11.5 million in two rounds. It wound up owning approximately 30 percent of YouTube before it was sold to Google for US$1.65 billion in stock.[6]
Ease of acquisition	Difficult. Institutional venture capitalists are choosy. Compounding the degree of difficulty is the fact that institutional venture capital is an appropriate source of funding for a limited number of companies.	KPCB led a US$75 million investment in Silver Spring Networks which is a leading provider of Smart Grid Technology. This unique technology facilitates efficiency in electric consumption, thereby reducing carbon emissions. Apart from that, it enables consumers to monitor their consumption levels.[7]
		As observed, ``green technology'' is a market with very bright prospects, and this global market trend is not a mere fad. In fact, there is pressing need for such technologies. Venture funds are particularly interested in such initiatives; Markets in the growth stage and with the potential to expand globally.

| Supply | Depends on these factors:[8]
- Tax rates on capital gains
- Health of public equity markets
- Government policy, including regulatory restrictions | "An institutional investor will allocate 2 percent to 3 percent of their institutional portfolio for investment in alternative assets such as private equity or venture capital as part of their overall asset allocation.

Currently, over 50 percent of investments in venture capital/private equity comes from institutional public and private pension funds, with the balance coming from endowments, foundations, insurance companies, banks, individuals, and other entities who seek to diversify their portfolio with this investment class."[9] |

strategic marketing, and planning of the firms they choose. They are entrepreneurs first and financiers second.

Both organizations and individuals can be venture capitalists. In the early days of venture capital investment, in the 1950s and 1960s, individual venture investors were the norm. While individual investment did not totally disappear over the next few decades, the modern venture firm emerged as the dominant vehicle for this type of investment. Then the cycle began to turn again, and individuals became a potent and increasingly larger part of the early-stage start-up venture life cycle.

More commonly known as "angel investors," individual VCs are especially inclined to mentor a company and provide needed capital and expertise to help it develop. Angel investors may either be high-net-worth individuals with management expertise or retired businessmen and businesswomen who seek the opportunity for firsthand business development.

Venture Capital as an Asset Class

Venture capital investing has grown from a small investment pool in the 1960s and early 1970s to a mainstream asset class that is a viable and significant part of the institutional and corporate investment portfolio.

Professionally managed venture capital firms generally are private partnerships or closely held corporations funded by private and public pension funds, endowment funds, foundations, corporations, wealthy individuals, foreign investors, and the venture capitalists themselves. As a general rule, venture capital firms engage in the following practices:

- Investing for the long term, taking higher risks with the expectation of higher rewards
- Purchasing equity securities
- Adding value to the company through active participation

Venture capitalists mitigate the risk of venture investing by developing a portfolio of young companies in a single venture fund. Many times, they will co-invest with other professional venture capital firms. Pierre Hennes of Upstream Ventures adds that the job of a VC is to reduce risk over time, keeping in mind the capital risk. "In the beginning, all risks are high. Building a company is heavily dependent on team in building revenue, markets, and products. A good team reduces the management risk. There is a technology risk. With a beta or a proof-of-concept, product risk is minimized. There is also market risk in that the market may not pick up product and also financial risk in that the venture may not be well-funded."

Recently, some investors have been referring to venture investing and buyout investing as "private equity investing." This term can be confusing because some in the investment industry use *private equity* to refer only to buyout fund investing. Strictly speaking, *private equity* refers to an asset class made up of investments that are not publicly traded. Venture capital is a broad subcategory of private equity that refers to equity investments typically made in young and emerging companies for the launch, early development, or expansion of a business.

Fund Partnership   VC firms typically manage multiple funds formed over intervals of several years. Funds are illiquid, but as companies in the portfolio go public or are sold, the investors realize their returns. Funds typically consist of limited partnerships invested in a number of companies. VC firms generally regard the following breakdown of returns as normal: a third of the investments they make will be complete losses, another third will be the "living dead," and the remaining third will generate returns on the original investment substantial enough to make it all worthwhile. The big winners yield 10 times the original investment, or more.[10]

Investment Philosophy Venture capitalists mitigate the risk of venture investing by developing a portfolio of young companies in a single venture fund. Many times, they will co-invest with other professional venture capital firms. In addition, many venture partnerships will manage multiple funds simultaneously. For decades, venture capitalists have nurtured the growth of high-technology and entrepreneurial communities worldwide, resulting in significant job creation, economic growth, and international competitiveness. Digital Equipment Corporation, Baidu, Focus Media, Apple, Federal Express, Compaq, Sun Microsystems, Intel, Microsoft, and Genentech are just a few famous examples of companies that received venture capital early in their development.

Types of Venture Capital Firms

Most mainstream VC firms invest their capital through funds organized as limited partnerships (LPs) in which the venture capital firm serves as the general partner (GP). Venture firms may also be affiliates or subsidiaries of a commercial bank, investment bank, or insurance company and make investments on behalf of external investors or the parent firm's clients. Some firms may be subsidiaries of nonfinancial industrial corporations making investments on behalf of their parent. These latter firms are typically called "direct investors" or "corporate venture investors." Many corporate venture investors are motivated by strategic reasons when injecting capital into investments. Corporate venture capital is often employed as a means to screen the surroundings for novel technologies that either form a threat or fit with the parent's primary business. Microsoft IP Ventures is an example of a corporate venture investor that licenses its technology to companies so as to cultivate innovation and accelerate product development. Other organizations may include government-affiliated investment programs that help start-up companies through programs organized at a variety of levels, from national to local.

Organizational Forms   In the United States, the tax code has allowed the formation of either Limited Liability Partnerships (LLPs) or Limited Liability Companies (LLCs) as alternative forms of organization. However, the limited partnership is still the predominant organizational form. Preference for the LP structure may be due to the "flow-through" taxation position in most jurisdictions and limited liability of investors. The advantages and disadvantages of each involve liability, taxation issues, and management responsibility.

Fund Structuring   Most venture capital firms organize their partnership as a *pooled fund*; that is, a group consisting of the general partner and the investors or limited partners. These pooled funds are typically organized as fixed-life partnerships, usually having a life of 10 years. Each fund is capitalized by commitments of capital from the limited partners. Once the partnership has reached its target size, it is closed to further investment from new investors or even existing investors. This is to create a fixed capital pool from which investments can be made. Venture Capital funds are highly illiquid. For example, 95 percent of venture funds are not liquidated for more than 10 years, and half last more than 15 years.

Fund Management   Like a mutual fund company, a VC firm may have more than one fund in existence. It may raise another fund a few years after closing the first one so it can continue to invest in companies and to provide more opportunities for existing and new investors. It is not uncommon to see a successful firm raise six or seven funds consecutively over the span of a decade or so. Each fund is managed separately and has its own investors or limited partners and its own general partner. These funds may employ an investment strategy similar to that of other funds in the firm. However, a firm can launch a variety of funds with different areas of focus and different levels of diversification. The decision depends on the strategy and focus of the venture firm itself.

Management Fees   As an investment manager, the general partner will typically charge a management fee to cover the costs of managing the committed capital. The management fee will usually be paid quarterly for the life of the fund, but it may be tapered or curtailed in the later stages of a fund's life. A ballpark figure that general partners usually charge for management fees is around one to two percent of the fund's net profit. This is most often negotiated with investors upon formation of the fund and stated in the terms and conditions of the investment.

Carried Interest   "Carried interest" is the term used to denote the profit split of proceeds to the general partner. This is the general partner's fee for carrying the management responsibility plus all the liability, and for providing the needed expertise to manage the investment successfully.

Generalist or Specialist?   Venture capitalists may be generalist or specialist investors depending on their strategy. Generalists invest in various industry sectors, or various geographic locations, or several stages of a company's life. On the other hand, specialists prefer to focus on one or two industry sectors, or may seek to invest in only a limited geographic area. The degree of diversification of investments also differs. Some venture funds are broadly diversified; they invest in companies in industry sectors as diverse as semiconductors, software, retailing, and restaurants. Meanwhile, other firms choose to invest in only one technology—Silicon Valley, for example, attracts many such specialist investors that invest in high-growth technology-based start-ups.

Stage of Investment

Not all venture capitalists invest in start-ups. While venture firms will invest in companies that are in their initial start-up modes, venture capitalists will also invest in companies at various stages of the business life cycle. A venture capitalist may invest before a real product or company exists (so-called *seed investing*), or it may provide capital to start up a company in its first or second stages of development (known as *early-stage investing*). Also, the venture capitalist may provide needed financing to help a company grow beyond a critical mass to become more successful (*expansion-stage financing*). Some funds focus on later-stage investing by providing financing to help the company grow large enough to attract public financing through an initial public offering (IPO). A notable case of a venture-backed stock offering is Baidu.com. It was named "Best Exit of the Year" in the China Venture Capital Ranking 2005, based on the success of its listing on NASDAQ. It was listed on August 5, 2005 with an offer price of US$25. It subsequently opened at US$66 and closed at US$122.54 per share. Alternatively, the venture capitalist may help the company attract a merger or acquisition with another company by providing liquidity and exit for the company's founders. At the other end of the spectrum, some venture funds specialize in the acquisition, turnaround, or recapitalization of public and private companies that represent favorable investment opportunities.[11] Table 1.2 traces the VC history of Focus Media, showing the impact of venture capital at various stages of its growth.

When Is VC Inappropriate?

Venture capital can be the answer to an entrepreneur's problems, but it is not always the ideal choice. The following sections spotlight some of the problems:

Too Early Stage   Without real customers, revenue, or product, anything on your business plan will be merely assumptions. VCs tend to favor deals that offer more market traction. To get a sense of the type of business plan and type of market traction that VCs are looking for, please refer to http://wayofthevc-vbp.easyurl.net. At the same site, I have also provided a simple tool to generate a business plan for your type of business.

Small Market   The economics should make sense. If the company cannot generate more than US$20 million in revenues, it probably does not have the scalability that VCs look for. As Kate Harnish and Tom Lister, authors of *Finding Money: The Small Business Guide to Financing*, note, "Venture funded companies are expected to be able to grow to US$30, US$50 or even US$100 million in five to seven years. This means that the industry has to be big enough to support such growth. But many venture proposals fail to adequately convince investors of the market potential while others naively project that they'll capture 10%, 20% and even 50% market share in a very short period. When the entrepreneur is projecting potential market share,

Table 1.2 Funding Focus Media

Stage	Start-Up	Early Growth		Late Growth
Year	2003, 2004	2005	2006	2007—Present
Milestones	Source for advertising space in areas yet to be occupied. Source for clients. Source for advertising materials.	Expand existing advertising channels (mobile handset, cinema, Internet).	Continual expansion in advertising channels. Broaden coverage in as many cities as possible.	Growing market share, albeit not as fast as before. Financial performance in revenue and delivering consistent value to shareholders.
Financing structure and development stages	First received seed capital from Softbank China Venture Capital. However, Focus Media ('Focus') was operating at a net loss and urgently needed more capital. In December 2003, CDH Fund injected US$12 million. Revenue started growing in 2004, attracting investors such as Goldman Sachs Group Inc., venture-capital fund 3i Group and United China Investment Ltd., which together, provided US$30 million.	July 13: Announced IPO at NASDAQ. Issued 10,100,000 American Depositary Shares (ADSs), at US$17 per ADS.[12] October 16: Acquired 100 percent of equity stake in Framedia for US$39.6 million in cash and US$55.4 million in the form of new Focus Media common stock.[13]	January 27: Follow-on offering of 6,787,829 ADSs at $43.5 per ADS.[14] February 28: Acquired rival Target Media for US$7 million in new Focus common stock.[15] March 21: Acquired Dotad, a leading mobile handset advertising service provider in China.[16] June 16: Follow-on offering of 6,700,000 ADRs, at US$54.00 each.[17] August 31: Purchased 70 percent of the equity interest in ACL, which	2007: Two follow-on offerings (1) 6,655,700 ADRs, at US$79.50 per ADS. (2) 13,720,873 ADSs at US$64.75 per ADS. 2007: Acquired Allyes Information Technology Company Limited, the largest Internet advertising service company in China.[19] 2008: acquired CGEN Technology, a leading operator of an in-store digital advertising network.[20]

(continued)

Table 1.2 Continued

Stage	Start-Up	Early Growth		Late Growth
Year	2003, 2004	2005	2006	2007—Present
			leases screen time prior to the start of every movie.[18]	2008: Announce plans to repurchase up to US$100 million worth of its issued and outstanding ADRs over the next 12 months.[21]
Analysis of financing stages	Most start-ups will face this initial problem; capital intensive yet revenues do not reflect high returns. Typically loss-making.	At this stage, revenue growth is not considered a milestone yet as Focus was trying to gain a foothold in the industry. Following a very successful IPO, Focus Media could embark on expanding operations. Given how rivals can easily copy its business model, Focus had to expand its service offerings swiftly to outdo them. In addition, Focus engaged in long-term exclusive deals which forbade entry of rivals.	Expansion speed is key at this stage. Apart from increasing advertising channels, Focus had to cast its net wider to include tier two cities in China in order to maintain a lead. Therefore, in 2006, there were multiple offerings to raise funds quickly. Each capital injection gave Focus the capacity to upgrade the battle fought.	In 2007, Focus is still strong on expanding operations. But come 2008, where signs of credit turmoil surfaced, growth slowed down. Share price inevitably plunged, leading to a decision to repurchase its ADRs, which signals that current prices are undervalued. Considering that Focus is now unparalleled in scale of network, it believes that it can still compete effectively in this challenging time.

be mindful that Apple's personal computer market share is less than 9%, despite Apple's marketing prowess."[22]

Businesses with the potential for long-term returns are more captivating. Contrary to the popular belief that VCs are more interested in quick returns, they usually are not dependent on short-term income (that is, three to six months); they tend to adopt a longer-term view, usually in the horizon of two to five years. "VCs never pressurise you for quick profits if you are able to explain when you aim to get profits and the details of how you are working toward it," says Quentin Staes-Polet, founder of Kreeda Games India.[23] Hence, companies with the best prospects to create the largest long-term increase in shareholder value will stand out.

No Barriers to Entry If the venture requires speedy execution to have any chance of success, VC may not come online fast enough. The VC fundraising process requires a minimum of six months, and if the venture is a pure execution play, where anyone who moves right now can get in, someone else will probably do so. Venture capitalists prefer to support companies with stronger fences: proprietary products or services that allow them to enjoy a desirable "unfair" competitive advantage by virtue of the exclusivity of their products. Patents, trademarks, copyrights, exclusive distributorships, or other special rights may protect a company's unique position in the market. Sometimes, a nonprotected product or service with an exceptional head start on potential competition can fit these criteria, as well. The point is that the company must have some significant advantage over existing or potential competitors so it can achieve and maintain a dominant position in its industry.[24]

What Star VCs Do: Winning Techniques

Tim Draper, founder of DFJ, highlights that the most common mistake VCs make is not investing when they see passion. The best VCs apply three winning techniques:

- Follow the romance, not the finance.
- Build a company around the entrepreneur.
- Source for deals in a densely innovative geography.

WINNING TECHNIQUE #1: Follow the Romance, Not the Finance

VCs love to build great businesses. The ultimate joy of a VC is in helping and seeing entrepreneurs realize their dreams. Most of our interviewees share that their passion was in seeing companies grow. Andy Tang, managing partner of DFJ Dragon, says it is a privilege to be in the VC industry, adding that he feels privileged because he enjoys taking part in the entrepreneur's dream. At any given time, he has seven dreams, as every portfolio CEO he is helping has a dream. A VC who doesn't feel privileged, he adds, "cannot endure the long journey of company formation with a CEO. In Silicon Valley especially, the passion of the entrepreneur is much greater than that of any other region. Passion is a powerful device—if you start a business purely based on passion, the impact is unimaginable." VCs look for entrepreneurs who love what they do and who are very good at doing it.

Bing Gordon, partner at Kleiner Perkins Caufield & Byers, who has been on the board of Amazon since 2003, agrees. "I love mentoring highly motivated people, but I also like being accountable for results. VCs get to mentor, but also have line responsibility for investment outcomes. It is the best of both worlds. My biological clock was also ticking. At this stage of my life, the opportunity to work side by side with a nucleus of brilliant people was irresistible."

WINNING TECHNIQUE #2: Build a Company Around the Entrepreneur

Soo Boon Koh, managing partner of iGlobe Ventures, explains, "The venture capitalist is a mentor to the CEO of the portfolio company. This is analogous to a coach training an athlete. A VC is most effective when working with a coachable CEO. The challenge of a VC is take the vision of an entrepreneur team and to work with this team to build a global sustainable business." The journey to build a successful business is not straightforward. It will see up times and down times. The key is the passion, dedication, and perseverance of the team, and some stroke of good luck.

Returning to the kitchen, imagine a chef assigned the task of cooking dinner. There are two ways the task could be organized. The host might ask the chef to look through the cupboards for ingredients and utensils and cook a meal. Here, the chef has to imagine possible menus based on the given ingredients and utensils, select one, and then prepare the meal. It starts with given ingredients and utensils, and focuses on preparing one of many possible desirable meals with them. Most venture capitalists adopt this approach—from the pool of companies that they see, they choose the best deals and invest, following which they assist the companies—with the wide range of outcomes discussed earlier.

Alternatively, the host might pick out a menu in advance and present it to the chef. All the chef needs to do is to list the ingredients and utensils needed, shop for any that aren't already on hand, and then cook the meal. It starts with a given menu and focuses on selecting between effective ways to prepare the meal. In the venture capital landscape, the best VCs choose their chefs—that is, they choose markets, choose the business model for it, and then assemble the team with a clear exit strategy in mind.

After first-round funding of US$10 million by Warburg Pincus, RDA Micro (led by CEO Vincent Tai) was on its way to grow into a leading global player in the IC design market. Particularly note-worthy was that Vincent Tai was scouted by Warburg Pincus before he'd generated a dollar of income or hired the first team member. Warburg Pincus saw the market opening: a vacuum in China's IC design market. It was not a difficult decision to occupy that vacuum. After deciding on the market, Warburg Pincus then found the CEO—Vincent Tai. It then assembled the team to complement him. Such was the confidence in Vincent and the market opportunity that Warburg Pincus took the lead in the investment.

Soo Boon Koh takes time to coach the teams in her portfolio companies. "Team stability is of greatest importance. Changes and new challenges need to be absorbed as soon as possible. The VC intervenes quickly in the case of conflicts among portfolio team members and uses informal contacts to sense team morale and satisfaction."

WINNING TECHNIQUE #3: Source for Deals in a Densely Innovative Geography

Innovation is not a unified phenomenon: some forms of innovation disrupt, destroy, and make obsolete established competence; others refine and improve it, and are incremental in their effects. Different kinds of innovation require different kinds of organizational envi-ronment and different managerial skills.[25]

Revolutionary innovation, applied to existing markets and customers, disrupts the industrial status quo and renders established technical and production competence obsolete. This mode of innovation is dominated by "technology push" and often follows on the heels of architectural innovation. Vacuum tubes, mechanical calculators, and the Disk Operating System (DOS) are examples of established technologies that have been overthrown through a revolutionary design.

Differences in the cross-border mobility of factors of innovation often determine the formation of disruptive companies. For example, Shanghai-based Focus Media, founded by ad veteran Jason Jiang in 2003, operates LCD screens displaying ads in elevator lobbies of office towers and upscale apartment blocks. In July 2005, the firm raised about US$120 million with a NASDAQ listing, turning Jiang into one of the richest men in China when he was in his early 30s.[26] Focus Media has established itself as an advertising powerhouse by recognizing that innovation generates profits. The company conveys clients' messages by way of 200,000 flat panel TVs. It also operates an advertising network for the Chinese mobile telecommunications market and recently acquired China's largest Internet advertising agency. Clients include Coca-Cola (KO), Yum! Brands (YUM), and Procter & Gamble (PG).[27]

What Focus Media accomplished was not via ground-breaking technology but an innovative business model. Among the innovations by Jiang are ones introduced to bring down the costs. Focus Media employees pedal their bikes to buildings to manually change flash memory cards containing ad videos, thus ensuring a very low-cost ad delivery that advertisers find appetizing. Focus Media's success stems largely from the fact that people don't mind staring at LCD screens to while away their time in the elevator.[28]

Scientific discoveries travel across national borders much more easily than context-specific know-how and marketing practices. Focus Media was the application of a scientific technology (LCD screen) in the context and local marketing practice of Asia (mass growth of commercial buildings in Asia). In these instances, the original developers capture a low share of the value of innovations vis-à-vis the agents who have applied the development locally. The growth of this "untraded" services sector has sparked excitement on the latent opportunities, which have at least partially offset the more intensive trading of goods.

Finding Innovation   Innovation in a geography can be difficult to measure directly, but a number of measures can serve as proxies for it:

1. *Patents.* While copyright only protects the expression of an idea, patents protect the idea itself, with a set of exclusive rights granted by a state to an inventor or assignee for a limited period of time in exchange for a disclosure of an invention. Although patent offices in Asia are generally reliable, many Asian technology firms actually file their patents in the United States due to the territorial nature of patents. (Many Asian firms want to enter the U.S. market, hence they end up filing their first patents in the U.S. Patent Office.)

2. *Ownership.* VCs will shift out of places where there is a decline in sense of ownership, to places where the idea of ownership with active leadership is thriving.

3. *Scientific publications.* The best way to find out if something has been accepted by the scientific community is through peer-reviewed publications. John Doerr, a partner at Kleiner Perkins, worked at this exhaustively, subscribing to thousands of dollars' worth of technical publications, all of which he dutifully read.[29] Outside of the peer review system, it becomes difficult to assess whether scientific discoveries are really up to accepted standards. These are not perfect measures—for example, Hwang Woo-suk's cloning paper, which *Science* published in 2004, sparked a growing controversy over the rigor of peer-reviewed journals like *Science, Nature,* and a host of lesser-known peer-reviewed publications. Nonetheless, such publications do reduce the chance of reporting something that has not been accepted as fact.

4. *Migration of scientists.* There is an increasing trend in the reverse migration of Asians trained in U.S. universities, particularly back to China and India. China's state media reported in January 2008 that China is setting up science research and development centers to convince the 200,000 Chinese studying abroad to return home. This is a manifestation of the *bandwagon effect* (where people have the tendency to do something because many people around them do the same thing); more important, it reflects an increasing awareness by overseas scholars and researchers of the opportunities in Asia.

5. *Cutting-edge design hubs.* Design and service innovation have become buzzwords and core themes in innovation. Designers of Web sites and consumer electronics are the global economy's translators of experimental technologies, ranging from software code to

earth-friendly plastics, into goods and services. Cities and corporations are paying attention to design as a gambit to attract the world's top innovators. The New York Museum of Modern Art, in a bid to help corporations unearth fresh development talent, assembled 200 projects by international designers and exhibited these designs to CEOs. The show includes displays on nanotechnology, data visualization (interactive graphs of statistics such as Web site traffic), and low-cost computers for developing nations. The designs are also showcased on platforms such as the World Economic Forum in Davos.

East versus West   Overcoming the bandwagon effect is essential to top returns for a VC. Top VCs take calculated risks to venture into unexplored frontiers before their contemporaries. Bobby Chao, founding managing director of DFJ Dragon, says,

> The VCs entered China and made the best returns on their investments when China was not all that solid and open for foreign investors. The VCs entered Google and Baidu when all the odds did not suggest that they made the right decisions. The definition of VC is to venture out ahead of the mainstream investors. While everyone went to Boston and New York, the ones who went to Silicon Valley ventured well. While everyone went to Silicon Valley, the ones who went to Shanghai and Beijing ventured well. While everyone is going to Beijing and Shanghai, the ones who are going to Chengdu, Xi'an, and Inner Mongolia will venture well. It doesn't mean that there is no gold left for New York, Silicon Valley, Shanghai, Beijing, and other places in the world. There are plenty of opportunities for late-stage investments, buyouts, and M&As. In my opinion, the contrast is more like the real VC creates the pie and enlarges it while the other kind of investors mostly rearrange the size of slices of the pie.

Chao's colleague Andy Tang (another managing director at DFJ Dragon) recalls that in January 2005 he was a principal at Infineon, the corporate venture arm of a German semiconductor firm, when the parent company decided to sell its venture portfolio to Cipio Partners. Tang decided to move to China because as a hardware investor, he saw a lot of CEOs coming back to China, and he thought that if customers were moving there, he needed to follow them.

VCs who explore new frontiers have to be realistic and patient. Andy Tang believes that the Silicon Valley model cannot be wholly replicated. "I am not sure whether China (or any parts of Asia) can replicate the SV model. SV is unique (in terms of its academic culture). It has not been replicated anywhere else. Israel, which has come the closest, still has some way to go. I think the culture is impossible to replicate. The level of innovation and disruptive flow is unparalleled. China has shown some early signs of success. China is successful in other ways. Chinese entrepreneurs have come up with interesting business models and technology which is unique to China and can possibly be extended past China." A lot of ideas in SV are replicated in China. SV copies China too, but the balance of exchange is not equal. China is not as fast as SV and there is still a long way to go in terms of the levels of tech and entrepreneurial spirit.

However, in a downturn, there is a real opportunity for VCs in the emerging geographies (such as China) to step into the limelight like their Western counterparts. Entrepreneurs will be less ambitious about looking for VCs in Sand Hill Road (the center of venture capital in Silicon Valley) and start looking for local money. It is likely to open the door for local venture capital. For example, Chinese RMB-denominated funds are likely to get superior pricing and a real boost to their profile. Robert Zhou, managing director of Northern Light, explains that China, as an emerging market, is different from the mature venture capital hotbeds. The VCs in China invest not only in the traditional VC-invested industries such as technology but also in traditional industries such as consumer products, retail, and professional services. Thus, on one hand, the average return on investment will be more modest than the typical VC return on investment. But on the other hand, the investment landscape is more stable. Consequently, VCs will not experience a major slowdown in China due to economic fluctuation

What Entrepreneurs Should Do: Commandments to Follow

Wise entrepreneurs abide by the following principles:

- Weigh the costs and benefits of venture capital.
- Remember that the right sector attracts the dollars.

- Be disruptively innovative.
- Position yourself in an intersection of markets and technology.
- Employ weapons of influence.

COMMANDMENT #1: Weigh the Costs and Benefits of Venture Capital

Finding the right VC can seed the ultimate success of the enterprise.[30] Companies that are funded by more experienced VC firms are more likely to succeed.[31] Top-quartile VC firms are better in identifying high-quality companies and entrepreneurs—these top-quartile VCs could actually add more value to the companies—by helping new ventures make customer contacts, fill key management positions, or set business strategy.

However, 99 percent of start-ups do not require venture capital. Similarly, VCs are very selective in the type of businesses that they look for—large market prospects, scalability, and capital efficiency. As a rule of thumb, a business should offer the prospect of significant turnover growth within five years before it is of interest to a venture capital firm.[32] Not all businesses are suitable for VCs. Some successful businesses may not fit this definition although they are profitable and generate healthy cash flows. "Many small companies are lifestyle businesses whose main purpose is to provide a good standard of living and job satisfaction for their owners. These businesses are not generally suitable for venture capital investment, as they are unlikely to provide high financial returns for investors."[33] VCs invest in companies with a threshold valuation because of the fund size they manage. They would rather focus both their expertise and funds on a few large portfolio companies than on many small companies.

Companies with a significant research and development component often seek venture capital funds, especially for sectors such as semiconductors, biotech, and data-communication equipment. In the United States, there were disproportionately more venture deals in heavy R&D industries like semiconductors and biotech than other sectors.[34] The only exceptional sector with low initial capital expenditure drawing VC funds is the software industry, which has seen more VC deals than any industry to date. In the fourth quarter of 2008 in the United States, there were 194 reported software deals, 109 biotech deals, 36 semiconductor deals, and only 4 retail deals.[35] Figure 1.2 traces this history.

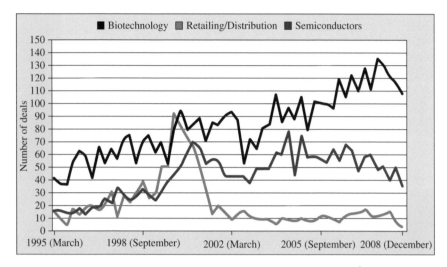

Figure 1.2 VC Deals in Various Fields

A start-up entrepreneur should also stop to think whether the current venture is a large opportunity requiring significant working capital. Reva Electric Car Company, for example, received US$20 million funding in late 2006 from Global Environment Fund (GEF) and Draper Fisher Jurvetson (DFJ). Reva had sought venture investment to increase its working capital for immediate expansion of production to enter international markets; it needed to expand the production capacity of its plant in Bangalore from 6,000 vehicles a year to 30,000, to enhance its global presence. At the time of writing, 1,800 Reva cars were on the road, and 600 of them were in the United Kingdom. Other than venture capital, Reva considered options such as debt financing, factoring, and organic growth bootstrapping. This choice boils down time horizons: an entrepreneur who chooses to grow big fast (thereby capitalizing on a narrow window of opportunity) rather than pursue long-term, organic growth needs capital on a scale only a VC is likely to supply.

It is often very difficult for a start-up with negative cash flows to obtain funds from bank loans as the prerequisite track record simply isn't there. As one wise VC told me, "Banks look at the past records of a company, venture capitalists assess the future potential." Entrepreneurs often try to borrow from families and friends, who are apt to ask less searching questions but are unable to supply funds in the quantities needed, and they can also opt to bootstrap, starting small and tapping the increasing cash flows to finance the operations. This is common in the service industry but impractical for businesses that require large capital investments, especially in the technology industry.

Despite its obvious advantages, however, it is also essential to weigh the cost of venture capital. One significant cost is dilution of founder stock. The average founder who seeks funding from a VC owns less than 10 percent of the business upon exit. Fred Wilson of Union Square Venture comments that founders who go all the way through the process of building a lasting and sustainable profitable business (as opposed to an early exit) will generally suffer the most dilution. In his experience, it will generally take three to four rounds of equity capital to finance the business, and 20–25 percent of the company to recruit and retain a management team. That will typically leave the founder or the founding team with 10–20 percent of the business when all is said and done. The final equity split will typically be 20–25 percent for the management team, 20 percent for the founders, and 55–60 percent for the investors (ranging from the original angel all the way to late-stage VC). Founders who opt for a "quick flip" or any form of early exit (to me, *early* means any time before the company becomes sustainable and profitable) can see much less dilution. For example, Joshua Schachter owned more than 50 percent of Delicious when Yahoo bought it. The four founders of FeedBurner owned more than 25 percent of the company when it was sold to Google. Those exits are generally for less money so the trade-off is more ownership times less total value, but sometimes the early sale is advantageous—especially if the entrepreneur has the next project in mind. This explains why early exits continue to be part of the venture capital landscape.[36]

It's worth bearing in mind that the founder might not always retain any practical control of the company. A partnership with a VC is analogous to a marriage. In the event of a divorce, the founder may not always get to keep the company—custody of children is not guaranteed to one spouse or the other in a divorce.

CASE STUDY: "The dream wasn't supposed to end like this."

One entrepreneur we interviewed founded an engineering solution company in Boston Harbor. Three years later, she had to seek financing for the launch of a new product, and with limited options, she returned to her original VCs. The firm offered a loan secured with the rights to two patents, her most valuable assets. Rather than close the company, the entrepreneur took the money despite the onerous conditions. Her control of the struggling engineering solution firm was quickly ebbing. With sales dead in the water, the VC—which owned 75 percent of the company's shares—ousted the entrepreneur and, in early 1995, made its newly hired vice president for sales and marketing the CEO. Today, the company is little more than a shell. And the entrepreneur has turned warrior, suing her former partner for breach of fiduciary duty. In court papers, the VC countered that it replaced the CEO only after she had ``four years to prove herself and failed to sell a single system.''[37]

COMMANDMENT #2: Remember That the Right Sector Attracts the Dollars

Most believe that VCs invest in good people and ideas.[38] The reality is that VCs invest in good industries—industries that are more competitively forgiving than the market as a whole. In the 1980s, more than 20 percent of venture capital in the United States went into energy industries. In 1999, at the height of the dot-com boom, about 60 percent of venture capital disbursements in the United States went to information-technology industries, especially communications, networking, software, and information services. About 10 percent went to life sciences and medical companies, while the rest was spread over the other industries. In 2008, the industry saw a much higher proportion going to renewable energy despite a global recession, with US$2.8 billion of investments made globally in the third quarter of 2008, according to the PricewaterhouseCoopers Money Tree Survey. This is a familiar winning technique among our star investors. Peter Lim, one of Singapore's leading angel investors, looks at prospective sectors and invests heavily where he sees long-term growth potential. His most successful investments include Wilmar, an agribusiness group that is today among the largest listed companies by market capitalization on the Singapore Exchange. He advises, "You may not have a lot of money, but you have a lot of time." Sumir Chadha, managing director of Sequoia Capital India, adds that entrepreneurs need to ask themselves if they are in a capital-efficient sector with a "significantly large market opportunity."

While high-technology investment makes up most of the venture investing in the United States, and the venture industry gets a lot of attention for its high-technology investments, venture capitalists also invest in other niches, such as retail company investment, "socially responsible" start-up endeavors, or fields such as construction, industrial products, and business services. One such company was Sahajanand Laser Technology Limited, one of the largest manufacturers of laser systems for diamond industry in India. It received Rs. 40 million (approximately US$8 million) in late 2007 from Gujarat Venture Finance Limited (GVFL), a fund started by Gujarat Industrial and Investment Corporation (GIIC) at the initiative of the World Bank. "Picking up innovative technology companies early and nurturing them to leadership is GVFL's forte." With India emerging as "the global destination for diamond cutting and adding value to small and very small diamond 'roughs,' Sahajanand has the potential to become a definite winner with GVFL's effective nurturing and constant support," says Vishnu Varshney, CEO of GVFL Ltd.[39] The common denominator in these types of venture investing is that the venture capitalist is typically not a passive investor but someone who takes an active and vested interest in guiding, leading, and growing the company (and thereby increasing the probability of a successful exit). These VCs seek to add value through their sectoral experience.

COMMANDMENT #3: Be Disruptively Innovative

Breakthrough innovations tend to be disproportionately developed and brought to market by individuals or new firms (even though the ideas behind the breakthroughs originate in larger firms or universities that do not exploit them because of their bureaucratic structures). Research suggests that entrepreneurial action occurs with firms whose organizational structures are not bureaucratic and rigid. The potential for stimulating breakthroughs is greatest among individuals who have prior experience in relevant technologies and insight about fresh roles for existing inventions and technologies, and who have the energy and means to act on their insight. For these reasons, smaller, younger firms produce substantially more innovations per employee than larger, more established ones. Look at your business model: if you have underlying core technology that can change the market complexion, you will be more attractive to VCs than of you're starting a me-too company.

Clayton Christenson, a renowned professor at Harvard Business School and founder of Innosight Ventures, argues that VCs look for disruptive innovation, not sustainable innovation. A VC employs several litmus tests to assess disruptive business. If a technology enables the larger population of less skilled and less wealthy people to do something that historically they could not do or that only specialists could do, it fits the mold of a disruptive business. This is especially so if the business model appears unattractive to the established players, and clearly isn't a sustaining technology to anyone else. For these businesses, the right strategy is unknowable in advance and disruptive ventures should realize that they should put in place a strategy to learn, rather than a strategy to implement.

Tim Draper of Draper Fisher Jurvetson adds, "VC makes money because large companies don't have all the answers. In fact, most large companies are risk averse, which allows small companies to jump in and try new things. I also believe that the entrepreneurs and the teams they build have more energy and put more effort into their jobs than employees of big companies. So more value is created there."

COMMANDMENT #4: Position Yourself in an Intersection of Markets and Technology

What are star venture capitalists and angel investors looking for? The collision of a technology and a market. Ron Conway, a legendary investor in some of Silicon Valley's most successful companies, including Google, looks for convergence of two apparently separate markets. For example, new online video is the convergence between wireless mobile devices and Internet video. Live content being posted by a mobile phone to Internet can serve extremely relevant ads, which in turn allows the content provider to monetize traffic.

Another convergence of two markets is bioinformatics. The massive knowledge base of genetic information needed major computational tools to decipher the underlying meaning. An exciting field of bioinformatics is thus born at this intersection. The science of genomics is intricately intertwined with robotic applications. Cell biology now relies heavily on imaging techniques, and biologists cannot live a day without their innumerable laser-based applications. Attractive themes can also boil down to structural change.[40] Possible changes suggested by DFJ Gotham Ventures include the decline of the firm and the rise of one-to-one commerce, the merging of cyberspace and real space, cloud computing, and the generational shift. The *generational shift* is defined as the difference between people who dated before they had their first computer and those who had their first computer before they started dating. Thatcher Bell, a partner at DFJ Gotham, thinks we still have a long way to go in terms of making the Web easy to use. For instance, Bell compares Google's current interface to the C: prompt days of the PC before Windows. According to Bell, this is a really good way for a search engine to get input from a human and for Google to make money. It is not the best way for a human to interact with a computer. He argues that more intuitive Web and search interfaces, like SearchMe, are needed.

In all such cases, sparks of innovation took place when the participating disciplines were ripe with their respective developments. Intersections thus do not represent forced marriages between disciplines but are natural outcomes when they come of age.

COMMANDMENT #5: Employ Weapons of Influence

VCs are typically busy executives, yet much of what they do for a living is sit through presentations—lots of them. The following weapons of influence could tip the scales in the entrepreneurs' favor.[41]

- Social Proof: "We're meeting DFJ next week, and we previously raised US$44M from Sequoia and others." People tend to be followers. Use testimonials, the more similar to the people you are trying to persuade the better. Likewise, draw upon people who are seen as having expertise or authority.

- Authority: "Ron Conway is an angel for us." "Our CFO has also worked in [a major VC firm]." "I was introduced to your partner by [someone the prospective VC knows and respects]." Build legitimacy and seem like an expert on the topic at hand. This can mean past experience, credentials, or perceived knowledge. Try to establish this early in the persuasion process to keep people listening to you. People will tend to obey authority figures, even when asked to do something they would normally resist.
- Scarcity: "There's only room for one investor in this round." People want more of what they can get less of. Show why your product or service is unique and scarce and people will want it.
- Desirability: "We had a great time pitching to you." Get people to like you and you are more likely to persuade them successfully. People are easily persuaded by other people they like— and they tend to like people who like them.

Pitfalls to Avoid

The road to acquiring venture capital support is not always smooth. Watch out for the following common pitfalls:

- Believing the herd is always right
- Overconfidence
- Concealing skeletons in the closet

PITFALL #1: Believing the Herd Is Always Right

The common gripe among entrepreneurs is that if one big-name VC firm funds a particular sector, the others follow. VCs either all fund something or none of them will. Therefore, an entrepreneur who has an idea that's too new and too different will face a serious struggle for funding.

There is a certain truth in that. According to Eric Tao, vice president of Keytone Ventures and formerly an associate at KPCB China, bubbles do tend to swell in certain sectors. For example, as of 2008, the Internet and mobile space in China includes no companies that are undervalued. However, there are verticals such as solar and retail chains, wireless communications, and wireless applications where ventures are currently doing well and still exhibit potential growth.

PITFALL #2: Overconfidence

As an entrepreneur, it is important to exhibit confidence in your company. However, overconfidence has downside repercussions. Note that three attitudes, anti-authority ("Don't tell me"), invulnerability ("It won't happen to me"), and macho ("I can do it"), were identified by the U.S. Federal Aviation Administration as hazardous to pilot decision making.[42] These same attitudes also affect an entrepreneur's chances of success. Overly optimistic projections may ruin an entrepreneur's credibility. Investors rely on credible financial projections, not expectations. Unless your assumptions on future earnings are backed up by credible sources, do not bring them up. It's better to present realistic figures that can be achieved by the business.

PITFALL #3: Concealing Skeletons in the Closet

All investors understand that businesses have problems. Attempting to avoid mentioning them will be futile. As Rick Segal, member of the BlackBerry Partners Fund, explains, "We're going to find out. We do background checks and real/paid reference reviews. We will know about jail time, know about bankruptcy, know you got fired despite the 'pursue other options' nonsense, so fess up."[43] This may sound intimidating but it reflects reality. As an entrepreneur, never try to provide incomplete financial information. Entrepreneurs ought to present both past and projected financial data, including balance sheets and income and cash flow statements to VCs. Relevant historical financial data will help give meaning and context, and will lend credibility to future projections. Be honest and clear about how you will manage each problem and solve it in the future. Owning up to past and existing problems is better than hiding them—just present a solution your investors will understand.[44] The key here is to communicate well.

Post-investment, entrepreneurs need to spend conservatively and control overhead. Make sure venture partners stay informed of progress—or glitches. Think early on about bringing in professional managers, or recognize that the venture firm may do that for you.

When seeking new sources of capital, it is important to alert venture partners early if the company requires more financing, and prepare to see your ownership stake cut. To minimize dilution, seek stock options or a performance-based compensation plan.

Endnotes

1. For definitions, see KPCB, "iFund™," n.d.; retrieved from www.kpcb.com/initiatives/ifund/index.html, June 20, 2009, and KPCB, "Kleiner Perkins Caufield & Byers Leads US$75 Million Investment in Silver Spring Networks, Smart Grid Technology Leader," October 7, 2008; retrieved from www.kpcb.com/news/articles/2008_10_07.html, June 20, 2009. See also "Nanosolar Secures US$6.5 Million in First-Round Financing," Nanosolar Inc., June 20, 2003, retrieved from www.ewire.com/display.cfm/Wire_ID/1649, June 20, 2009; and "V.C.'s Deliver US$20 Million to Goodmail," *New York Times*, June 20, 2003; retrieved from http://dealbook.blogs.nytimes.com/2008/11/24/vcs-deliver-20-million-to-goodmail/, June 20, 2009.

2. "eBay Inc. Announces Third Quarter 1998 Financial Results," eBay, October 27, 1998); retrieved from http://news.ebay.com/releasedetail.cfm?ReleaseID=210560; June 20, 2009.

3. "Amazon.com Announces Financial Results for Second Quarter 1997, Amazon, October 7, 1997; retrieved from http://phx.corporate-ir.net/phoenix.zhtml?c=97664&p=irol-newsArticle&ID=231874&highlight=, June 20, 2009.

4. "V.C.'s Deliver US$20 Million to Goodmail," *New York Times*, June 20, 2003; retrieved from http://dealbook.blogs.nytimes.com/2008/11/24/vcs-deliver-20-million-to-goodmail/, June 20, 2009.

5. "Nanosolar Secures US$6.5 Million in First-Round Financing," Nanosolar Inc., June 20, 2003, retrieved from www.ewire.com/display.cfm/Wire_ID/1649, June 20, 2009.

6. Michael Arrington, "Sequoia Could Take US$480 Million from Google/YouTube deal." TechCrunch, October 9, 2006; retrieved from www.techcrunch.com/2006/10/09/sequoia-could-take-480-million-from-google-youtube-deal/, June 20, 2009.

7. KPCB, "Kleiner Perkins Caufield & Byers Leads US$75 Million Investment in Silver Spring Networks, Smart Grid Technology Leader," October 7, 2008; retrieved from www.kpcb.com/news/articles/2008_10_07.html, June 20, 2009.

8. Paul Gompers and Joshua Lerner, *The Venture Capital Cycle* (Cambridge, Mass: MIT Press, 2004).

9. Chaoyang Wang, "Primer on Venture Capital" (unpublished manuscript), p. 3, December 2007; retrieved from www.softwareap.net/docs/Primer_on_Venture_Capital.pdf, January 2008.

10. "Venture Capital," Investor Home (n.d.); retrieved from www.investorhome.com/vc.htm, June 20, 2009.

11. Gary Dushnitsky and Michael J. Lenox, "When does Corporate Venture Capital Investment create Firm Value?" April 1, 2005; retrieved from www-management.wharton.upenn.edu/dushnitsky/documents/Dushnitsky_Lenox%20(JBV%202006).pdf, June 20, 2009. See also Microsoft, "Intellectual Property Licensing," n.d.; retrieved from www.microsoft.com/iplicensing/InformationalPage.aspx?content=IPVentures, June 20, 2009, and Zero2ipo Venture Capital Research Center, "China Venture Capital Had a Winning Streak; IDG VC Won the Award of Venture Capital Firm of the Year 2005"; retrieved from www.zero2ipo.com.cn/f/research/2008112617522853535.pdf, June 20, 2009. There are many variations of this profit split both in the size and how it is calculated and accrued.

12. "Focus Media Announces Pricing of Initial Public Offering of American Depositary Shares," Xinhua, July 13, 2005; retrieved from http://ir.focusmedia.cn/phoenix.zhtml?c=190067&p=irol-newsArticle&ID=729592&highlight=, June 20, 2009. See also "Focus Media Announces US$100 Million Share Repurchase Program," Xinhua, July 16, 2008; Retrieved from http://ir.focusmedia.cn/phoenix.zhtml?c=190067&p=irol-newsArticle&ID=1175487&highlight=, June 20, 2009.

13. "Focus Media to Acquire Framedia," Xinhua, October 16, 2005; retrieved from http://ir.focusmedia.cn/phoenix.zhtml?c=190067&p=irol-newsArticle&ID=768091&highlight=, June 20, 2009.

14. "Focus Media Announces Follow-On Offering of 6,787,829 ADSs," Xinhua, January 27, 2006; retrieved from http://ir.focusmedia.cn/phoenix.zhtml?c=190067&p=irol-newsArticle&ID=809558&highlight=, June 20, 2009.

15. Xinhua, "Focus Media Completes Acquisition of Target Media," February 28, 2006; retrieved from http://ir.focusmedia.cn/phoenix.zhtml?c=190067&p=irol-newsArticle&ID=823180&highlight=, June 20, 2009.

16. Xinhua, "Focus Media Completes Acquisition of Dotad," March 21, 2006; retrieved from http://ir.focusmedia.cn/phoenix.zhtml?c=190067&p=irol-newsArticle&ID=833820&highlight=, June 20, 2009.

17. Xinhua, "Focus Media Announces Follow-On Offering of 6,700,000 ADSs," June 16, 2006; retrieved from http://ir.focusmedia.cn/phoenix.zhtml?c=190067&p=irol-newsArticle&ID=873351&highlight=, June 20, 2009.

18. Xinhua, "Focus Media Completes Acquisition of ACL," August 31, 2006; retrieved from http://ir.focusmedia.cn/phoenix.zhtml?c=190067&p=irol-newsArticle&ID=900665&highlight=, June 20, 2009.

19. "Focus Media to Acquire Allyes," *China Daily*, February 28, 2007; retrieved from www.chinadaily.com.cn/bizchina/2007-02/28/content_6336782.htm, June 20, 2009.

20. Reuters, "Focus Media Completes Acquisition of CGEN," January 2, 2008; retrieved from www.reuters.com/article/pressRelease/idUS79221+02-Jan-2008+PRN20080102, June 20, 2009.

21. Xinhua, "Focus Media Announces US$100 Million Share Repurchase Program," July 16, 2008; retrieved from http://ir.focusmedia.cn/phoenix.zhtml?c=190067&p=irol-newsArticle&ID=1175487&highlight=, June 20, 2009.

22. Kate Lister and Tom D. Harnish, *The Naked Truth About Making Money at Home* (New York: Wiley, 2009).

23. "Entrepreneurs Focus on Building Long Term Value, *Economic Times*, December 21, 2007; retrieved from http://economictimes.indiatimes.com/articleshow/msid-2639068,prtpage-1.cms, June 22, 2009.

24. Kate Lister and Tom D. Harnish, *The Naked Truth About Making Money at Home* (New York: Wiley, 2009).

25. Frankie Tan, "Innovation Ventures," n.d.; retrieved from www.innovation-ventures.sg/Entrepreneurship-resources/Home/innovation-and-entrepreneurship, June 20, 2009.

26. Li WeiTao, "AD Vantage," *China Daily*, April 30, 2007; retrieved from www.chinadaily.com.cn/bw/2007-04/30/content_863939.htm, June 20, 2009.

27. "Young Entrepreneurs Go After China's Gold," *Wall Street Journal Asia*, May 11, 2006, p. 1.

28. Larry Schutts, "Through The Fly's Eyes: Focus Media Holding," October 8, 2007; retrieved from http://theflyonthewallblog.blogspot.com/2007/10/through-flys-eyes-focus-media-holding.html, June 23, 2009.

29. Tom Perkins, *Valley Boy: The Education of Tom Perkins* (New York: Gotham, 2007).

30. Paul Gompers, Anna Kovner, Josh Lerner, and David Scharfstein, "Skill vs. Luck in Entrepreneurship and Venture Capital," October 2006; retrieved from www.haas.berkeley.edu/groups/finance/wl2592.pdf, June 23, 2009.

31. Paul Gompers, Anna Kovner, Josh Lerner, and David Scharfstein, "Skill vs. Luck in Entrepreneurship and Venture Capital: Evidence from Serial Entrepreneurs," NBER Working Paper No. W12592, October 2006. Available at SSRN: http://ssrn.com/abstract=937293.

32. Tutor2u. "Introduction to Venture Capital," n.d.; retrieved from http://tutor2u.net/business/finance/raising_finance_venture%20capital.htm, June 23, 2009.

33. "Is Venture Capital for You?" Startups, n.d.; retrieved from www.startups.co.uk/6678842908273525147/is-venture-capital-for-you.html, June 23, 2009.

34. PricewaterhouseCoopers, "Venture Capital Investments by Sector," March 31, 2009; retrieved from www.frbsf.org/csip/data/charts/chart23b.cfm?init=1&selectedstate1=Semiconductors&selectedstate2=Biotechnology &selectedstate3=Software&selectedyear=allyear&datachoice=p3moachg (http://tinyurl.com/sectorchart), June 23, 2009.

35. You can download the data set at www.frbsf.org/csip/data/files/chart23b.zip.

36. Fred Wilson, "Founder Dilution—How Much Is 'Normal'?" February 21, 2009; retrieved from www.avc.com/a_vc/2009/02/founder-dilution-how-much-is-normal.html, June 23, 2009.

37. Richard A. Melcher, Ann Therese Palmer, and Gregory Sandler, "Venture Capital: Not a Love Story," *Business Week*, May 13, 1996; retrieved from www.businessweek.com/archives/1996/b3475156.arc.htm, June 23, 2009.

38. Bob Zider, "How Venture Capital Works," December 1998; retrieved from http://web.mit.edu/peso/Pes1/HBS,%20Zider%20-%20How%20VC%20works.pdf, June 18, 2009.

39. "GVFL invests in Sahajanand Laser Technology, October 24, 2007; retrieved from www.ciol.com/ec/bfsi/news-reports/gvfl-invests-in-sahajanand-laser-technology/241007100994/0/, June 25, 2009.

40. TechCrunch, "Structural Change Is Always an Attractive Theme to Invest In," talk by DFJ Gotham partner Thatcher Bell, June 25, 2008; retrieved from www.techcrunch.com/tag/dfj-gotham/, June 25, 2009.

41. Robert Cialdini, *Influence: The Psychology of Persuasion* (New York: Harper Collins, 1998).

42. Adam Breindel, "Hazardous Attitudes: Disregarding VC Due Diligence," November 30, 2007; retrieved from http://skipmeamadeus.blogspot.com/2007/11/hazardous-attitudes-disregarding-vc-due.html, June 25, 2009.

43. Rick Segal, "The Due Diligence Dipsey Doodle," November 25, 2007; retrieved from http://ricksegal.typepad.com/pmv/2007/11/the-due-diligen.html, June 25, 2009.

44. Barbara Angius Saxby, "Top Ten List on Pitching VCs," April 2005; retrieved from www.cob.sjsu.edu/svce/resources/bpr/files/The%20Top%20Ten%20List%20on%20Pitching%20VCs.pdf, June 25, 2009.

2

Finding the Right Partner at the Right Time

FOCUS ON THE FOREST, NOT THE TREES

Great venture capitalists, like great chefs, are often shrouded in mystery. Nonetheless, the key elements of their "cuisine"—successful companies—are easy to define. Using the same analogy, the great world cuisines came into being when people experimented with limited regional food resources and technologies over long periods of time. For example, the Chinese method of stir-frying developed where large populations made firewood scarce. Brief cooking over a hot flame, stirring constantly to avoid burning, maximized fuel efficiency. The Greeks create equally wonderful but different dishes with olive oil, mint, marjoram, and other locally available ingredients.

Similarly, winning investments by VCs stem from the convergence of markets and technology, typically under constraints of factors of production (such as cash flow and manpower). The best companies are concocted when entrepreneurs in diverse sectors and geographies cross-pollinate disruptive ideas and technologies, guided by the wisdom of the right partner.

The Math of Venture Capital

How VCs make money: *Is it just speculating on the bubble or is there more to it than that?* As Figure 2.1 illustrates, it's a matter of knowing where and how to look.

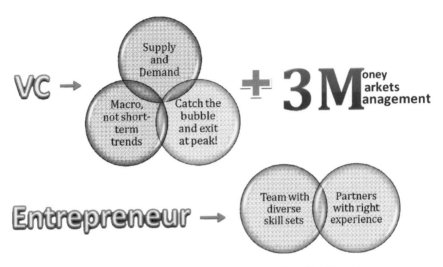

Figure 2.1   The Gamble: Focus on the Forest, Not the Trees!

"When you see venture capital more than double from one year to the next, and IPO values double from one year to the next, that's the sign of a bubble in the making," says Matthew M. Nordan, president of Lux Research.

Over the past 15 years, the global venture capital industry has seen a tremendous boom. *Business Week*, for example, reported in February 2007 that venture capitalists put US$920.7 million into Chinese information technology companies in 2006. Venture capital's recent global growth has outstripped that of almost every class of financial product. Even with the recent global economic meltdown, overall commitments into venture capital only declined gradually over the course of 2008 and 2009 due to the long latency of the asset class (limited partners typically commit funds for a 10-year period). Despite the recession, cleantech investment has been robust globally, supporting the overall investment ecosystem. (However, should the recession persist, the venture capital asset class will not be spared indefinitely.) More important, the role of venture capital is not only confined to the realm of finance—venture capital is widely seen as the bridge between innovation and finance as well as the catalyst for entrepreneurial growth. Indeed, venture capital's role in unshackling entrepreneurial spirits and developing high-tech clusters like Silicon Valley and Zhong-guan-cun Science Park (in Beijing) cannot be denied.

Yet the VC market, like any other asset class, goes through short-term cyclical ups and downs despite exhibiting overall long-term growth. A running joke among Silicon Valley venture capitalists: these days, you're far more likely to run into a colleague at a hotel bar in Beijing or Shanghai than at a local haunt in Northern California.[1] Min Zhu, founder of Cybernaut, a Hangzhou-based venture capital firm, and also a former partner at New Enterprise Associates, warns of the overconfidence, "Most VCs are unqualified because they are using Valley thinking to manage their funds in China."

Another top-tier VC interviewed for this book elaborates, "The underlying grammatical structure of the venture capital business does not vary very much between places and businesses. But it is important to have people who are part of the local community in the business who understand the nuances of the local scene."

Sound familiar? In the dot-com bubble, a lot of companies raised large amounts of venture capital and built up big cost bases on the assumption that they would be able to raise more money in the future. In the United States alone, the venture industry accumulated over US$200 billion in committed capital and invested almost the same amount from 1999 to 2001—this was as much as the industry had raised and invested in the prior 20 years. The assumption collapsed when the bubble burst and some of these companies either went under or had to endure painful restructurings and down rounds. The U.S. venture capital industry suffered three sequential years of negative returns from 2000 to 2003.

But what exactly is a bubble? One definition of a bubble is speculative market or stock in which prices rise very rapidly and then fall sharply. The classic example, the one that more or less defines the phenomenon, is the tulip mania that convulsed the Netherlands in the 17th century. Eric Janszen, a venture capitalist and proprietor of iTulip.com, lays out a common framework for analyzing bubbles and defines various stages within a bubble: normal, formation, hyperinflation, dissipation, and overshoot.[2] In the boom years (formation and hyperinflation), new VC funds are successfully raised, and hence investment activity is robust. In the bust years (dissipation and overshoot), VC firms have difficulty raising new funds and investments by the VC firms slow down, so as to stretch out the remaining funds while awaiting an upturn in the industry.

In China from 2004 through 2006, it was easy to see signs of overheating and the beginnings of a bubble. VC grew globally from

US$30 billion (in investments actually made) to US$125 billion, only to retreat to US$25 billion as public markets collapsed in 2008—all in the space of just three years.[3] (There is, however, substantial "dry powder"—that is, funds committed to venture capital but undeployed to specific investments, waiting to spring into action as promising new prospects appear—so, as an industry, VC remains larger than the figures indicate.) The VC economy's gradual saturation and a slowdown in growth manifested itself when the supply of funds was more than what local markets could absorb, with too much money finding too few deals and immense competition among VCs. In a bubble, VCs make mistakes. VCs fund deals where they should not. VCs decide not to invest in firms that would have been good prospects. In a hyped environment, deals are overpriced and you only discover the problem after the fact.

Are VCs just speculating on the bubble or is it something more than that? Do some VCs thrive in bubbles? Is venture capitalist decision making as poor as some academics suggest? How do you overcome behavioral biases in a bubble?

If decision-making errors are common in the venture capital industry, then one might also expect that venture capitalists, or firms that employ biased venture capitalists, should be competed away by market selection pressures.[4] In practice, however, the people my colleagues and I interviewed left us with the impression that individual cognitive shortcomings are prevalent in the venture capital industry, and that succumbing to these biases results in good money being left on the table at best and bankruptcy at worst.

Harvard Business School professors Paul Gompers and Josh Lerner explain why venture capital is a market response to capital market imperfections.[5] Venture capitalists operate very differently from bankers or institutional investors. Collateral is not a relevant consideration. Venture capitalists typically have substantial representation on the board of directors and closely monitor the firms they invest in. This allows them to reduce information asymmetries and opportunistic behavior on the part of the firms. In addition, venture capitalists typically infuse funds into a firm in stages rather than all at once, thereby keeping the recipient on a very tight leash.

Given the advantages of venture capital, it is not surprising that a large fraction of the high-tech firms that went public in the United States in 1980s and 1990s were backed by venture capitalists. Over the time period 1972 to 2000, 2,180 firms went public after receiving their private funding from venture capitalists, and by the end of 2000, the total market value of venture-backed firms was US$2.7 trillion dollars, or 32 percent of the total market value of all public firms in the United States.

The VC industry has been on a growth track since the end of 2004. In 2007, venture capitalists put more than US$40 billion to work in innovative companies globally.

Several themes often appear in the venture capital cycle. In 2000, the venture cycle was predicated on the dot-com boom. In early 2008, the venture capital cycle was characterized by substantial acceleration in cleantech investing, the maturation of the venture capital ecosystem in China, and growing venture capital investments in India. Corporations were becoming bullish investors and the robust innovation pipeline was also a major driver of the global venture industry in early 2008. Figure 2.2 traces VC activity around the world this decade.

This promising tide began to subside sharply and take on a more severe note in late 2008. VCs now want the companies to cut costs, to figure out ways to survive and emerge at the other end of this downturn, which could last years. Mike Moritz of Sequoia Capital, someone who likes to get ahead of a fire and not fight it from behind, says, "It's pretty clear that demand is going to soften across the board for every company—it doesn't matter if you're selling to consumers or companies." iGlobe Partners held a meeting for its portfolio companies and explained that the firm had forecast the downturn in late 2007. Subsequently, it advised its portfolio companies to freeze hiring and trim travel expenses—essentially a haircut on the companies' budget.

What Star VCs Do: Winning Techniques

The best VCs are clear about several insights. They are willing to enter and exit within a bubble, although long-term principles apply. They invest with less confidence in good times, and invest with more confidence in bad times. For first-time funds, they prefer to make good (not fast) investments without falling prey to newcomers' syndrome (faster expansion and bigger funds at the expense of low-quality investments). They apply the following winning techniques:

- Gauge supply and demand.
- Catch a bubble at its formation and exit at the peak.

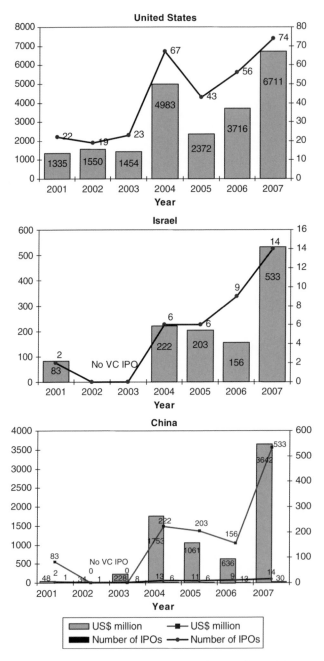

Figure 2.2 Venture-Backed IPO Activity in Three Countries

Source: Ernst & Young Venture Capital Report 2008

- Apply the funnel model.
- Monitor macro conditions, not short-term trends.
- Remember that star first-time funds can overcome newcomer bias.
- Pursue the 3M of venture capital (money, markets, and management).

WINNING TECHNIQUE #1: Gauge Supply and Demand

Bing Gordon, a partner at Kleiner Perkins Caufield & Byers who has been on the board of Amazon since 2003, summarizes the math of venture capital: "Buy low, sell high, and make sure other investors get to sell even higher." The following factors are distilled from interviews with Gordon and other top VCs.

Supply of Venture Funds   When there is a lot of idle cash in the economy or when other forms of investment are not creating adequate returns, the supply of funds flowing to venture capital increases.[6] That is, the desire of investors to place their money in VC funds increases. A decrease in the capital gains tax rate can have a similar effect, as investors look for ways to move income out of their regular bracket.

Demand for Venture Funds   Demand for VC funds—that is, the desire among entrepreneurs to attract VC funds into their companies—also changes over time. There is an increase in demand for VC funds when professionals have more incentives to be entrepreneurs. In certain geographies, this coincides with a downturn, where more people start businesses to replace jobs they've lost.

Short-Run Factors   In the short run, intense competition between venture capital groups may lead to a willingness to pay a premium for certain types of firms (for example, in recent years, firms specializing in tools and content for the Internet). This is unlikely to be a sustainable strategy in the long run: firms that persist in such a strategy will eventually achieve low returns and be unable to raise follow-on funds.

Long-Run Factors   The types of factors that will determine the long-run, steady-state supply of venture capital in the economy are likely to be more fundamental. These most likely will include the magnitude of fundamental technological innovation in the economy, development of regional agglomerations, and the presence of liquid and competitive markets for venture capitalists to sell their investments (whether markets for stock offerings or acquisitions), and the willingness of highly skilled managers and engineers to work in entrepreneurial environments. (The last factor in turn will be a function of tax policy, legal protections, and societal preferences.)

Patenting   The clearest indication of innovative output levels is in the extent of patenting. The greater the rate of intellectual innovation, the more fertile the ground for future venture capital investments. Much of the growth in patenting appears to have been spurred by the growth in the number of VC-backed firms.[7] In short, there seems to be somewhat of a "virtuous circle," where the growth in the activity of venture capital industry has enhanced the conditions that drive the long-run value creation of this capital, which has in turn led to more capital formation.[8] However, the growth in entry by inexperienced investors can create negative pressure on value creation in ventures financed by (regular) venture capitalists.[9]

Agglomeration Economies   Another change has been in the development of "agglomeration economies" in the regions with the greatest venture capital activity. The efficiency of the venture capital process itself has been greatly augmented by the emergence of other intermediaries familiar with the workings of the venture process. The presence of such expertise on the part of lawyers, accountants, and real estate brokers, among others, has substantially lowered the transaction costs associated with forming and financing new firms. The increasing familiarity with the venture capital process has itself made the long-term prospects for venture investment more attractive than they have ever been before, regardless of the country you consider.

WINNING TECHNIQUE #2: Catch a Bubble at Its Formation and Exit at the Peak

Mayer Amschel Rothschild, the founder of the Rothschild international banking dynasty, once described investment as "like a cold bath, in and out quickly.'' That's still good advice almost 200 years later, though it's important not to leave the bath too quickly. Successful investing consists essentially of catching a bubble at its formation stage and not jumping ship too early or too late.

Supernormal profits can be made from good bubble handling. Yan Huang, partner of CDH Venture, one of China's top-performing funds, keys into this observation, describing VC in China simply as, ''VCs starting with a pot of cash and going back to the limited partners with a larger pot of cash.''[10]

There is often an element of opportunism in investing, However, for a few defining companies, investors can hold their equity for a long time and can make more money in the public market than in the private market. For example, a well-known company wanted to acquire one of the portfolio companies of a top-rated venture firm for cash. The partner insisted on stock of the company instead of cash, because he thought the fundamentals of the company were outstanding.

The venture capitalists who get it right more often have a tendency to underestimate how much they know and are under-optimistic about their chances for success. On an upturn, they made the best investments on a reliable bull market, not bubbles. On a downturn, they are also less pessimistic when there is no guarantee that any particular trend will reach a stage of dissipation. The ability to predict when these cycles will occur is extremely rare, but a good indicator of the cycle is how difficult it is for firms to raise new capital.

WINNING TECHNIQUE #3: Apply the Funnel Model

The valuation of deals follows the laws of supply and demand. The more potential investors there are, the higher the valuation. The market determines what the value is. When the market is good (the upside of the funnel), a good VC resists the tendency to indulge in irrational exuberance and invest in overvalued deals, instead reserving funds for the downside. For a valuation calculator, please refer to http://wayofthevc-calc.easyurl.net.

In Good Times. . . .   In a hot market, valuations can be stratospheric. For example, Goldman Sachs and its partner CDH China Growth Capital Fund II won their joint bid for meat processor Henan Luohe Shuanghui Industry Group in April 2007, after offering to pay

2.01 billion yuan (US$251 million). The price represents 19 times the company's net profit last year. Another comparable company, China Yurun Food Group, a meat products supplier, is trading at 16 times its 2006 profit. "[In an upturn], prices overall are higher than they used to be and there is no such thing as a cheap deal [in a boom]," a veteran VC from CDH China, one of China's most successful VC funds, comments, "the market is pretty crowded, so differentiation of experience and brand is important."

The situation reverses in a downturn. A top-rated venture capitalist that we interviewed adds, "Venture industry is much like other industries. The best will still continue to survive, the rest will struggle and some will wither. When the economy is flourishing, blemishes and flaws are concealed. In a downturn, spotlight shines on you and exposes all the flaws." He remarks that it is also easier for the VCs who survive in a downturn like the one experienced in late 2008 and early 2009. "The people we are meeting are the genuine article as opposed to the pretenders. The only people who venture out are on a mission, which is what you need."

Another of our interviewees, veteran venture capitalist Robert Ackerman, co-founder of Allegis Capital, told us, "You can start companies in a downturn economy. In fact, I think it's a better time to start one." Every dollar goes further, Ackerman points out. As failed start-ups shut down, vacated office space is cheaper. Lawyers work for less. The best executives are easier to recruit and more moderate their salary requirements. Companies that start during a downturn are born with a frugal streak. Developing careful cash management habits from day one is a good long-term strategy. Although frugal spending means companies may not have the same kind of explosive growth that the market has come to expect from tech start-ups, thrifty and lean companies can out-survive their spendthrift competitors.

Comforting as that advice is when you're *in* a downturn already, there's no need to wait for one. In a strong enough wind, even pigs can fly. Time and place often give the advantage to the weak over the strong. In a boom, solid high-potential companies will have a slightly stronger hand during negotiations with VCs. Principles of supply and demand tell us that when demand is high (excess money in VC funds), demand will be strong (for good deals). It becomes a sellers' market when it comes to entrepreneurial deals being peddled to the

VC "road show" market. Yan Huang, partner at CDH Venture, one of China's top-performing funds, believes that a sellers' market is "not good news" for the venture capital field. "Entrepreneurs find it easy to raise money in their sector. Entrepreneurs have a lot of choice in terms of VCs and exits, and VCs face a competitive market. They ask, 'Why should I go to NASDAQ when I can get a good price-earning ratio in Asia?'"

In good times, venture capitalists will not be able to be as selective in their investments. They are more likely to invest more in earlier-stage ventures (as opposed to late-stage deals), and may even become less selective in the industries that they are willing to look at investing in.

And Bad. . . .   When you enter a storm, talk to your clients.

When the market is sluggish (the downside of the funnel), deals undergo a Darwinian process of self-selection, and the ones that survive generally have high potential. Hence, it is critical for a good VC to have funds to invest in these deals.

In a downturn, our interviewees advise their portfolio companies to enhance their communication with customers, adopt acceptable ideas from them, and explain to them where the company is going to be at end of the crisis. One portfolio CEO (who wishes to remain unnamed) elaborates, "Otherwise, the cash flow projection is going to be wrong. Communicate to the key management that this is going to be a team effort—talk to your team immediately instead of procrastinating on delivering the bad news. Sell—pick up the phone and go sell yourself. The corporate Web site assumes greater importance. Cut marketing cost but do not cut cost on the Web site—engineer direct communication to clients and provide direct communication through newsletters, so that it is cheap and helpful to get feedback. Freeze any development which is not self-financed and not bringing revenue to the company. Tap government grants, tap tax incentives, and explore strategic partnerships."

Focusing Effect   Market forces play a significant role in determining the behavior of VCs. Humans are susceptible to the *focusing effect*—in this case, the judgment bias that occurs when VCs place too much importance on adverse market conditions, resulting in errors in predicting the utility of a future outcome.

CASE STUDY: Alibaba

In 1999, an English teacher in Hangzhou, Jack Ma, saw the future of business in China—building on the Internet as a convenient meeting place to connect with other buyers and suppliers. Alibaba was born. From 18 angel investors, Jack managed to put together US$60,000 in seed funding to start the company. Alibaba allowed businesses to create a profile and display their product listings, so that users could search for a particular business with ease, saving precious time in the process—in short, Alibaba paired non-Chinese companies with Chinese suppliers. Jack Ma explains his secret for success:

> There were three reasons we survived. We had no money, we had no technology, and we had no plan. Every dollar, we used very carefully.

Alibaba was able to secure first-round financing quickly with the rise of the dot-com boom and rising importance of Asia and China as an export hub to the world. Goldman Sachs injected US$5 million into the company. Shortly after that, in early 2000, Softbank Corporation provided an additional US$20 million. The capital infusions and the optimism for dot-com companies allowed Alibaba to do well.

The journey was not all smooth sailing. The dot-com bust struck in 2002, forcing Jack Ma to revise Alibaba's revenue model. Fortunately, Alibaba was able to weather the storm, and this resulted in a strategic trade sale. At that time, Yahoo was having difficulty breaking into the Chinese market on its own, so it decided to acquire a 39 percent stake in Alibaba for US$1 billion, of which more than US$700 million went to buy out the venture capitalists and employee stock option.[11] The remainder reflects the strategic partnership that Yahoo wished to form with Alibaba. Yahoo was willing to pay the high price as it would be able to tap into Alibaba's Asian network for its consumer-to-consumer market. Through the partnership with Yahoo, Alibaba got access to Yahoo's technology and resources. This allowed the company to improve its service to businesses and consumers in China and around the world. The partnership also saw the addition of an online search engine to the group's e-commerce portfolio of businesses. This made Alibaba one of the largest Internet companies in China, with leadership positions in business-to-business, e-commerce, consumer e-commerce, online payments, Web-based software solutions, communications, and search.

As the Chinese economy expanded, Internet usage in China and Asia continued to rise, and Alibaba decided to list itself on the Hong Kong Stock Exchange. Over the span of two years, the company's profitability grew by 13.7 percent. In 2007, Alibaba was valued at US$21.5 billion and the company was able to raise a total of US$1.5 billion through IPO. Shares of Alibaba soared more than 120 percent to about HK$33 a share, up from about HK$13 during the first day of trading. After Alibaba was listed, it was able to expand the company's operations aggressively to other markets. It upgraded and re-launched the Alibaba Japan marketplace, and it opened offices in Taiwan and India.

Kelvin Chan of Partners Group comments: ``A true VC identifies something which is promising and which nobody can discover. The problem in Asia is that there is insufficient breakthrough technology. VCs tend to depend a lot on the market. In a poor market, the VC may not feel confident enough. For example, a lot of VCs who invested in the earlier rounds of Alibaba did not follow on after the NASDAQ crash.'' This is a manifestation of loss aversion, where there is a tendency for VCs to strongly prefer avoiding losses over acquiring gains. In bad times, overcoming loss aversion is difficult for VCs. ``A true VC must have holding power,'' Kelvin Chan maintains. ``It depends on the individual skill. When a VC believes that company is going to be wildly successful, a true VC must be able to follow on with conviction. Those who believed in Alibaba were rewarded handsomely.''

In a downturn, there are certain advantages to venture capital. First, venture capital doesn't rely on leverage to originate deals, which means that in spite of the credit crunch, VC funds are still capable of deploying capital to deserving young companies. Second, venture capital investments typically take anywhere from three to seven years to gestate, so the current state of the financial markets shouldn't matter that much in the whole scheme of things as far as building sustainable businesses. That's not to say, of course, that VC-backed companies are immune to the day-to-day economic woes.[12]

In an upturn, VCs do not mind investing in a bubble. Market growth is of utmost importance to VCs. A portfolio company's fast growth, fueled by the market, is what provides the high returns that VCs look for. VCs acknowledge that high growth in any sector is unlikely to be sustainable over the long term, so they invest as long as they figure it will last at least five or six years. An IPO would then provide the exit for the VC and supply further funding for the company to push into new growth opportunities. "Both the VC and the investee would then avoid being hurt if the bubble were to burst," says Lin Hong Wong, VC veteran and former managing director of Temasek Capital.

WINNING TECHNIQUE #4: Monitor Macro Conditions, Not Short-Term Trends

"A bubble will burst before you can adapt," explains Jeff Chi, partner of Vickers Venture. "Unlike a hedge fund with liquidity, which can enter and exit a market, a VC firm must adopt a strategy which is fundamentally bubble-independent. A VC must be able to ride out the bubble; what happens if the bubble bursts?" Our interviewees uniformly assert that the salient principle is to invest in the long term. Good VCs are here for the long term and will stay with their companies regardless of the economic cycle and wider macroeconomic conditions, provided always that the company retains its potential. The corollary is that great companies always get financed, while poor companies will find it almost impossible to be financed in a downturn. Some points to keep track of:

- *Not losing sight of the big picture.* The people interviewed for this book maintained that a quality VC paints a picture of the market and builds a company with an end market in mind. A VC grows specific technologies by focusing resources. A VC eyes long-term markets and builds long-term relationships.

• *VCs put too much money behind companies.* Ho Nam from Altos Ventures comments, "VCs are trying to force growth by overinvesting in companies. You cannot use brute force. Explosive growth happens when a market takes off and a company is well-positioned, with the right products—in the right place at the right time. Until the right conditions are in place, you have to remain patient."

• *Stagger investments in pilots.* iD TechVentures described a company it funded in 2000: In the course of a year, this company changed its product road map four times and went through three CEOs. iD TechVentures tried to rescue the money left in the company, but the attempt failed—and the newly renamed company burned through the rest of the cash, plus a new infusion, for a total US$2.5 million loss. In hindsight, the capital injection should have been conducted in tranches (installments keyed to milestones). In addition, a closer and more decisive relationship between the VC and the entrepreneurs would have yield a better result.

• *Speedy trails and successes.* Randy Komisar's Rocket Ship model of investing also illustrates the model of learning by speedy trials and successes. His analogy: fill each start-up with rocket fuel as fast as possible and blast it into space. Monitor the ones that fly—and if the rest of them blow up, *c'est la vie* (that's life). In fact, the Rocket Ship model of start-up investment has been touted as producing many of the most prominent Silicon Valley successes. When too much money is pumped too fast into a start-up, there's no room for mistakes and no time to stop and reconsider. Once the market is understood and the product is fully developed, then move fast and hard. The initial product and the initial fix on the market have to be right. But for every rocket that takes off and flies to success, there are many potentially viable companies that might have prospered eventually if they had been incubated longer and at a lower temperature.

• *Avoid arrogance.* VCs have to be open-minded and humble. As soon as you think you know everything you need to know, you put yourself in danger. Ho Nam of Altos Ventures adds, "It is difficult to predict the future. Many VCs say that they know how to pick the home runs. If that were true, they should get into the hedge fund business because most of the value is created post-IPO. That way, they can manage a lot more capital and make a lot more money. Their probability of success should go up since they will be picking among much larger companies. If you get arrogant in this business, you are in trouble.''

• *Market conditions play a large role.* ''In a downturn, entrepreneurs have no choice. They are largely thankful and appreciative to any funds to slash their burn rate,'' says York Chen, president and managing general partner, iD TechVentures. Johan Stael of IQUBE, who made his first billion in a dot-com, adds, ''In good times, VCs are squeezed by the entrepreneurs. In bad times, it is the other way round.'' Professor Poh Kam Wong, a renowned angel investor in Singapore, witnessed firsthand the chilling effect of the global financial meltdown in early 2009.[13] One of his portfolio companies received a term sheet from an Asian regional office of a blue-chip, Silicon Valley-based VC firm about three months before the economic meltdown, and despite the fact that it cleared all their due diligence checking, the VC firm walked away from the deal. He found out later that its U.S. headquarters had told it to hold all investment indefinitely, period.

WINNING TECHNIQUE #5: Remember That Star First-Time Funds Overcome Newcomer Bias

''VCs who have not been through cycles are urged to make investments quickly as they are rewarded by investing quickly and in a bigger fund,'' says Andy Tang. This is why some first-time VCs fall prey to newcomer's phenomenon—the urge to expand bigger with faster investments but not necessarily good investments. On the other hand, GPs starting a first round fund tend to be more hardworking, both to prove their worth and to build a track record. Our panel of top-quartile VCs advises newcomers to channel the diligence into making better, not necessarily faster investments.

WINNING TECHNIQUE #6: Pursue the 3M of Venture Capital (Money, Markets, and Management)

With venture capital, good things come in threes. The trio of smart money, large growing markets, and experienced management is a winning combination.

Money   "Money is smart, and the more money there is, the smarter it becomes," says Peng Tsin Ong, serial entrepreneur and founder of numerous companies, including Match.com, Interwoven, and Encentuate and currently chairman of Infocomm Investments Private Limited. Money is only one element of succeeding in a start-up, however important it is, and the A-list VC must structure the deal carefully to allocate the right amount of cash. The VC cannot give the entrepreneur too much money or too little. Orna Berry of Gemini Israel Fund has been an entrepreneur and understands innovation as a chief scientist managing a US$500 million research budget. "I had worked in a former investment field so I had a fair understanding of people, markets, and innovation. As a venture capitalist, structuring and allocation of capital is important. Sometimes Company A is sold for US$600 million with a US$20 million capital gain, while Company B can be sold for a lesser value at US$300 million but with a US$30 million capital gain. The company gains more in the sale of company B. As a venture capitalist, one sees opportunity and momentum in a different way."

Markets   Marketing experience, that is, the ability to recognize market characteristics and potential, is a critical skillset for a VC. A VC who settles in to assist the start-up in sourcing and penetrating the right markets can be more useful than a VC with a well-known brand name. A VC can assist the entrepreneur in many ways when the entrepreneur rolls out new products:

- Positioning of product
- Working with channel partners
- Direct sales

The measure of VCs' contribution is their value creation. The entrepreneur can spend 99 hours on product development while the VC spends only 1 hour introducing the product to customers—and nonetheless, the VC has created more value than the entrepreneur.

To understand the pulse of the market, a VC cannot depend solely on industry surveys (just as you cannot judge would-be employees by the résumés they send in). Any industry survey is a representation of the past, and the window of opportunity is apt to have narrowed by the time there is clear data. Surveys may be marginally useful for long-term trends but have limited value for short-term trends. Finding the right people to talk to is critical. A VC cannot be an expert in every field. A simpler way is to know the experts and pick their brains. For example, a VC can talk to marketing companies to learn marketing. Tim Draper learns about the sector by interacting with people who work with great venture capital firms or people with great enthusiasm for the business and great knowledge of the industry the business is pursuing.

Management   Start-ups derive a lot of benefit from having capable mentors to help them succeed, that is, to commercialize their technology and refine their marketing strategy. Lin Hong Wong adds,

> Technology start-ups are typically weak in marketing and business strategy. They would benefit from having mentors with senior executive experience and preferably with some marketing expertise and good understanding of technology. They should avoid VCs or other investors who only have financial backgrounds. VC firms therefore usually have a balanced team of investment staff with technical, marketing, consulting, and financial experience at senior levels to mentor and add value to investee companies. However, the mentors must resist reverting to their executive past and taking over the running of their investee companies. Investment firms in Asia that are mainly staffed by financial people would tend to steer away from start-ups and do more later-stage deals as such firms would already have management teams in place.

Johan Stael, whose IQUBE is a disruptive incubator based in Sweden, empowers the entrepreneur by saying, "I cannot build the company for you. If the company is to be built at all, you have to build it." Other renowned VCs take a minority stake to ensure that they don't have to be the one waking up in the middle of the night worrying about the company—the entrepreneur is. Andrew Braccia, a partner at Accel Partners, says that the most important thing about investing in start-ups is placing value on company culture.

An important part of management due diligence is people judgment. You would need a network to validate the integrity and track record of the management team. A VC would have to possess the sufficient experience to appreciate the challenges of company-building to ask the right questions. Here are the top three questions a VC would ask:

- What is the market size and growth (which is usually the upper bound for company growth)?
- How would the company exploit the market?
- What is the level of competition with incumbent firms? What are the techniques and tools that companies can use for their competitive advantage?

What Entrepreneurs Should Do: Commandments to Follow

In this section, I discuss the principles gleaned from the people consulted for this book. They have two basic commandments:

- Choose a diverse team (with diverse skillsets).
- Choose the partners with the right experience. This falls into three models:
  - The Winner
  - The Apprentice
  - The Corporate/Government Combination

COMMANDMENT #1: Choose a Diverse Team (with Diverse Skillsets)

VCs are not all created equal. An entrepreneur shopping for venture capital support needs to look for more than the money; the skills and insights of the VC can make a huge difference in the effectiveness with which the funds are deployed. Here are some examples of what the top VCs can offer:

Born and raised in Shanghai, and armed with a master's degree in economics and finance from the University of York in the United Kingdom, Ken Xu, now partner of Gobi Ventures, had wide experience—including IT, financial services, real estate, and construction—prior to venture capital. Most, notably, he was part of Shanghai Golden Point Investment Corporation, a personal finance management and investment consulting firm where he was responsible for personal finance management and investment consulting services. Xu joined Gobi Partners in 2003 and focused on wireless and broadband applications, e-learning, and the digital TV sector within the digital media value chain. Xu helped Gobi invest into a leading Beijing-based LBS player in 2004.

At Gobi, he was complemented by a good team with three other partners with different skillsets. His partners, Thomas Tsao, a former investment banker at Dresdner Kleinwort Benson (China) and Merrill Lynch, along with his colleagues, Wai Kit Lau, a former managing director of Wi Harper, and Lawrence Tse, a Stanford graduate who had experience in several high-tech companies such as Sybase, collectively hold the title of the earliest VCs to hit the ground running in China's Information Technology sector with a particular interest in "ambient media"—a field whose name they coined.

In addition, Xu equipped himself with additional skillsets by learning on the job: "I had to learn a lot by myself—via meeting people and companies—triangulating three or four ideas from different sources helped to sharpen my analysis and thinking. Between our partners, we also divided up our sector focus. This minimized the chance of a blindspot bias by any one partner." The team collectively possesses substantial investing experience and *guanxi* with new tech companies in China. This effectively prevents what Tim Draper, founder of Draper Fisher Jurvetson, believes to be one of the most common mistakes made by VCs—groupthink.

Another of our star VCs, Lip Bu Tan, chairman of Walden International, was in the process of finishing his Ph.D. in nuclear engineering at MIT when the U.S. government decided to stop building nuclear power plants after the Three Mile Island leak. As a result, he decided to drop out of the Ph.D. program and look for ways to combine his engineering background, his physics training, his skills in finance, and his enjoyment of building companies. In 1984, he stepped into the venture capital business and never looked back. His love for building great businesses, entrepreneurial instincts, self-belief, and work ethnic were critical factors for his success as a VC.

Tan is one of the few who had diverse skillsets entering the venture capital industry. In reality, VCs are seldom born into the industry. For example, Fred Wilson, now a general partner at Union Square Ventures, entered the VC circuit as a young professional without significant operational experience. (From 1987 to 1996, Wilson was first an associate and then a general partner at Euclid Partners, another New York–based early-stage venture capital firm.)

He says he wouldn't recommend that anyone try it the way he did it. "If you choose to get an MBA," he adds, "get a real job out of business school. Help to build a few businesses in an industry sector you really like. Become an expert in that industry. Then try your hand at venture capital. You'll be much better at it than I was my first 10 years in the business."[14]

Dixon Doll, co-founder of top-tier venture capital firm DCM, has been fascinated throughout his career by the combination of business and technology. Equipped with a Ph.D. in networking and data communication (earned when the sector was just getting started), Doll founded a strategic consulting firm focusing on data communication. As his profile grew, Doll was increasingly called upon to teach, present, and give keynotes. "I enjoyed the educational aspect of my work. The field was exploding and yet there was a lot of misinformation and lack of understanding. My consulting practice developed in parallel with my activities in education and lecturing and it was a subject where I was recognized as an area industry expert and visionary." As his stature as a leading consultant grew over the next 10 years, Doll fielded numerous calls from entrepreneurs in Silicon Valley who asked him to become a board member for emerging start-ups. When Doll became involved in several venture-backed deals, he met and built ties with many premier VCs and started to work closely with them. He started Doll Capital Management (which later became DCM), an early-stage venture capital firm focused on supporting entrepreneurs building world-class technology businesses, together with David Chao in 1995 and 1996. The firm operates out of offices in Silicon Valley, China, and Japan.

With regard to why he became a venture capitalist, Doll says, "The whole entrepreneurial process is exhilarating. I enjoyed working with entrepreneurs who were mostly risk takers (I was not a risk-averse person)." After finding success in a first few exciting businesses, he changed his career to venture capital. Initially, he did not know the business, financial engineering, and legal side, so he set out to find a firm that would bring him on board. The venture firms wanted to utilize his industry expertise in communication. In turn, Doll worked with them to learn financial engineering, legal, negotiation, and fundraising. In 1985, he became partner number three in Accel Partners, a group that had been in the venture industry for 15 years and was raising its third fund. With Doll, the Accel team raised US$40 million on a fund focused on telecommunications.

"Following that, I had a couple of successful private investments that I had made on my own and had a good reputation in the communications industry. Eventually, LPs committed to a telecommunication fund I raised due to the combination of my prior experience and own expertise. DCM has backed such well-known entrepreneurial companies as About.com, @Motion, Clearwire, 51job, Foundry Networks, Internap, IPivot, Neutral Tandem, PGP Corp., Recourse Technologies, Semiconductor Manufacturing International Corporation, and Sling Media.

COMMANDMENT #2: Choose the Partners with the Right Experience

Besides looking for range and scope, entrepreneurs need to look for the right match for their own business. Based on our interviews and analyses, my colleagues and I identified three common models of VCs, which we have called the "Winner" model, the "Apprentice" model, and the "Corporate/Government Ventures" model. Even though this list is not exhaustive, it is advisable to pay attention to the peculiarities of each model in choosing a partner.

MODEL #1: "Winner"   *Strong domain knowledge.* When asked for what qualities he looked for in the senior management he recruits, Lip Bu Tan replied that he looks for people who can eventually become partners at the firm. They either have an operations background and a track record of successfully running a company, or they have a management consulting or investment banking background. Of the first type, he cited fellow partner Mary Coleman, who had 25 years of management experience and financial expertise in new business development in technology companies like Baan, Aurum, and Rightworks before she stepped into the VC industry. Yimin Zimmerer used to work for Ericsson. Ultimately, the critical skill she looks for is strong domain knowledge.

Prior relevant experience. The general road map for this model looks like this:

1. Start company.
2. Raise venture capital for company.
3. Exit successfully with significant investor return.
4. Repeat steps 1–3. (That is, be a serial entrepreneur.)
5. Join VC firm as partner (or start a fund).

Dixon Doll says he prefers to work with partners who have strong operating expertise. Since building a portfolio is both a rewarding task and an arduous one, it pays off for a partnership to focus on building companies that leverage their area of experience. For example, at DCM, Dixon Doll's co-founder David Chao gained deep operational expertise and industry know-how in the information technology sector from having worked in marketing and product management roles at Apple Computer, where he was instrumental in the success of Apple Japan's One Billion Dollar Revenue Plan. David Chao also worked as a management consultant in McKinsey & Company in San Francisco, where he helped communication and software firms develop their technology, marketing, and financial strategies.

Doll describes Chao as one of the smartest, hardest-working, and most enthusiastic people he has ever met. In 1996, their shared beliefs and unique view of the world prompted them to set up the Silicon Valley–based VC firm that focused on investments in China and Japan. They recognized the importance of building their practice in Asia and opened offices in Beijing and Tokyo to gain access to a vast network of resources that greatly benefited their portfolio companies. DCM has been a VC of choice to entrepreneurs who value the distinctiveness of establishing connections in Asia and DCM's proven track record of making successful investments in the United States.[15]

A VC who was a former CEO could value-add more substantively to operations and also has credibility when communicating with the entrepreneur. Operating experience includes senior management experience at large companies and line management experience with P&L responsibility. When working with growing companies, and often with first-time CEOs, it's helpful to see the challenges in advance and be able to provide relevant experience and advice. VCs would have the relevant expertise to help portfolio companies to resolve challenges and generate greater success. Having fresh relationships, both within their old company and with senior management peers in other big companies, allows them to introduce start-ups to the CEO of a big portal or media company, often in the capacity of a board member. However, line experience can be even more valuable, because it is actually more effective to get introduced directly to the real decision maker a couple of levels deeper in the organization, especially when the introduction comes from someone the decision maker already has a relationship with.

After selling his first company in 1993, Seth Levine dabbled successfully in angel investing from 1994 to 1997 before co-founding

Mobius in 1997. He cautions, "[There] isn't an obvious path, and the road to a VC career is more often random, haphazard, and fraught with uncertainties. Great CEOs are a scarce commodity." Successful entrepreneurs who made a VC wealthy (those who led firms that a VC backed and that culminated in a successful exit) end up being partners at VC firms because VCs love to back successful CEOs again. For example, Neil Shen, managing director of Sequoia, was formerly CFO of NASDAQ-listed Ctrip, China's most popular travel portal. Hurst Lin, general partner at Doll Capital, was formerly CEO of the large Chinese portal and NASDAQ-listed SINA Corp. Deng Feng, founding managing director of Northern Light Ventures, had co-founded and served as the vice president of engineering, chief strategy officer and board member of NetScreen Technologies, which went public on NASDAQ in 2001 and was acquired by Juniper Networks in 2004 for US$4 billion.

Example is more powerful than precept. All too many VCs below the top tier have a tendency to emulate Aesop's mother crab. (The one in the millennia-old fable, who said, "Why do you walk so one-sided, my child? It is far more becoming to go straight forward." To which, Aesop reports, the young crab replied: "Quite true, dear Mother; and if you will show me the straight way, I will promise to walk in it.") Unfortunately, many CEOs lack the young crab's perceptiveness, and they put a lot of time and effort into things that are actually impossible to accomplish.

A wise entrepreneur seeking funding from a venture capitalist will seek advice from an experienced mentor rather than from a young person with limited experience. Money is a commodity with many potential sources; experience is individual and impossible to duplicate. As Guy Kawasaki of Garage Technologies famously noted, "Venture capital is something to do at the end of your career, not the beginning."

Venture capitalists with entrepreneurial experience face problems of their own. They must withstand the temptation to fall prey to *déformation professionelle* tendencies. Former entrepreneurs find it easy to see the role of a VC from the vantage point of an entrepreneur, forgetting the broader operations of a venture capital fund. For example, entrepreneurs might be too focused on operations, neglecting exit. Lip Bu Tan also reports success recruiting Winners with profound domain knowledge. However, he warns that they can be so intensely involved with operations that they forget they are the coach, not the player. VCs who were formerly in operations can get frustrated and paralyzed by a one-track mind in operations. It is very hard for them to be objective in their judgment. They tend to be overconfident during investment, making an investment in the belief that they can fix operational issues that are actually beyond fixing. This may sound attractive to entrepreneurs who see the VC's overconfidence as smoothing their way to the money, but it reduces all participants' chances of a successful exit. Hence, entrepreneurs should look for VCs who draw clear boundaries between the roles of coach and player.

Winners who start their own funds may address the monetary aspect but not necessarily have the knowledge or experience aspect of how to be a VC. For that, our interviewees recommended that would-be VCs start in an environment with other experienced VCs so as to learn the business. As a corollary, entrepreneurs should be wary of solo VCs whose experience too closely tracks their own.

MODEL #2: The "Apprentice" Model   The traditional path for aspiring VCs is to work up the hierarchy as an analyst, associate, principal, and then partner.[16] Venture finance is largely an apprentice business—to really be a good venture capitalist requires a broad set of skills that one is unlikely to pick up in other jobs. (As noted, people typically enter the industry with a subset of those skills, but there is no substitute for spending a lot of time with an experienced and successful partner to learn the ropes.) While some do leverage their own money into angel investments and sometimes into a fund, these people have missed a few of the important steps along the way that they would have learned by spending time with more experienced VCs.

This is the general road map for this model:

1. Work in brand-name consulting firm.
2. Get brand-name MBA.
3. Intern at a VC or otherwise get involved with venture capital.
4. Enter investment banking or corporate development firm, or the merger and acquisition arm of established technology firm, or both.
5. Network effectively.
6. Join the industry as a VC analyst or associate.

Despite the advantages Winners bring to the table, it is desirable for an entrepreneur to seek out a VC with some Apprentices in its ranks, bringing consulting and especially investment banking to the table. Some examples:

Lip Bu Tan from Walden International has a couple of staff with finance expertise, and had worked in other fields such as investment banking and engineering prior to venture capital. For example, Hock Voon Loo, managing director in Singapore, is an engineer by training. Tan also has a couple of former management consultants, who contribute significantly because of their training in analyzing different sectors and their ability to pick out winners from the different sectors. Tan adds that the best of the former consultants usually complement their background with investment banking skillsets, are well-honed in finance, and have an ability to analyze sectors in-depth and identify winners. Orna Berry of Gemini Israel Ventures agrees: "I have only hired two staff without an MBA. Most are engineers with an MBA who are analytical and well-versed in dealing with people and technology. Financial savvy is helpful when dealing with financial documents."

In essence, the venture capitalist buys a stake in an entrepreneur's idea, nurtures it for a short while, and then exits with the help of an investment banker. The investment banker knows what the capital markets are looking for and shares the venture capitalist's interest—both parties have exit strategies in mind. As a result, an investment background equips the VC with an exit-focused orientation. Investment banks can also invest upstream.

Hans Tung, a partner at Qiming Venture Partners, worked at the investment banking division of Merrill Lynch in New York and Hong Kong after completing his undergraduate study at Stanford, before moving into private equity at Crimson Asia Capital. After spending three years in private equity, Tung co-founded two award-winning Internet start-ups: Asia2B in Hong Kong and HelloAsia headquartered in Silicon Valley. "I liked financial engineering and thus private equity. But it was during my start-up days that I realized my true love lay elsewhere. I knew then I would love to work with entrepreneurs and help them to build great companies."

Before joining Qiming in 2007, Tung spent almost three years with a leading VC firm in the US, Bessemer Venture Partners. "It takes time to learn the VC business. My training in investment banking, growth capital PE, and equity research, as well as my startup experiences, all prepared me well to be a venture capitalist. But I really learned the VC business from my days at Bessemer."

When interviewing entrepreneurial ventures, the legendary Arthur Rock is particularly interested in the kind of financial people companies recruit. So many entrepreneurial companies make mistakes in the accounting end of the business. If the start-up doesn't have someone who will scrutinize the operations closely and impose appropriate controls, it is unlikely to succeed.

In 2000, Soo Boon Koh explains, iGlobe participated in the Series B investment in Televigation Inc. (Later renamed Telenav Inc.) H. P. Jin and Bob Rennard had founded the company in 1999 with Y. C. Chao, with the vision to provide real-time voice-activated navigation services to mobile consumers. The company worked hard to deliver its business plan. In March 2001, it contracted a leading investment banker to launch its series C financing, with the promise that major U.S. mobile carriers were close to signing major contracts.

On 9/11, when the Twin Towers collapsed, Telenav had no visibility in its business. Its potential customers—the major mobile carriers—reneged on their earlier promises and new investors did not show up. The 9/11 event had a severe impact on the company. A majority of the board members decided to resign and the suggestion was made to wind the company down and file for Chapter 11. Koh continued to show support to the founding team and stayed on the board while the founders were fighting to save the company. The founders appealed for continuous support from iGlobe and vowed that they would do whatever it took to turn around the company.

After careful evaluation, iGlobe took a calculated risk to continue to back Telenav with additional funding, with the proviso that the company must move part of its software development to Shanghai to take advantage of lower costs. In early 2002, Xiao-Bao Hu (chief adviser to Telenav Shanghai and now venture partner of iGlobe) helped Telenav start its software development center in Shanghai.

In the second half of 2003, Telenav started to sell its navigation services with U.S. mobile carriers. By 2006, Telenav was profitable and achieving decent revenue growth. Koh attributes the successful turnabout to the dedication and fighting spirit of the Telenav founders. Their flexibility in moving swiftly to Shanghai to take advantage of China's low-cost in-sourcing center played into a capital-efficient investment business model.

Lip Bu Tan emphasizes that a good VC has an optimistic personality. The fortunes of a portfolio company may vacillate, but a good VC cannot be depressed when a company is going through difficulties—nor succumb to elation when it reaches a smooth patch.

VCs with an operational background tend to be pessimistic in the downswing and overconfident on the upswing. When a company is going through difficult times, it is critical to rally the morale of the staff and maintain the belief that the company can do better.

Lip Bu Tan summarizes the advantages of the Apprentice model: "In general, a good VC has to be able to multi-task, have good interpersonal skills, and (most critically) be able to pick winners with . . . accurate business acumen. It is also a profession which one has to work hard over long hours and sit on a couple of boards."

MODEL #3: Government/Corporate VC model A number of today's top VCs have come from stable organizational structures in both government and the private sector.

Government Venture Capitalists Former high-ranking officials bring tremendous value to a government contractor seeking new work or a private equity fund looking for companies to buy. "You understand the decision-making process inside the Beltway [that is, in Washington, D.C.], and that is liquid gold," says Roger Cressey, who worked in President Clinton's National Security Council as deputy director of counterterrorism and is now a partner in Good Harbor Consulting, a company he founded with his former boss at the NSC. At Kleiner Perkins, Colin Powell (formerly U.S. secretary of state) is a strategic limited partner and Al Gore (Bill Clinton's vice president) is a partner.

Government investors also sometimes choose venture capital as an alternate career path. Most have prior backgrounds at sovereign funds, are analytically sharp, and equip themselves with the relevant investment skillsets. Their understanding of the inner workings of government is also helpful in tightly regulated industries. Some success stories:

Lin Hong Wong started work in 1970 in the Singapore Economic Development Board, heading the electronics group, where he spent 11 years promoting the development of the electronics industry, now the largest industrial sector in the economy. It was here that he had his first taste of venture investing. The Economic Development Board at that time had a venture fund called the Capital Assistance Scheme (CAS), which offered equity and loan financing to promote the start up of manufacturing projects critical to Singapore's economic development. Wong was instrumental in promoting the establishment of the first semiconductor wafer fabrication plant in Singapore, incentivized by an interest-free loan from the CAS. He also negotiated a joint venture with Hitachi Ltd. with equity funding from the CAS to set up the first color television picture tube plant in Singapore. Building an intimate knowledge of setting up electronics manufacturing operations and an extensive contact base in government and industry, Wong then became the CEO of several U.S. subsidiaries manufacturing disk drives in Singapore. During the same period (1981–1990), he started up Computer Memories Far East Ltd., which was sold to Micropolis Ltd. for about US$30 million in 1986, resulting in a significant capital gain for the owners of Computer Memories. Wong and his management team restarted under Micropolis in 1986 and grew the Singapore operations to achieve an annualized revenue run rate of US$400 million at the time of his departure. This paved the way for his entry into the venture capital world as EVP of Transpac Capital Pte. Ltd., from 1990 to 2000. Transpac was established in 1986 (under the name Transtech) and grew to become one of the largest venture capital firms in South-East Asia, managing more than US$820 million of funds in 2000, which were invested in a broad range of companies in Asia and the United States.

York Chen had a similar journey. Upon graduation, Chen joined the Taiwanese government in the ministry responsible for entry and exit visas and passports as the prevailing preference was for a safe and well-respected government job. At 33, Chen joined the International Trade Institute and joined Acer two years later. After spending 10 years in a variety of roles involving computer operations, channel development, and setting up new operations, Chen decided to move into uncharted territory following a reorganization in Acer. Fortunately for Chen, at this time Acer decided to finance a venture capital fund. Accordingly, at the beginning of 2000, Chen and several other Acer veterans were asked to set up Acer Ventures, with an initial fund of US$260 million raised from Acer and from other limited partners such as Singapore's Government Investment Company, TIF, DBS, and Temasek. Two separate teams were set up, one in the United States and the other in Asia Pacific, each able to draw upon the US$260 million capital. Chen joined the Asia Pacific fund, which had operations in Taipei, Shanghai, Singapore, and Bangalore, and moved to the Shanghai office.

A second fund of NT$70 million was raised for investments in Taiwan, then in 2004, a third fund of US$30 million was raised to focus solely on investing in Greater China. In 2006, this was supplemented by a new sequence of funds called IP Cathay Fund 1, which closed at US$175 million and also targeted investments in greater China. Since the first closing in July 2006, this fund has made eight investments.

Though these are success cases, the civil servant mind-set has blind spots that entrepreneurs should keep in mind. For example, the civil service tendency to emphasize procedures will obscure tacit knowledge. In certain cases, following procedures strictly may not be the best option and often it is necessary to go beyond the procedures when they do not apply.

In addition, government VCs may not necessarily be profit driven and are susceptible to risk aversion. When faced with two options, one with a higher upside but higher associated expected risk and one with a lower upside but lower associated risk, government VCs may choose the latter, which may not yield the best overall outcome. Damien Lim of BioVeda Ventures explains, "As a money manager, I won't get fired buying IBM. If the stock performs well, it was because I chose good stocks, if the stock doesn't perform well, it is attributed to portfolio theory."

Roger Cressey, a terrorism consultant for NBC News, points out that retired officials have a short shelf life—that is, their influence lasts only a limited time after they leave office. He explains, "You have 18 to 24 months to translate your Rolodex into real services."[17]

Government funds often invest strategically for their nation's interest. For example, Cap Vista is the strategic venture investment arm of Singapore's Defence Science and Technology Agency, a statutory board under the Ministry of Defence. Its mission is to identify and execute strategic investments in early-stage high-tech companies to serve Singapore's defense initiatives. SITRA, a fund operating under the auspices of the Finnish Parliament since 1967 with operations funded with endowment capital and returns from capital investments, focuses on venture-capital investments in the health care, food and nutrition, and environmental area for Finland.

In terms of the returns, the magnitude of government funds appears to have a smaller correlation with success than the quality of due diligence that the outfit performs. Government funds sometimes succeed when they focus on an underfunded industry independent of region. Policy fails when the government tries to stimulate growth in geographic regions where there is little private-sector investment.

CASE IN POINT: In-Q-Tel

For example, In-Q-Tel is the strategic investment arm launched by the Central Intelligence Agency (CIA) in 1999 as a private, independent, not-for-profit organization. It helps deliver technology solutions to the Central Intelligence Agency and the broader U.S. Intelligence Community (IC) to further their missions. In-Q-Tel confers certain key benefits that help explain its success:

Corporate customer and investor. For start-ups, working with In-Q-Tel is like working with a corporate customer that is also an investor. During product development, In-Q-Tel portfolio customers work closely with CIA employees to learn the agency's requirements. The system pays off because a funded start-up can build what people need and want.

Rigorous due diligence. In-Q-Tel's screening process is more rigorous than that of most corporate customers. There is an incentive to make sure it works for corporate customers because commercial products are cheaper to upgrade than custom ones. In-Q-Tel's demanding technical testing process also increases the potential for additional sales. If the CIA buys a product, the FBI may follow suit.

Share leads with VCs. In-Q-Tel shares leads with about 80 VC firms, as well as investment banks, universities, and research labs. With a US$30 million a year budget, it's not in competition with anything in venture capital (smaller amount than its private sector co-investors, some of which like co-investing because of its thorough due diligence).

Corporate Venture Capitalists Corporate venturing first became popular in the 1980s and has recently regained popularity. Corporate venturing is also termed "direct investing" in portfolio companies by venture capital programs or subsidiaries of nonfinancial corporations. These investment vehicles seek qualified investment opportunities that are congruent with the parent company's strategic technology or that provide synergy or cost savings.

Most corporate VCs are loosely organized programs affiliated with existing business development operations; some are self-contained entities with a strategic charter and mission to make investments congruent with the parent's strategic mission. There are corporate venture firms that specialize in advising, consulting, and managing a corporation's venturing program. In certain cases, companies specially established a venture capital entity such as Applied Materials

Ventures or Koor Corporate Venture Capital; in others, venture investment may be conducted through a firm's business development unit as is the case with IBM and Bezeq. In either form, corporate venturing units benefit their parent companies by providing exposure to new technologies and a means to keep research and development spending under control. For certain corporate venture firms, the benefits of relationships forged are often not immediate, but are also manifested in acquisitions in the long term.

Differences Between Corporate VCs and Mainstream VCs   Corporate VCs generally differ from typical VCs on two fronts: First, corporate venturing tends to be performed with corporate strategic objectives in mind, while other venture investment vehicles tend to have investment return or financial objectives as their primary goal. Second, corporate venture programs usually invest their parent's capital while other venture investment vehicles invest outside capital. For example, Xilinx, the world's leading supplier of programmable logic solutions, launched its Asia Pacific Technology Fund, a US$75 million corporate venture capital fund focused on accelerating programmable systems innovation and development within the Asia Pacific technology market. Unlike traditional venture capitalists, Xilinx does not invest solely for financial return—it also needs to establish a strong strategic link to its core business, market, or technologies. Once a strategic link is established, the company analyzes all the same attributes that a typical venture capital firm would consider, including a sound business plan, solid management team, and a reasonable exit strategy.

CASE IN POINT: Semiconductor Corporate Venture Firms

Semiconductor firms, in particular, have established high-quality venture capital arms. Infineon Ventures is the venture subsidiary of Germany's semiconductor giant, Infineon Technologies. UMC Capital is the corporate venture arm of UMC, a leading semiconductor foundry based in Taiwan; it invests in innovative technology companies worldwide.[18]

Upon graduation from Wharton with a newly minted MBA, Andy Tang joined the corporate finance arm of CSFB in Palo Alto, California, in 2000 and worked on transactions for semiconductor and hardware systems companies. An opportunity to work in corporate venture capital came along when Infineon, a German-based semiconductor company, thought it would be easier to cover China from California than from Munich and came looking for someone with industry experience and a financial background who wanted to work with early-stage companies. Andy liked the broad charter as a corporate venture capital arm to invest throughout the hardware value chain at any stage was attractive, and he stayed with Infineon Ventures from 2001–2005. As a principal and member of the investment committee, he oversaw and managed investments in Broadbus, Imago Scientific, Zettacom, NuTool, and Corrent. Broadbus, which Infineon Ventures invested in when the portfolio company employed just two entrepreneurs, was an especially successful venture. It provided video-on-demand equipment and within three years acquired 10 major customers, including the biggest cable television providers in the United States. In July 2006, it was acquired by Motorola for US$186 million.

CASE IN POINT: IBM Venture Capital Group

San Mateo-based IBM Venture Capital Group has the mandate of "equity for value."[19] The corporate venture arm of IBM does not provide cash for equity, but it provides other valuable service to start-ups, including access to IBM's Rolodex file, if the technology is a fit for Big Blue—or more specifically for the needs of its big name customers.

IBM has made investments in both start-ups and locally based venture firms. Its last direct start-up investment was in Aduva, made at the end of 2001. But IBM is still very actively searching for new companies that can bring it strategic advantages. IBM has a broad scope of activities, but currently has particular interest in the enterprise software and storage sectors. Cash investments are possible if the investment is right, but according to Zippi Dekel, IBM's local investment chief, "We're looking for equity for value."

Technologies that can help make green data centers, as well as hardware and software for other energy-efficient applications, are also of particular interest for IBM, as well as for the utilities, computer storage firms, and other companies that it works with.

IBM acts as a mentor, working with venture capital companies and their portfolio firms to get the technologies ready for market. While it's not a direct financial relationship, there is a financial incentive for IBM, which hopes that these start-ups will become valuable suppliers for IBM's customers, who will want to integrate the new technology into IBM systems.

IBM's Venture Capital Group has had more than 1,400 venture-backed companies come through its operation over the last few years, and it works with over 120 venture capital firms around the world.

Drew Clark is the co-founder and director of strategy at IBM Venture Capital Group. "We're part of IBM's corporate staff, so we don't report to the CFO. We're not a financially driven or financially measured organization, but rather we're strategic."

The IBM Ventures mandate is to drive top-line growth to IBM, in terms of helping push strategic growth initiatives, rather than, for example, an equity arm, or something more conventional like a VC. IBM Ventures doesn't have a fund because it decided back in 2000 that there was plenty of capital in the market, and the real need seemed to be a company like IBM to help in the rest of the life cycle of a start-up.

Beyond the initial capital infusion, who's going to help that company get pulled into enterprise solutions? Who's going to help that company mature and grow into a great ISV (independent software vendor) or a participant in the IT ecosystem? And that kind of role falls to IBM Ventures. Its expertise is not around managing minority ownerships in small companies, but around markets and customers and deep technology.

It's a partnership with the VCs, rather than competition with VCs. Most would term IBM Ventures more of a venture technologist than a venture capitalist. IBM VC does pro bono advisory work for VC, where IBM Ventures gives venture partners value in return for early access to high-quality new partners for IBM, termed a "give to get" arrangement.

Over 30 percent of IBM VC's revenues come from partner channels. By working closely with VCs and their invested companies, IBM VC can access potentially great new partners and new technologies more effectively. There is alignment of interest to help the start-ups succeed, because when they succeed, IBM VC succeeds. IBM VC creates business for IBM and the start-up in a complementary arrangement, where IBM VC surrounds the technology with IBM's processes and business know-how and positions the tiny start-up in front of major customers.

Additional Value-Add   Generally, corporate VCs offer several advantages to their portfolio companies. In addition to credibility and respectability, corporate VCs may provide technological assistance, a clear and knowledgeable assessment of the market, and established contacts to enable market penetration and widespread distribution.

While, overall, the advantages to a start-up having a major corporate investor often outweigh any downside, teaming with a corporate partner is not necessarily for everyone; corporate objectives may differ significantly from those of entrepreneurs or traditional VCs. For example, a corporate VC might discourage acquisition interest from competitors or not sufficiently staff up to work with their portfolio companies as traditional VCs can. Financial gain is an important consideration for corporate investing, but more often the underlying reason for the investment is strategic. Corporate ventures also have a tendency to succumb to the tendency to look at things from their own corporate perspective, which is often at odds with the perspective of start-ups. A corporate VC may not be able to fully appreciate the disruptive innovation a start-up often epitomizes, being bogged down in the incumbent corporate mentality.

Definition of Success   Asked whether any of the three models shows a clear superiority, Bobby Chao replied, "It really depends on what the definition of 'success' is. Government-sponsored fund managers promote business for government's sake. If clearly the monetary return on investment is the goal, then the 'winner/entrepreneur' type of VC will likely succeed, especially in early-stage deals. The corporate finance type and the 'apprentice' with formal academic training may also score well in the bean-counting environment of late-stage deals.''

Barry Drayson of Nanoholdings, an early-stage venture fund focusing on nanotechnology, elaborates, "If the government-turned-VC model comes with university contacts and credibility with funding agencies, the VC can stay the course and succeed in a niche (such as nanotechnology); the Ex-CEO/Winner model is also infectious in motivating entrepreneurs. Hence, a hybrid model might work well."

Pitfalls to Avoid

Choosing a partner has pitfalls of its own:

- Forgetting that the devil is in the details, and the details are in the term sheet
- Getting blinded by the VC brand

PITFALL #1: Forgetting That the Devil Is in the Details, and the Details Are in the Term Sheet

Love it or hate it, a term sheet is a step toward the actual deal. An entrepreneur must think hard about VC contracts. These contracts have to address the differing interests of entrepreneurs and investors. To protect investors from the "take-the-money-and-run" syndrome, various terms have been introduced. Here are working definitions for the key features to be found in VC contracts:

Term	Definition
Nondisclosure*	Investor will retain confidential information as confidential. (Note: VCs typically will not sign nondisclosure agreements. This affords them protection if they like your ideas, but the downside for the entrepreneur is that there is a possibility for the VC to fund someone else to execute the business plan.)
Noncompete*	Investor will not compete for a certain period of time. (Note: These terms are seldom accepted by venture capitalists.)
Tag-along rights	Investor can sell shares when the entrepreneur, or anyone else, sells shares.

Pre-emptive rights	Investor can invest in additional rounds to maintain percentage ownership.
Registration rights	Investors can register their stock in the event the company goes public. This term is typically required by investors.
Royalty rights	Investors earn a percentage of revenues. This is a tricky condition that entrepreneurs should be wary of.
Dividend rights	Investors get a preferential dividend, sometimes cumulative, sometimes deferred.
Board rights	Investors have the right to appoint one or more members of the board.
Information rights	Investors have the right to get certain internal information, sometimes in a structured report with deadlines.
Liquidation rights	Investors get whatever they invested plus their promised return on the investment first before others. (Note: Protection is the name of the game. Mark Peter Davis of DFJ Gotham Ventures writes, ``The main reason (for liquidity preference is) incentive alignment. Liquidity preference ensures that the entrepreneurs are focused on realizing a big exit. Early-stage VCs invest in companies because they believe they can exit for several hundred million dollars or more. Without the liquidity preference, entrepreneurs may be tempted to pursue US$10M exits—seeking a US$5M personal payout before they realize the full potential of the company.[20]
	For further elaboration on liquidation preferences, please refer to http://wayofthevc-lp.easyurl.net on the book's companion site.
Anti-dilution protection	Investors have the right to maintain their share of ownership. In *full ratchet* protection, the first investors will receive a number of shares by applying the price of the second round. For instance, if in the first round, shares given to the first investor were at US$1.00 per share and in the second financing round, shares prices are US$0.50, with full ratchet protection, the investors can convert their shares at the US$0.50 price, thus increasing the number of shares they hold. If *weighted average* is used instead of full ratchet, the first round investors can adjust the option price based on sale price and number of shares sold by the company.

(continued)

Term	Definition
Co-sale rights	Investors have the right to sell shares in the same quantity and at the same price at which the founder or management is selling to a third party. Investors and founders will sell to the third party together.
Drag-along rights	Investors may be able to force other shareholders to sell shares to a buyer if more than a certain percentage of the shareholders agree.
First refusal rights	In the event of a sale of shares to a third party, preferred shareholders get a right to buy those shares on the same terms.
Price conversion	Investors can convert their holdings into equity at a set price, such as US$2/share.
Future price conversion	Investors can convert their holdings into equity at a price based on a future round, usually at a discount to that round (most popular = 10–15 percent discount to the VC round).
Interest payments	Investors get an annual interest payment, which is sometimes deferred. This can motivate the entrepreneur to create an exit event.
Warranties and representations	Entrepreneur is held liable for making any false statements.
Entrepreneur compensation rights	Typically done through board. Motivates entrepreneur to get an exit from shares, important when a lifestyle or empire builder entrepreneur may be present.
Special voting or consent rights	Investors have a veto on major undertakings, such as a new share offer, debt, or sale of the company.
Redemption rights	Investors can redeem (``buy back at the original purchase price plus an annual carrying cost'') the preferred stock. Investors sometimes seek redemption rights as a way of obtaining a return on their investment if the company does not go public or get acquired. Theoretically, one can come up with a situation where a fund is late in life, and it has a good company but no liquidity. In this event, it is useful to have an alternative to get liquidity, or to have some leverage to have some control on the situation. That being said, redemption rights are fairly benign. They look scary, but few VCs, if any, have ever actually used them. For further elaboration on redemption rights, please refer to http://wayofthevc-redempt.easyurl.net.

PITFALL #2: Getting Blinded by the VC Brand

Do your due diligence on the VC—do not be blinded by brand. Venture capitalists will help companies grow, but never forget that they plan to exit the investment with a profit for themselves. An early-stage investment may take 7–10 years to mature, while a later-stage investment many only take a few years, so the appetite for the investment life cycle must be congruent with the limited partnerships' appetite for liquidity. The venture investment is neither a short-term nor a liquid investment; it is investment that must be made with careful diligence and expertise. To anticipate and defuse potential tensions with a venture partner, entrepreneurs should check references and reputations of venture firms before engaging them. Establish clearly what management role the financiers expect to take. Invite outsiders with no ties to the company or the venture capitalists to sit on the board. For example, one of the most highly valued telecom start-ups in the United States, backed by more than US$272 million of venture-capital funding and reaching a valuation of more than US$1.5 billion, was ultimately sold to an industry behemoth for a disappointing price of less than US$100 million. It was widely believed that had the VCs had a longer time horizon, the company could have tackled its issues patiently instead of selling out.

Endnotes

1. Greg Cruey, "A Venture Capital Bubble in China," October 2007; retrieved from www.chinaventurenews.com/50226711/a_venture_capital_bubble_in_china.php, June 23, 2009.
2. Eric Janszen, "The Next Bubble: Priming the Markets for Tomorrow's Big Crash," *Harper's Magazine*, February 2008; retrieved from www.harpers.org/archive/2008/02/0081908, June 23, 2009.
3. Ernst and Young, "Global Venture Capital Insights and Trends Report," forthcoming, p. 3. Please write to the author to request the document.
4. Peter Knez, Vernon L. Smith, and Arlington W. Williams, "Individual Rationality, Market Rationality, and Value Estimation," *American Economic Review* 75, no. 2 (1995).
5. Paul A. Gompers and Josh Lerner, "What Drives Venture Capital Fundraising?" August 1998; retrieved from www.hbs.edu/research/facpubs/workingpapers/papers2/9899/99-079.pdf, June 23, 2009.
6. Jeff Cornwall, "Supply of Venture Capital Funds Is High," January 29, 2007; retrieved from www.drjeffcornwall.com/2007/01/supply-of-venture-capital-fund.html, June 23, 2009.

7. Samuel S. Kortum and Josh Lerner, *Does Venture Capital Spur Innovation?* (Washington, D.C.: National Bureau of Economic Research, 1998).

8. Paul A. Gompers and Josh Lerner, "The Future of the Venture Capital Cycle," November 23, 1999; retrieved from http://hbswk.hbs.edu/item/1165.html, June 23, 2009.

9. Holger M. Mueller and Roman Inderst, "Venture Capital Contracts and Market Structure," New York: Center for Economic Policy Research, CEPR Discussion Paper No. 3203, 2002.

10. He made this remark at a VC and entrepreneur summit I hosted at Knowledge Innovation Community, Shanghai, China, April 6, 2007.

11. Assuming that $700 million was used to buy out venture capitalists' share only, the estimated IRR of both venture capitalists can be estimated at 60 percent, for an estimated combined stake of 39 percent.

12. Eric Manlunas, "Why Venture Capital Still Matters: The Real Value of Venture Capital Investing," Vator News, February 12, 2009; retrieved from http://vator.tv/news/show/2009-02-11-why-venture-capital-still-matters.

13. Poh Kam Wong, "Innovated in Asia: Globalization's Next Tidal Wave," March 12, 2009; retrieved from http://connect-the-dots-singapore.blogspot.com/, June 23, 2009.

14. Nicholas Carlson, "How Not to Become a VC," May 30, 2008; retrieved from http://valleywag.com/394288/how-not-to-become-a-vc.

15. "Doll Capital Management," n.d., retrieved from www.dcm.com/index.php, June 23, 2009.

16. Brad Feld, "How to Become a Venture Capitalist," January 26, 2007; retrieved from www.askthevc.com/blog/archives/2007/01/how-to-become-a.php, June 23, 2009.

17. Tim Shorrock, "Former High-Ranking Bush Officials Enjoy War Profits," May 29, 2008; retrieved from http://americasprotector.blogspot.com/2008/09/former-high-ranking-bush-officials.html, June 23, 2009.

18. UMC Capital Corporation (Taiwan, Republic of China) is a major player in the global contract manufacturing industry, with operations in a wide variety of fields; see www.umc.com. SNG Networks, Inc. "UMC Capital Corporation: 2006 Contract Manufacturing Profile," SNG Networks, Inc., 2006.

19. David Ehrlich, "Startups Get Big Help from Big Blue," August 11, 2008; retrieved from http://media.cleantech.com/3217/startups-get-big-help-big-blue, June 23, 2009.

20. Mark Peter Davis, "Why Liquidity Preference Exists," July 23, 2008; retrieved from www.markpeterdavis.com/getventure/2008/07/preferred-sto-4.html, June 23, 2009.

3

Transitions in Partnership

A BRIDGE OVER TROUBLED WATERS

How VCs can get the entrepreneur out of (and occasionally into)
hot soup. . . .

The decision criteria used by venture capitalists in making investment decisions are widely debated and analyzed, with VCs often
proclaiming that they have the secret recipe. Anecdotal evidence
suggests that venture capitalists tend to screen investment proposals
rapidly and rely heavily on intuition, focusing on factors such as a
new venture's overall fit with their firm's lending guidelines, the
profitability of the industry targeted by the new venture, and the
source of the business proposal.

In a rapidly changing, intense venture investment environment,
cognitive biases and errors made by venture capitalists are unlikely to
be corrected for a number of reasons:

- The counterfactual (that is, what would have happened if a
  different investment decision had been made) is never considered and estimated.
- The reliability of feedback is variable.
- Outcomes are commonly delayed and not easily attributable to
  one particular action.
- Most important decisions are unique events (like IPOs and
  bankruptcy).

Less sophisticated VCs typically do not contemplate their cognitive biases and only ask three key questions: How much money do you want? What are you going to do with it? And how and when do I get my return?

What Star VCs Do: Winning Techniques

Unlike their lesser cousins, the star VCs my colleagues and I interviewed took a more complex and nuanced approach. They employed the following winning techniques to reduce cognitive biases:

- Be less confident in good times, more confident in bad times.
- Maximize chances in a lottery.
- Prioritize risk; invest cross-spectrum to reduce risks.
- Maximize exposure to successful entrepreneurs.
- Manage talent.
- Maintain strength in character.
- Network for success.

WINNING TECHNIQUE #1: Be Less Confident in Good Times, More Confident in Bad Times

"VC is an art (but not a black art). There is fundamentally no scientific rule," says one leading VC, who adds a dose of caution: "Investing in Internet start-ups (to me), is a black art, where the returns are arbitrary. An entrepreneur writes something [on a Web site], it may be cute but it is essentially an eyeballs game, and the replay of the Internet bust in 2000. The Chinese guys have not gone through the bust. After sensational start-ups like Baidu and Shenda, some entrepreneurs think their companies can walk on water. This also applies to the video and audio start-ups. A model which is successful in the U.S. does not mean that it will be successful in China. Political uncertainties like Tibet all contribute to market uncertainties."

Overconfidence VCs are prone to overconfidence. Professors Zacharakis and Shepherd studied 51 U.S. venture capitalists in 2000 by asking them to rate 50 potential ventures' success chances and their confidence in that assessment, both on seven-point Likert scales. The authors found that 96 percent of the participants had confidence levels greater than their accuracy rate and that this overconfidence reduced their decision accuracy. Additionally, the availability of more information did not lead to better-informed assessments by venture capitalists. Rather, more information resulted in higher levels of confidence and decreased accuracy, which suggests that cognitive overload might be to blame for overconfidence. As Guy Kawasaki cautions, "Management consulting [as a background for VCs] is bad because it leads you to believe that implementation is easy and insights are hard—when the opposite is true in start-ups."

The myth is that more information leads to better sensemaking. The truth is that more information only helps with some types of uncertainty, not others. More information can even increase uncertainty and reduce performance because the marginal value of additional data points keeps getting smaller, but the interconnections and complexities keep increasing. Under complex conditions, VCs need to manage uncertainty as much as to reduce it. Such sensemaking informs every move a top VC makes and pays off handsomely.

Accountability mechanisms improve the quality of their judgment and decision making. In venture capital investment decisions, venture capitalists may anticipate the objections of their partners, preempting their recommendations with self-criticism, and thus striving to maintain the social approval of their peers.[1] Although accountability pressures can be stressful, tiring, and annoying for individuals forced to justify their decisions, advance accountability mechanisms may improve the quality of their judgment and decision making. One managing partner of a venture firm described his firm's decision process: "Our approach is that you have to have a co-sponsor [internal to the firm]. So, you know, the deal doesn't get done unless you have at least one other person." Most firms we surveyed do not invest unless all, or nearly all, of the partners reach a consensus.

IPO Market Entrepreneurial drive, combined with venture investors' money and experience, plus access to the public markets, equals a tech revolution and a world-class industry. An IPO generally means that the founders can continue to run the companies they have painstakingly built, except with greater resources. (In contrast, an acquisition generally means that the founders move on, see projects they championed get axed, and watch old colleagues get fired.)[2] Robert Zhou explains that when the IPO market is in a cooling-down period, there are significant impacts on both venture capital and private equity funds. If the market continues to be weak, valuations will decrease. If the market remains slow, start-ups will face challenges in their capital-raising efforts. In overheated regions, underperforming VCs might be confronted with tougher challenges when they have to start raising their next fund.

CASE IN POINT: Blogging in China

iDT VC entered China in 2000 at the trough of the dot-com bust. During 2001–2003, the firm strategically increased its investment volume and invested in seven deals (totaling about US$20 million investment) in a downturn. The investments were well planned and the firm invested in good undervalued deals such as Linktone and E-ton. An investment space that iDT VC passed on was the nascent blogging space. In the second half of 2005, the Web 2.0 blog business model was generally perceived by VCs in China as an attractive market, following the success of the U.S. blogging sector.

BlogCN is one of China's largest blog sites. Established in November of 2002, BlogCN is the first free blog hosting service provider in China. It built the world's largest Chinese blog community, blog hosting service, and blog search engine from its base in Hangzhou, using its proprietary blog management software RABO. The Internet portal offers free blog space, but began to charge for value-added services, including mobile phone features, in 2005. BlogCN simultaneously introduced a virtual coin system to purchase such services. About 70–80 percent of its revenue comes from advertising.

China's other top blog site was Blog China. Both BlogCN and Blog China were valued at approximately US$30 million post money and raised US$10 million. Both were bankrolled by large coffers; Blog China was financed by four VCs Softbank Asia Infrastructure Fund (SAIF), Global Granite Venture Capital (GGVC), Bessemer Venture Partners (BVP), and Mobius Partners. BlogCN was also financed by four VCs, including IDG, DFJ, and GGVC (Granite Global Ventures) in late 2005, when the blogging still had no revenue model.

However, with prices soaring, BlogCN and Blog China have yet to articulate a sound business and revenue model. A planned IPO in NASDAQ was abandoned. In 2007, it seemed that the investment in the Chinese blog sites was proving to be a mistake. The valuation was too high and ventures had to go through a down round. Previously, the burn rate had drastically increased as the ventures jacked up their scale of operation and expanded to bring in manpower and changed management. As the realization of an overvaluation set in, the ventures scaled down operation and retrenched staff to cut down burn rate.

Most regrets resulted from acts of omission and not commission. For blogging, however, it appears that iDT VC was prudent to have come down on the side of omission.

Assume the Worst—Have a Plan B   When public offerings vanished during that earlier tech bust, Allegis Capital's Robert Ackerman reassessed his firm's game plan. "No one knew when the next IPO market was going to be," he says. "So we did our analysis: Let's assume there are no IPOs. That means starting with more conservative fundraising. Large funds only work when there's a robust public market and the potential for a huge payoff is greater, so raise small ones."

WINNING TECHNIQUE #2: Maximize Chances in a Lottery

The VC industry can also be compared to a lottery—VCs invest in many companies expecting to hit the jackpot on just one or two. Business as a whole actually works like that; for every success, there are many failures. The difference is that VCs are aware that they are in the lottery business, whereas entrepreneurs need to believe they can win with the ticket they have. Raj Kapoor, managing director at Mayfield, based in Menlo Park, California, says, "It's an extremely hit-driven business that's becoming more and more like the movie industry."

Doing Good Deals—Deal Filtering   Sean Dalton, general partner at Highland Capital, counsels a simple, head-down approach: "Do good deals. Focus on what you can control." Star VCs do not dismiss deals because other VCs have passed on them—a gem can be overlooked by one miner and found by another. In September 2005, two young Harvard undergraduates, Mark Zuckerberg and Eduardo Saveri, met with a senior associate at Battery Ventures of Waltham to pitch Facebook.[3] Zuckerberg struck some partners at the firm as a little too brash. In addition, Battery had already made an investment in an earlier social networking site, Friendster, which was foundering. No one was sure whether Facebook would appeal to anyone other than college students, its target. There were also turf issues with Battery's Silicon Valley office, which had invested in Friendster. "There was a question about whether we on the East Coast side were going to lead an investment with a sophomore in college who was considering a move to the West," says the senior associate. The firm eventually passed on the deal. However, Accel Partners subsequently invested US$12.7 million, and then the two students picked up US$27.5 million more from Greylock Partners. The result: Battery Ventures missed out on an online phenomenon worth up to US$6 billion and now known as Facebook. Similarly, John Doerr admitted in a National Venture Capital Association conference that one of his biggest regrets was not investing in VMware (due to its high valuation), which eventually turned out to a successful company.

How Do VCs Filter Deals?   Peter Thiel, investor in PayPal, Facebook, and Slide, and chairman of Founder's Fund, believes that the best predictor of start-up success is low CEO pay.[4] Thiel believes that in practice, if you can only ask one question, ask about the CEO's salary. The lower it is, the more likely the business is to succeed. The CEO's salary sets a cap for everyone else. If it is set at a high level, the start-up ends up burning a whole lot more money. But it reflects a larger point of whether the mission of the company is to build something new or just collect paychecks. Ideally, everybody should be working toward the same goal (and payday): the exit—which is aligned with the equity holders. VCs we interviewed suggested that if the CEO had quit a regular job to start the company, they would be highly skeptical if the CEO were to receive a higher paycheck in the start-up.

WINNING TECHNIQUE #3: Prioritize Risk; Invest Cross-Spectrum to Reduce Risks

Risks are gambles. A venture capitalist would need to calculate and decide the potential for losses and gains, given the possible outcomes and the likely probabilities. Following this overall assessment, the first question to ask is: Is the worst case tolerable? If not, abandon that plan. If the threat is manageable and the benefits are worthwhile, proceed to prioritize and reduce risk. The common fallacy is for venture capitalists to be overconfident in assessing failures and breakdowns and rush to identify the list of risks factors in order to quantify and prioritize them.

In decision making, the best venture capitalists follow a two-stage process. For example, for a software start-up launching a beta version of the product, the entrepreneur has sufficient information from the beta to scale up or abandon. To reduce risk, it is often not a good idea to compete with incumbent producers. Instead of contesting in Bangalore or Shanghai, the entrepreneur might be better off exploring the rural cities in ASEAN and second- and third-tier cities in China.

A VC firm's ability to cross the investment spectrum is a huge advantage (in terms of returns for VCs and ultimately for limited partners). In addition, venture firms improve the probability of success by creating synergies between companies they have invested in; for example, one company that has a great software product but inadequate distribution technology may be paired with another company in the venture portfolio that has better distribution technology.

Star VCs cultivate relationships that confer strategic value, that is, relationships that generate deals and then help the companies in which VCs have invested. The most successful VCs invest time to cultivate a broad set of relationships with later-stage private and public company executives and also relationships that help early-stage companies and source new deals. Zac Boon of McLean Watson adds, "There is a broad set of risks in every venture, but if you co-invest with the right set of venture guys (who can find good deals) and concentrate the bets, you significantly lower the attendant risks."

But to get "the right set of venture guys" together, you need to know who they are—and they have to know who you are, and trust you. That takes identifying and nurturing the right relationships.

WINNING TECHNIQUE #4: Maximize Exposure to Successful Entrepreneurs

Harvard Business School professor Josh Lerner found that successful entrepreneurs have a 34 percent chance of succeeding in the next venture-backed firm, compared with 23 percent for those who failed previously, and 22 percent for new venture-backed entrepreneurs.

VCs are generally more motivated by the person writing the business plan than by the business plan itself—they also perceive their portfolio company CEOs as partners who can weather a storm with them. For a VC, investing in quality and passionate management probably has the highest correlation with the success of the company. As VC legend Arthur Rock describes it, "Strategy is easy but day-to-day and month-to-month decision making is hard."[5]

The litmus test of a VC is the ability to maximize exposure to available deals in a market in a period of time. How many companies has the VC considered when making an investment decision? A VC who is exposed to a large number of deals can be a chooser and won't have to chase to participate in deals. The VC can then pick the best deal.

In a good market, an investment decision is not restricted by financial constraints.

The follow-on decision would then need to optimize the return to the fund. A top VC is one who knows the market and can organize the best team to yield the highest return on investment.

A star VC would also possess business intelligence to tap available funds for the work. According to Orna Berry of Gemini Israel Fund, "Venture capital is like shooting. A VC's goal is to hit the target as often as possible and counts the success by the number of targets hit. The VC industry is also analogous to baseball where the wins are in the form of home runs, with the portfolio also having a couple of base hits and misses."

WINNING TECHNIQUE #5: Manage Talent

Talent is the hardest aspect of a business to duplicate and arguably the most important driving factor behind the success of top VC firms. Many top VC firms have successful entrepreneurs as general partners. Vinod Khosla of Kleiner Perkins Caufield & Byers (KPCB) made his mark as an entrepreneur by co-founding Sun Microsystems. Jerry Colonna co-founded Flatiron in 1996. Ann Winblad of Hummer Winblad Venture Partners co-founded Open Systems (starting with US$500 in investment, she sold it for US$15 million after six years), and Heidi Roizen of Softbank Venture Capital co-founded T/Maker, which made software for the Apple Macintosh. These entrepreneurial experiences provided the VCs with the required vision and instincts to filter potential winning ideas from losing ones. Don

Valentine, founder of Sequoia Capital, was known for having a perfect sense of when a technology and a market were about to collide.

When *Forbes* polled VCs, investment bankers, and entrepreneurs to identify the best VCs in the industry, it also found that top VCs scored highest in industry knowledge, involvement in the company (recruiting, support during crisis), openness to new ideas, fairness in negotiation, and honesty. Other characteristic traits of top VCs:

- John Doerr: An excellent judge of character
  "I never invest in someone who says they're going to do something; I invest in people who say they're already doing something and just want funding."[6]
- Irwin Federman and Heidi Roizen: Analytical, sharp and observant
  "Even if he doesn't fund you, you would have learned volumes about your company, your business, and yourself."
  "Listen to her go through a set of problems or evaluate an opportunity, and she's razor sharp."
- Vinod Khosla: Competitive, strategic thinker; relentless
  "He's so competitive that when you walk out with him to the parking lot, he tries to beat you to the car."
  "He really helped me and the company to think about things in a non-conventional way."
  "He pushed us to think differently about strategy and to be very aggressive and innovative."
  "I was pretty excited about the role, but then the phone rings at home at 7 pm and it's Vinod telling me he's got a great opportunity for me. . . . He made up his mind early on. . . . He was relentless over four months."[7]

International mobility of talent is high, and top VCs know how to restrict damages caused by staff attrition. As Soo Boon Koh of iGlobe explains, "Due to the cyclical nature of the VC industry, not many VCs are going to stick around during this prolonged period of harsh times. Some VC partners may leave the VC industries to become entrepreneurs, or some of them may go into teaching. This movement is positive if you can continue to maintain relationships with departing VC partners, as a few years later, they may be back to the VC industry again, hopefully much wiser." This would result in choice bracketing—the departing VC may narrow the time horizon, dividing the time into short-term considerations (before departure), and long-term considerations (after departure). The partner might also time a move so as to receive the short-term gains right before departure (hyperbolic discounting), knowing that the long-term potential losses wouldn't be felt until later in the future.

Portfolio companies of venture firms also experience shortages of talent. In a study of the largest VC firms in Ireland, the most serious internal challenge facing venture-backed companies is the availability of experienced international sales executives, highlighted by over half the respondents (55 percent), followed by a lack of qualified senior management in general (40 percent). And lack of an experienced management team is the main reason VC applications are turned away. VC investors continue to look at the people rather than the idea.

WINNING TECHNIQUE #6: Maintain Strength in Character

Strength of character is another desirable trait. Soo Boon Koh was a board member of GRIC Inc. In March 1997, Hong Chen (then CEO) was asked by his Board to get a first-tier investment banker (no longer around) to assist in raising additional funds from U.S.-based strategic corporate investors after Singapore Telecom has made their pre-IPO investment in GRIC. In the nine months following, the company was not able to raise money. In December 1997, Koh decided to work with the CEO to change the company's CFO and investment banker. Within a span of a week, they fired the investment banker and successfully recruited Joe Zaelit as the new CFO.

Koh pulled out her Rolodex file and found Asian and European investors to complete a US$24 million pre-IPO funding.

WINNING TECHNIQUE #7: Network for Success

A wide-spanning network is another major determinant in the success of top VC firms. A recent study has shown that the better networked a VC firm is, the better investment performance it tends to produce.[8] Top-tier venture capitalist firms often build on their reputation to create quality relationships that enjoy more influential network positions than others. Often, their more influential positions have led them to enjoy benefits including investment opportunities and access to crucial information.

VCs typically have outgoing personalities and are not introverted. The more connections VCs make, the more networks they belong to. Tim Draper highlights that one of the most common mistakes that VCs can make is that they don't build as big a network as they possibly can. They must not only be able to judge numbers but also people. A network is also critical for conducting reference checks. Lousy management can kill good technology. Lousy technology can be saved by good management.

Choose the Right Network   A network relevant to the firm's needs optimizes value. If the focus of the fund is technology, it would make sense for the VC to network with the right technology sector. The second differentiator is the level of network. Might the VC be able to access the CEO level to find out more information, or only the sales division?

The types of working experience matter in generating dealflow and other areas of a VC's work. For example, if the VC has worked at a bank, his former clients at the bank would have provided him the industrial knowledge and network and some of them could be his potential portfolio companies. Wise VCs put in effort to expand their networks. For Lin Hong Wong, having been director of electronics at the Economic Development Board of Singapore (EDB), he formed his initial network there, forging deep ties with Singapore manufacturing companies, both foreign-based and local. He knew almost every company in the electronics and supporting industries. This made it easier for him to find someone to provide information on industry and technology developments and for reference checks on entrepreneurs. "Company CEOs remember EDB officers; they are appreciative of the support they received from EDB." Wong's subsequent experience as a CEO of manufacturing companies gave him operational and senior executive experience, including setting up operations from scratch in Singapore. His wealth of past experience proved valuable in his work as a VC.

Skilled performance in making the right judgment (especially about people) depends on tacit knowledge and intuition. Tacit knowledge is difficult to identify or even specify and teach. It is a sense of typicality or anomaly and requires perception skills, pattern recognition, and mental models.

Networking with other VCs is also important. A VC who has not forged a strong network with other VCs will have limited opportunity for syndication, which can often lead to better deals with more effective due diligence. For example, Walden International prefers to work with one or two specific VCs, usually by association of friends and former colleagues. Syndication often confers benefits such as portfolio diversification, reduction of risk, and decreased workload by getting others involved in due diligence and the reduction of information asymmetry. Dixon Doll adds that he picks people rather than firms when he syndicates. He picks people he knows and has worked with in the past—people he trusts—which helps him better understand how they think and behave. "I look for people who do not panic at the first sign of trouble and work very hard to fix a problem. People with a good reputation and plenty of capital from first funds to support the deals." He asks himself, "If the deal was successful, would syndicate partners be viewed favorably if the company were to do an IPO?"

Bing Gordon of Kleiner Perkins elaborates, "It is easier to work with people you know and trust. In a great transaction, both parties can share a beer two years later and agree that it was the right thing to do at the time, and they hope to work together in the future. The wonderful thing about Tech and Moore's Law is that many businesses can have win-win relationships, because of the miracle of constantly improving price-performance. 'Do they have resources? Do I trust them?' I always ask myself if this is a person I would pay to take to dinner. Because in the end, that's what you do."

Gordon adds, "Ultimately, the best way to network is to do successful projects together. I am not a believer in getting to know people over lunch. I have my own short list of company makers I'd love to work with. There are entrepreneurs and investors on the list, and I try to stay in touch with them. And I try to meet their best business friends, as well."

Networks via Spanning Ties   Professor Toby Stuart of Harvard Business school found that the venture capital world, like personal networks, is connected through spanning ties.[9] In addition to person-to-person social networks, firm-to-firm networks are vital in both contexts. Stuart and his colleagues found that about two-thirds of venture capital financing rounds involve syndicates of investors rather than single firms. And most young companies are very narrow in terms of the scope of their internal activities, which means that they need to partner other companies to bring their product to market. These syndicates and partnerships weave together firm-to-firm networks.

In the case of venture capital, spanning ties enable investors with fixed locations and industry expertise to learn of opportunities outside their geographic and industry domains.

Firms with broad, far-reaching networks are often more comfortable investing in a start-up from a distance because they have reliable local partners to advise and monitor the new venture. These ties are more likely to form between VC firms in the context of certain events, such as a hot IPO market. "A market bubble can effectively rewire some of the links in the network," says Stuart. "That sort of heated environment creates a rush of investment activity that increases the number of participants hoping to quickly take a company public. It results in some unlikely bedfellows in the syndicate network."

Another factor that can reconfigure a network is risk, Stuart adds. "The general reluctance in doing business with strangers revolves around trust," he says. "You don't know how to assess their competence and don't have a sense of how to read them." Evil companions bring more hurt than profit.

However, spanning ties are more likely to form between the lead venture capital firm and distant investors as the size of the syndicate grows, thus decreasing the risk associated with each organization's investment. The lead VC also perceives less risk in forming a relationship with a distant syndicate partner when seeking investment at a later stage of a company's financing, or when located near the start-up in question, or when holding specialized knowledge of the start-up's industry.

A Second Opinion in Early Stage   Under these low-risk circumstances, a firm starts small by engaging partners that look likely to be useful to work with in the future. "The next time around, that entity is part of their working set," Josh Lerner from HBS argues. He adds that an important rationale for venture investment syndication is that syndication can provide a valuable second opinion that helps to improve the quality of project selection. Venture capitalists tend to choose experienced venture capitalists to syndicate investment in the early stages of the enterprise when information asymmetry is the greatest. Venture capitalists are less selective in their syndicated partners as the enterprise progresses toward later stages. Foreign VCs in unfamiliar territory are also more likely to syndicate to mitigate risk.[10] Hans Tung typically syndicates by geography and by experience. However, the entrepreneurs are often the ones who decide who are in the syndicate. "It doesn't make sense for a venture fund to underwrite all the risk associated with a start-up. That's not efficient deployment of capital nor optimizes a portfolio." Tung has often seen "five or six VCs, sometimes more, circling around a deal at the same time. Sometimes, the entrepreneurs would choose two VCs—based on geography, industry experiences vs. brand, or personality fit of the VCs involved—to share a deal. Other times, one VC would do Series A, and other VCs would continue to follow the company's progress, and try to do Series B."

Build on Strengths   Raphael "Raffi" Amit, Wharton's Robert B. Goergen Professor of Entrepreneurship, believes that VCs syndicate because each one has different skills and information, so each can add value to an investment in different ways. "What we found is that syndication pays off—if you do it to add value," Amit says. "But if you do it to help select companies, it's not a good idea." When investments are obvious winners, venture capitalists don't need second opinions, nor would they want to share their returns. Likewise, when investments are obvious duds, they can reject them without consulting colleagues. It's the ones with unclear prospects that induce a venture capitalist to seek out a colleague's review. Thus, they end up sharing the investment by syndicating.

What Entrepreneurs Should Do: Commandments to Follow

When approaching potential VC partners, entrepreneurs need to keep several things in mind.

- Focus on the fundamentals.
- Reduce technical and market uncertainty.
- Remember that money is blood.
- Separate price and value: price is what you pay, value is what you get.

COMMANDMENT #1: Focus on the Fundamentals

Figure 3.1 outlines the fundamentals. The most essential step when approaching venture capitalists is to put together a founding team they will find attractive. VCs use simple pattern-matching to classify teams into two buckets. A founding team is deemed "investable" if it includes either of these two elements:

- One or more seasoned executives from successful or fashionable companies (such as Google). VCs like to see people with previous management experience who can execute and achieve the critical milestones to the next stage of funding.
- One or more entrepreneurs whose track record includes at least one past hit (an earlier entrepreneurial success). VCs like to work with people who have been high-achievers in the corporate setting or in running a start-up. In the absence of work experience, academic qualifications can be used as a proxy to gauge a prospect's attitude toward quality of work. This is, however, frequently not sufficient.

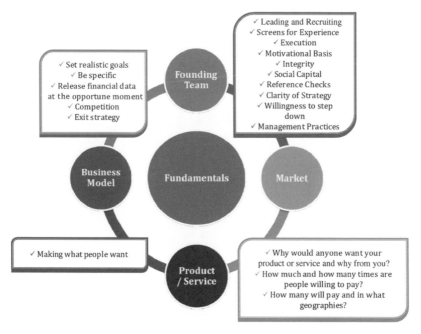

Figure 3.1 The Fundamentals

Key pillars of senior management include the founding CEO who can lead the team and a C-level management team (CFO, CTO and CMO). Dixon Doll, co-founder of DCM, pays a lot of attention to "both solid operational experience and academic track records—people who stood out in academic performance and also bring deep sector expertise that they can apply in the firm."

Zac Boon of McLean Watson is of the personal opinion that you cannot teach someone to be an entrepreneur. He adds, "You can help them by adding clarity to their vision and share your experience in the entrepreneurial journey, but if they didn't have you, a real entrepreneur will still find his or her own way, perhaps it will just take a little longer to get there. One of the greatest challenges is to identify these *real* entrepreneurs. Ultimately, it boils down to them [the entrepreneur]. If you find a capable leader whose team is (almost) willing to die for, place a bet on that entrepreneur. All things being equal, a lesser product with superior management will almost always win over a more superior product with inferior management. Finding a strong and resilient entrepreneur with a loyal team of people to address a large opportunity and compete in the marketplace is extremely rare."

The team should be committed to building a company, passionate, accomplished, have a history of working well together, and have a good set of references. Most VCs will look at management capability, trustworthiness of the management team, and (most important) passion. Charles River Ventures places a high premium on the team, its authenticity and empathy for the user experience. Do the founders speak the language of their customers? Do they empathize with their customers' pain? Do they feel passion for their users? The entrepreneur should assess the sum of the collective abilities and attributes of the members of the management team before pitching to a venture capitalist.

Leading and Recruiting Attracting talent to the venture is imperative for the venture to be able to grow into a viable business. In a start-up, talent would frequently include both managerial and creative types. Top CEOs we interviewed created an exciting work environment and motivated their people to work hard and long hours (often voluntarily)—this in turn built a positive reputation in the local community. Another way is to be nimble in recruiting. This means responding quickly to interviewees and being more flexible in assessing the fit of the candidates. Working in a start-up has several benefits: the breath of exposure, the flexible work environment created by relatively flat operating structures, and the possibility of acquiring an equity stake as part of the compensation package.[11]

The most important lesson that Vincent Tai, founder and CEO of RDA Micro, learned was in building the right team. Choosing China was the right market. His team has good technical ability, excellent teamwork, and, what is most important, consistently high performance. He attributes that to treating each employee fairly. Apart from the typical stock options in a start-up and giving each employee an equitable return, he strives to expand the potential of each employee, quoting the maxim, "The mind is a terrible thing to waste." He trusts his employees even though they make mistakes. Rather than firing an employee who has made a mistake, he prefers to sit down together and ask why it happened and what lessons can be learned from the experience.

Screens for Experience   The entrepreneur has to know the industry very well. If an entrepreneur cannot tell a VC a lot more than what the VC already knows about the industry, it is a warning signal. A star VC that we interviewed visited 200 cement factories to do the due diligence for one cement deal. He shares with us a simple gimmick that he employs to test the industry knowledge of the entrepreneur: He will ask the entrepreneur to teach him the industry. Using these inputs, he will then ask a competitor in the same space. If the entrepreneur can explain things better than the competitor, that's a good sign.

Here are the two most important questions that VCs ask to screen for experience:

- Please think of the most significant accomplishment in your career. What can you tell me about it?
- What roles have you played in past organizations?

VCs look for consistent answers from the entrepreneur. If they sense deviations, exaggerations, and attempts to snake around in the answers, it indicates a red flag. For example, if an entrepreneur claims to have been the vice president of sales who increased sales from US$1 million to US$5 million, the VC would validate the numbers to see if the scale is correct and talk with former colleagues and supervisors to find out what role the entrepreneur actually played in the increase—if any.

Execution   Having a high execution speed would allow the team to accelerate the process of feedback and learning. This, in turn, creates a virtuous user feedback cycle as users are encouraged by the rapid response to feedback. The key to the success of Asian Food Channel (AFC) was quick feedback. Hian Goh, managing director of AFC, showed some content (of what was to evolve into AFC) to five carriers. Three signed on the spot immediately. This gave him the resources to fine-tune the idea, which led to a successful VC funding. Anil Kumar Murthy, a civil-servant-turned-entrepreneur, spotted a pain-point of INSEAD students in finding housing in Singapore, so he sent a mass e-mail to provide one-stop-shop residence for INSEAD freshmen. He received 100 e-mails almost immediately and decided to start his business.

Most people think that money (or the lack of it) is the Achilles heel of entrepreneurs, but counterintuitive as it may seem, most often the real problem is the execution of good ideas. China has numerous self-made entrepreneurs who started with little money but bootstrapped themselves to prosperity. The start-up needn't pay huge wages nor hire many workers—the average start-up in Silicon Valley has only seven employees. Leonard Lin of Tyler Projects adds that most typical VCs expect the entrepreneurs to ask "What is the minimal revenue I need to generate for you to invest?" A top-quartile VC, Giza Ventures, explains that "this is an irrelevant question. I focus on the value of team."

Time is of the essence in the success of a start-up, as start-ups have a slim head start vis-à-vis larger incumbent firms. Venture capitalists will look at the speed of execution of the management team. A swift and decisive team with high execution speed will constantly learn, incorporate feedback, and create a virtuous user feedback cycle. One way of testing a team's execution speed and reliability is to give reasonable deadlines to execute suggestions on improvement of an idea and observing if the entrepreneurs keep to the deadlines. If results are not produced by the deadline when the management team has promised to deliver, it signals a red flag. VCs glean insights into entrepreneurs' ability to execute by assessing their willingness to make a promise and their ability to keep to the promise. When entrepreneurs agree too readily to suggestions by the VCs, it often signals that they have no focus. Before funding a business venture, venture capitalists will scrutinize the team's execution ability and road map, as it demonstrates their serious intention to start the company irrespective of VC funding.

Motivational Basis   In assessing whether entrepreneurs had the right motivational basis, our star VCs stressed that it was important to ask probing questions and to pay attention to detail.

- Top VCs ask the entrepreneur, "Tell me about a time when you really felt motivated, totally committed to a task?"
- When VCs visit the office or go for a site visit, do they feel the energy of the team? Are the employees working or surfing the Web? Is there a sense of organized hurry?
- Top VCs look out for tell-tale signs. Is the office spic and span? Organizational and administrative messiness and haphazard processes are red flags. It is difficult for entrepreneurs to dress up processes.

Integrity   Kathy Xu, founder of Shanghai's Capital Today Group, stresses, "We only give them [the entrepreneurs] money if they are trustworthy and have management integrity. We only take a minority share; the founder has a majority shareholding. Since we have handed over money and only have minority shareholding, we have to trust the entrepreneurs." It is useful to ask the seemingly innocuous question, "What do you think most entrepreneurs feel about hiding a problem from venture capitalists?" This actually leads entrepreneurs to reveal their own thoughts without realizing they are doing so. Most of the time, questions on integrity are asked with the objective of getting entrepreneurs to talk about their own personal agenda without involving the company.

Social Capital.   Social capital is the resources available in and through the team's shared network and the team members' own networks. These determine the size of the pool of people who will be willing to do the entrepreneur a favor. In fast-emerging markets like China, knowing the right people *(guanxi)* and being tapped in to the ecosystem will allow you to start a business there a lot faster and more effectively than if you were coming in as an unknown outsider.

CASE STUDY: Sakae Sushi, Douglas Foo

Douglas Foo. founder of Singapore's largest sushi chain, says, ''The human race is very interesting. With the globalization plus Internet, everybody knows everybody. When this is applied to business, this is very important. When I was studying in RMIT, I networked with people, and collected name cards. I attended conferences, talked to people, and got to know them. Academics only learn the foundation of knowledge. The application of knowledge is a whole new paradigm shift. By networking, (an entrepreneur) can understand what people do and how people see things in different perspectives. For example if (entrepreneurs) go to other cities and operate in Beijing rule, it will not work. There are different structures. (An entrepreneur) has to talk to different people there. It requires building a network there. Local network is more important than country network. Entering Sichuan was easiest compared to Shanghai and Beijing primarily because we know people there (even though they were not as close). Building a relationship is helpful and useful (for Sakae Sushi) in entering Sichuan.''

Reference Checks   Venture capitalists check references as part of the extensive due diligence they conduct on the management team. They test the company's services as a client, talk to customers to enquire about their experiences with the company and the management team, and call employees to find out about their perspectives on the management team, pursuing the maxim, ''The best predictor of future behavior is past behavior.'' VCs typically find out from people independently about the entrepreneur's track record. If ever an e-mail sent to the company requesting a reference gets rejected or ignored, or a reply such as ''call me and let's talk'' comes back, a potential red flag is raised. What is unsaid is often as important as what is said.

Focused Strategy   One of the best ways to get the most from your energy is to focus it. Robin Li, founder of Baidu, comments, ''An IQ of 150 becomes 75 when you try to do two things at once.'' Venture capitalists assess the focus and clarity of the entrepreneur's strategy and focus. ''The best answer (from an entrepreneur to most questions) is a no." Although entrepreneurship is never predictable even with the best-laid plans, there is a need for the entrepreneur to remain focused as the journey is fraught with distractions.

Willingness to Step Down   It may be cruel, but venture capitalists typically prefer founders who are willing to step aside when they have outlived their usefulness or when they are not the best for the job. VCs frequently bring in professional management to assist the founder. An ideal CEO would periodically ask the VC, "Am I still the best CEO for the job? If one day when I am not as good anymore, be honest about it and I will resign. It would be best if it is done in private, so that my credibility is still intact."

Management Practices   Entrepreneurs expanding into unfamiliar territory should also be mindful of the differences in management style between their home geography and the new one. For example, there is the dichotomy of management style between Asia and the West. Americans believe in results—the bottom line—and it does not matter if people are present at the workplace as long as they produce the desired results. In the Asian context, however, traits such as hard work and effort are highly valued and a colleague who is perceived as idling might be ostracized despite constantly high productivity.

In the West, the common belief is that expansion entails delegation and empowerment. Innovation, creativity, and ideas are what drive the workplace in the Western world. These corporate values can be easily observed in American companies like Google, IDEO, or Apple. In Asia, empowerment can lead to fragmented cliques as employees often form their own fiefdoms. Structure and hierarchy are usually at the core of the business in modern Asian companies. In general, innovation and creativity exist to a much lesser degree in Asia.

Cai Yong Cheng, general manager of a venture-backed logistics company, laments that foreign Western management often do not have a clear understanding of how the Chinese do business. "Foreigners probe every chain in the business (which is perhaps what they should do). However, they are indiscreet and not tactful." He cites the example where the foreign CEO probed into the accounts of a factory operator and upon detecting a fraud, he announced, "Chinese are cheats." The factory management, including the whole operations staff, resigned. The CEO found it hard to replace these workers because he lacked institutional knowledge and also faced a shortage of skilled people in the logistics industry. As a result of the disruption to operations, the company lost US$1 billion. "The key is people. Talk to them discreetly, personally, and find out what motivates them. This should include all ranks of the value employee chain (including the driver). After ascertaining the information, you need to be decisive in firing and incentivizing the right way. However, fire when necessary only after you have transferred the know-how."

Market   The opportunity to build a company starts with the attractiveness of the market opportunity. The most important metrics in determining the attractiveness of a market are its size and growth rate. Other key parameters, which may vary from sector and geography, include the industry structure, barriers to entry, customer switching costs, competitive landscape, and behavior of incumbents. Small markets seldom deliver the opportunity to build big companies.

VCs often ask whether the addressable market is a big market.

- If the entrepreneur is off target in a big market, the venture might still be successful.
- However, if the entrepreneur is off target in a small market, the prospect of survival is slim.

Another key question is, What is the adoption rate in the market? For example, for IT start-ups, how much will shift to the Internet? In the early days of the Internet, it was unclear whether consumers would buy items such as property, automobiles, and luxury items online, but start-ups, encouraged by the success of Amazon.com, fervently set up me-too sites for other product categories and encountered various issues with consumer adoption. Consumer behavior is hard to predict. Another example is of Web surfers' rapid adoption of Firefox, despite the availability of Internet Explorer on almost all Microsoft Windows PCs.

Union Square Ventures looks for start-ups that have the potential to change the structure of markets. Charles River Ventures advises start-ups to imagine that VCs are the most cynical financier possible and the one and only thing that matters to them is delivering economic returns to the LPs.

David Weiden of Khosla Ventures looks to disrupt large existing markets—that is, breaking monopolies or finding a billion-dollar market (instead of a million-dollar market) with a credible path to grow. Following that, he then assesses whether significant technology or business model innovation has the potential for disruption, either by contrarian approaches to existing markets or by a protected technology or other sustainable advantage.

Jeff Chi from Vickers VC cautions, "Look for markets with price-insensitive customers." He has realized that customers can be very price sensitive. A retail expert in China told Jeff that IKEA did a favor to China. When IKEA first opened its outlet in China, people were excited, rushing off with their catalogues and pictures of the furniture. Then they went back to their hometowns and provided their local carpenters with the picture to build the furniture with the exact design but at a cheaper rate. VCs like markets where people are not that price sensitive. These would be areas like education or health and wellness where quality is essential. Media are also attractive because when customers get more affluent, advertisements increase to encourage spending. In the most extreme case, VCs are looking for businesses that serve the entire world population and whose customers are completely price insensitive.

Before you consult a VC, ask yourself, Why would anyone want your service or product—and why would they want it from you?

People have no hesitation paying to fill a need—when it is raining, for instance, people will not take a bus but readily pay for a taxi. The trick is to develop the acumen to identify a need. More important, identify the difference between a need and a nice-to-have. Better still if the product or service fulfills a need *and* creates pleasure. Xu Ning Wang, CEO of Joyoung Group, one of China's largest distributors of household electrical appliances, says the key is to focus on what you are good at and to be laser clear about your areas of superiority—and channel resources to that area. In areas where you are not so good, collaborate, form a partnership, or build on what is out there in the industry. Knowing what not to do is as important as knowing what to do.

The best answer (among our entrepreneur interviewees) to the "Why You?" question comes from Dr. Xiucai Liu, CEO of Cathay Biotech, a pharmaceutical company with a long-chain dibasic acids production technology. Cathay Biotech raised US$78 million in Series A and B funding in 2006. Dr. Liu, a former tenured professor, has taught at Yale, Columbia, and Stanford, and at every place he has guided 10–15 Ph.D. students. Under the stringent graduation requirements he imposed, every Ph.D. candidate had to produce a significant breakthrough in technology. It was a simple matter for him to accumulate the breakthroughs to develop the building blocks of a credible company with high barriers to entry. Two (often deceptively simple) questions that the entrepreneur has to ask in the later stages of company building:

- Do I see this company listed in NASDAQ?
- Can I make improvements in this company for shareholder value?

Another key marketing question is, How much and how many times is a customer willing to pay?

The answer lies in the value the company or service delivers and whether it is sufficient to attract repeat customers. The corollary to that is that building a company is eventually *building a brand*. Building a brand is more long-lasting than building a company. William Kupper, president and publisher of *Business Week*, puts it succinctly: a brand is a promise and a promise is emotional. The only thing that doesn't depreciate in the long term for a company is the brand. This is particularly true in brand-conscious Asia, where entrepreneurs ought to leverage the value consumers place on brands.

Related to how much and how often, ask how many will pay and in what geographies?

Many entrepreneurs fail to think globally: two people created Skype; why not two Singaporeans? The interview in the sidebar with the co-founder of Skype, Toivo Annus, illustrates some of the challenges.

Interview with Skype's Co-Founder

Toivo Annus was the co-founder of communication software company Skype, where he built and led a world-class engineering organization. He co-founded Ambient Sound Investments together with three other Estonian Skype co-founders to continue joint partnership after Skype's sale to eBay, to invest and to manage assets together. Toivo has a key role in ASI's technology investments both in analysis and post-investment management. He has extensive experience with emerging technologies and maintains a very broad as well as deep understanding of the tech sector. Toivo is a MBA/CS graduate from Tallinn Technical University.

Q: What is your background?

Toivo: When I left Skype at the end of 2005, I devoted a significant time to build Ambient Sound Investments. We are a private equity partnership of four founders, investing our own assets. We have not taken outside money and so have unusual amounts of freedom and flexibility. Unlike standard VC funds we are not accountable to LPs in terms of scope of investments. We do invest into seed-stage technology projects including ICT, cleantech and biomedical sciences. It is a diversified portfolio.

We have been doing this for two or three years. We have an operational team of about 10 people overlooking investments, managed by Tauno Tats and Margus Uudam. By mid-2009, we have about 30 investments. Our typical amount of investment is about half a million to two and a half million. We do not focus on specific industries—as said and visible from portfolio—we are rather flexible.

Q: How did you come up with the name Skype?

Toivo: The name was originally "Skyper," and we changed it around 2003 due to finding a company providing pager service under a similar brand. It had to do with telecommunications (hence the reference to "sky") and the domain name was available. Other than that, there is no specific story how the name came about.

Q: So are you investing across Asia or globally?

Toivo: We have 30 investments in total, about 3 (10 percent) in the United States, 4 in Asia (10 percent), and rest of it is evenly split between Western Europe and Eastern Europe (latter would be our home region).

Q: What is your size of investments?

Toivo: Our average investment is US$500,000, larger ones are up to US$2.5 million, smaller ones (early stage—pre-revenue) are around US$10,000–20,000. We separate the companies stagewise, for example, Pre-revenue stage.

Q: Is there high-tech in Asia?

Toivo: There are very many interesting technology companies in Asia.

Q: How do you explain the success of Skype compared to other companies?

Toivo: There were a number of VoIP start-ups, but they were all based on the standard protocols, which were developed by technology corporations for large enterprise-class customers that naturally wanted to control the information and users. We realized that consumers needed a different solution; they needed a username and the ability to pass firewall, a solution that just works. And that's what we in Skype could offer over our competitors. We wanted to make Skype so simple that even soccer moms could use it, we were targeting the consumer segment. I think we were successful because we focused on that segment without getting distracted and we were fanatical in pushing the end-user simplicity.

Q: What did you look for (technology, and so on) when looking for an acquirer?

Toivo: Financial viability for sure. And eBay was a good choice because of their success and style when acquiring PayPal. Skype also had a technology platform which could complement eBay, whereas other interested companies had their own communication platforms where integration would not have been easy. (Google Talk, MSN, and so on.)

Q: How did it feel to get the check from eBay?

Toivo: Literally, I was working on a Friday evening and the Skype CFO wrote in Skype chat and told us to check our bank accounts and it was there!

Q: Do you think it was right for eBay to buy Skype?

Toivo: Now this depends on who you ask—the amount of answers and opinions are endless. There are many measurements—financial markets were one of the indicators: after the announcement to acquire Skype, eBay's value dropped by US$1 billion. Another view would be that by acquisition, eBay blocked several scenarios (Skype growing independently or being sold partially or fully to someone else) where the outcome maybe was in the end very favorable to eBay versus some of the alternative scenarios.

Q: Were they paying for technology or user base? What were they looking for?

Toivo: Skype was one of the fastest-growing start-ups, much like early successes like PayPal. The revenue growth and potential was a huge attractive factor for Skype. eBay was mostly interested in fast-growing user base.

Q: How do you see the success of the Skype phone?

Toivo: On desktop computers, Skype's value proposition was unique—you could call another user for free and also hassle-free. That was virtually unexisting combination, for regular consumers just having the ability to make PC-PC calls was unheard of. Now on the phones, the ability to call other phone owners is virtually available for everyone, there are thousands of competing companies both global and local. I think Skype will have a very hard time breaking into the handheld market, and the user intake will be far from quick.

Q: Any advice for entrepreneurs when working with VCs?

Toivo: Entrepreneurs should do their due diligence, read a lot of materials, and understand the terms well and how to prepare the presentation and how to find the right VCs.

Q: Skype started in a very small country, so how did you overcome the initial difficulties?

Toivo: We were an international team from the start and that helped a lot. I think that there were lot of coincidental factors that helped Skype as a team to grow and become successful and I don't necessarily see a repeatable pattern of behavior. For example, we had excellent market opportunity, we had excellent experience in building similar technology before (real-time massive data transfers in P2P network between consumer endpoints), we had a very good international team that we were able to extend even further, and as a team, we had clear focus on core features so we spent time efficiently. On all key positions, we were able to put in extra long hours; we had basic financial backing that allowed us to take risk, yet all of us were hungry to go the extra mile for more, and we had the global international market in mind from the start.

Q: Why did Media Ring, a company that also does voice over IP, lose out to Skype?

Toivo: They lost out in number of users and revenue projects.

Q: What's the next big thing?

Toivo: I am also constantly looking for the answer. Possibly highly replicable business models over the Internet.

Q: Any categories you're looking for?

Toivo: I think categorizing is the wrong approach to look at investments, because you may miss out certain innovative products, and you cannot categorize them. This being said, industries like clean energy are potential markets.

Q: How important was the company culture?

Toivo: Hugely important. I attribute the success of Skype largely to the ability to hire people who were able to think and work fluently together—who have the same values, and best of all, know each other's abilities, skills, ways of communication already from times before. Having tens of like-minded getting-things-done people pulling toward the same goal—you get amazing results.

Q: Did you have also investors and partners in mind when you built the team—what was valued by investors in your team?

Toivo: Yes, for example, financial management, software security, and so on were areas where hires were done with long-term and investor relationships in mind.

Q: How many iterations did it take to perfect Skype?

Toivo: We were constantly improving the interface. We interacted with the public for feedback to improve Skype, so we were able to find exactly what they wanted. In the beginning, we released new UI iterations every week or so, over time, this became less frequent as the complexity of new releases grew. Right now, Skype releases a new version every few quarters or so.

Product or Service YCombinator, a disruptive incubator in California, advises start-ups of the brutality of markets. Markets are not forgiving. Customers don't care how hard you worked, only whether you solved their problems. Investors evaluate start-ups the way customers evaluate products, not the way bosses evaluate employees. If you're making a valiant effort and failing, maybe they'll invest in your next start-up, but not this one.

The product or service offered should solve a customer problem and resolve a pain point. What is the unique selling proposition (USP)? Is the USP clearly communicated? Does the product require significant behavioral change on the part of the customer? (It shouldn't.) VCs are looking for what the trade calls an "unfair advantage"—something that will be hard for competitors to match or top. What is the elusive secret sauce that sets this start-up apart from all the competition? What is the disruption? What about the business and approach can't be done by anybody else? Unfair advantage can manifest itself as proprietary and differentiated technology, a superior business model, an incredible team building on past success and solving similar customer pain, or a network of relationships that drives down customer acquisition costs.

Business Model   In the words of Peng Tsin Ong, a serial entrepreneur who started Match.com, Interwoven.com and Encentuate.com, the business model is the means by which you can "make money repeatedly." Ideas are, in themselves, worth nothing. People come up with ideas every day. What really makes an idea stand apart, and what poses the highest barrier to entry, is the team that can implement that idea with high-quality execution. While some investors will have an appetite for businesses needing significant capital injection, most VCs prefer businesses and business models that are capital efficient, with high and sustainable gross margins. The combination of these two factors with a high-growth market supports a high, internally sustainable growth rate. For example, Union Square Ventures looks for a technology-enabled service business, information technology leverage, and companies that have a data asset (defensibility). Union Square's view is that the most valuable data assets are created when users interact with services on the Web.

Set Realistic Goals   Dixon Doll, co-Founder and general partner of DCM, advises entrepreneurs to focus on business fundamentals, particularly in a downturn. He encourages entrepreneurs to set realistic goals, keeping in mind that achieving and sustaining high growth rates depend on numerous factors that cannot be taken for granted. "In a slowing economic environment, some of your customers may be tightening budgets, so set realistic goals that you can exceed.'' In light of the capital market uncertainties, he advises entrepreneurs to overcapitalize their companies, more than they might otherwise be inclined to do. He warns entrepreneurs not to scrimp, but to implement business plans that have large cash reserves and contingency plans, particularly since today's start-ups almost always include multiple locations right from the start.

Dealing with Data   It is the job of a VC to look for evidence, as it is not uncommon for entrepreneurs to hide facts. Specific questions prompt entrepreneurs to isolate key facets of their business and ponder deeper and harder. The following are questions that entrepreneurs who are looking to raise professional capital should ask themselves:

- Can I secure clients in the next 60 days?
- Can I have 15–20 million paying customers, and in the process generate US$2 to US$3 million on new products?
- How many outstanding shares of stock are there?
- What is the monthly burn rate?
- How much cash is in the bank?
- When will the company achieve positive cash flow?

Strategically, there are two reasons for start-ups to release financial data. Entrepreneurs who have plans to raise venture capital should release financial data. Equitas Micro Finance India, a start-up that offers micro-financing solutions, released its financial reports and published its credit rating report from CRISIL (a Standard & Poor's company). This in turn increased its credibility when Equitas Micro Finance India was fundraising. Second, entrepreneurs should release financial data if they are experiencing rapid growth without outside capital. This often attracts the attention of external investors even though the company is not in the process of fundraising.

Tactically, companies that intend to reveal financial data should simplify the due diligence process. One way is to create a secure online data site that contains all the relevant corporate documents.

On the other hand, start-ups can be justified in their reluctance to release financial data. First, they have already raised professional money and are enjoying rapid growth. Reporting their figures then may alert unwanted competition. Hence, they would rather keep a low profile and commit themselves to their business. The next reason is quite apparent and straightforward—no one will be proud of their results if they are poor.

Competition At the busy start-up phase, where entrepreneurs are perfecting their business's internal operations, it is easy for entrepreneurs to neglect the external threat—competition. It is imperative for the management team to appreciate the competitive landscape, understand both present and future direct and indirect competitors, and grasp their core competencies in order to build sustainable competitive advantages.

When the entrepreneur says that the start-up faces no competitors, two inferences can be made: The entrepreneur did not perform due diligence on the market or the due diligence done was not thorough. Alternatively, there is no market.

Competitors do not merely include players within the industry; firms from another industry can also pursue the same customers. For example, in the game console space, Sony PlayStation, Microsoft Xbox, and Nintendo are direct competitors, whereas external competitors include board games and Internet games. An entrepreneur therefore has to acknowledge competitors in different fields in order to form effective strategies.[12]

Exit Strategy Most top-quartile VCs are primarily interested in management teams with a company-building mind-set—rather than build-it-to-flip mentality. VCs are drawn to entrepreneurs who wish to build a company that can independently thrive and have an IPO scenario. However, VCs are also realistic and understand that most successful investor exits will be the result of M&A. Key questions that they ask include "What potential exits do you see for the company, and when?" The best VCs strive to understand expectations of the entrepreneur with regard to exit, especially if they have a few potential acquirers in mind.

COMMANDMENT #2: Reduce Technical and Market Uncertainty

Uncertainty goes with the territory, and VCs are always alert for ways to reduce it, as Figure 3.2 illustrates. Early-stage companies go through predictable phases. The company manufactures the *product*. Then the company has to acquire early *customers*. Then it is about finding and choosing *partners*. Then the company has to plug into

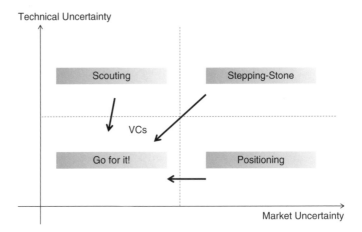

Figure 3.2 Assessing a Portfolio Prospect

the *investment community*. The team is constantly changing in composition and function, expanding, and improving. Successful early-stage companies either get acquired at nice prices or they go public.

Entrepreneurs in these different phases of the start-up process face different risk profiles. At the product formation phase, the entrepreneur may be facing technical complexity and be scouting customer needs, and will often elicit feedback by giving away alpha versions of the product. By introducing an alpha version product or service with features that some people may want, the entrepreneur tests at a low cost to gauge market response. When there is market uncertainty, the entrepreneur is positioning the product and looking for market reaction by conducting a small, bounded experiment. This often happens when an entrepreneur combines well-known technologies (such as a toaster and a tablet). The stepping-stone option is most useful when the entrepreneur faces both market uncertainty and technical uncertainty. For example, Kyocera was planning to produce a high-tech ceramic that was strong as steel and half the weight of steel, but had high production costs and unclear market demand. VCs often advise entrepreneurs to keep their business plan short and stick to a steeper curve of learning: how can I learn faster and cheaper than the next guy and have a higher chance of success. The process in the start-up should allow for fast decision making, a short planning horizon, and hard targets. The rationale is that everyone has a dollar to invest, and whoever recycles the dollar fast enough wins.

The optimal strategy for an entrepreneur is not to solve problems all at once. Put up a good enough product—don't wait for a perfect one. The more arrows you shoot, the more likely you are to succeed. By shooting more arrows, you can push back the boundary of ignorance.

However, there is often a disconnect between advice and attitudes. Advice that most Fortune 500 CEOs gave was: be innovative, willing to take chances, make deals, be achievement-oriented and aggressive. Risk-averse managers are "chicken, nervous, unsure, passive, slow and pessimistic." However, in practice, their approach is to "let others sign on to your decisions, don't gamble, arrange for a blanket, and pad yourself."[13] CEOs viewed risk as a bad thing, whereas financial investors viewed it as a necessary aspect of making gains. The strategies employed by CEOs for dealing with risk are to learn more, find a less pessimistic angle, and not to rely on the estimates of others.

Consider the case of a consumer Internet company with a low burn rate. The team projects its next build to cost US$2 million. Assume it has a 1 in 20 (5 percent) chance to succeed on the US$2 million raise, and a 95 percent chance of nothing. The chance of success if you raise US$4 million is 9.75 percent.[14] This is because you can iterate twice at 5 percent probability each. In the same vein, the chance of succeeding after raising US$20 million is 40.1 percent. However, each US$2 million dilutes the founder's share. The risk-adjusted ownership (diluted ownership times probability of success) increases as you raise more money.

The key to this thinking is to resist the temptation to spend like a lottery winner. Raising the big VC round isn't winning the lottery; it is the purchase of a deck of weekly lottery tickets. Failure is baked into the calculus of the opportunity. The key is to fail fast, fail cheap, and try again. Set metrics ahead of time and be decisive, because time really is money. Entrepreneurs who practice this discipline are just doing what VCs do every day. Venture capital is a hit business, too. Companies often fail. Failure is part of the process.

COMMANDMENT #3: Remember That Money Is Blood

In a downturn, Deepak Natarajan, who directs Intel Capital's investments in South East Asia, Australia, and New Zealand from a base in Singapore, says, "We're doing the hard work of finding the right companies. In a high tide, start-ups have less difficulty finding investments. In an economy like this when water leaves the shore, you find a lot of start-ups with their trousers down and left naked. It is going to be hard to raise money in the private market in 2009 and 2010. It is not going to be easy. Make sure you conserve cash. Run expenses tightly; in some cases, cut expenses. Companies should continue to make investments that will pay off when the market recovers. Do not stand still in a bad economy; continue to invest in R&D, build good products and channels to capitalize on the upswing."

It is important to have the optimal number of branch offices. Deepak's algorithm for the number of locations for start-ups is $n - 1$, where n is the digit count in the number of employees the start-up has. For example, if a start-up has 100 employees, the number of cities that a start-up should be in is $3 - 1 = 2$. If you have 1,000 employees, the number of locations is $4 - 1 = 3$. The benefits of multiple locations more than offset the overhead of commuting among the employees.

COMMANDMENT #4: Separate Price and Value: Price Is What You Pay, Value Is What You Get

When VCs invest, an agreed-upon value is set for the company. In subsequent quarters, the venture investor will usually keep this valuation in place until a material event occurs to change it. The venture investor is usually conservative in the valuation of companies, but it is common to find that early-stage funds may have an even more conservative valuation of their companies due to the long lives of their investments when compared to other funds with shorter investment cycles.

The classic venture model has been to fund to milestones 12–18 months out. In consumer Web services, there are only two meaningful milestones—getting a lot of users and making money. You're either hot or not. Second place does not have much intrinsic value. VCs use other metrics in other sectors (like management, product, and so on) as proxies for real economic progress. VCs also use them because of their residual value in an asset sale or merger.

However, it is hard for entrepreneurs and VCs to know a priori if something is going to be a hit. The only way to know is to try, and trying takes time and money. That's the real rationale for why it makes sense for these companies to raise a lot of money and run lots of experiments.[15] Although software is cheaper than ever to produce, it takes several iterations to hit it big.

Like a mutual fund, each venture fund has a net asset value, or the value of an investor's holdings in that fund at any given time. However, unlike a mutual fund, this value is not determined through a public market transaction; it is determined through a valuation of the underlying portfolio. As the investment is illiquid, the partnership may have both private companies and the stock of public companies in its portfolio. These public stocks are usually subject to restrictions for a holding period and are thus subject to a liquidity discount in the portfolio valuation.

Hence, although a secondary market for venture investments does exist, the reason they have not been securitized is that the underlying cash flows are irregular, and this is the kind of asset that requires active management. An active securitized market is possible only for investments that can be passively managed and have predictable cash flows. According to Dr. Oliver Gottschalg, assistant professor of strategy and business policy at HEC School of Management and co-director of the HEC-INSEAD Buyout Research Group, the venture capital industry will eventually move to more objective and reliable performance measures, a ratings-type model. This will result in a more liquid secondary market, which opens up a whole new toolbox for how you invest in this sector and changes how you think about investing in this area. Inefficiencies in the market help top private equity (PE) firms get great returns.[16] In addition, ratings are particularly likely to spur responses from firms that feel their legitimacy is threatened—and thus are shamed—by these ratings.

Pitfalls to Avoid

When it comes to forming partnerships, there are as usual pitfalls to avoid:

- Inability to confront difficult issues
- Distraction and overcommitment
- Lack of alignment among board members and investors
- Temptation to make excessive capital investments in the initial phases of a business
- Failure to focus on market and industry analysis

PITFALL #1: Inability to Confront Difficult Issues

Entrepreneurs should avoid board members who are tied to initial or outdated perspectives and who inhibit new members from offering important observations. Such a problem may arise when a former CEO is on the board. According to Pascal N. Levensohn, president and CEO of Levensohn Capital Management LLC, "It is naturally very difficult to move a CEO aside, have him remain a voting board member, and proceed to undo major projects that this person has previously done with the board's blessing. When more than one former CEO remains on the board, this problem is magnified. Retired senior executives have a natural tendency to glorify their exploits and to treasure past contributions as well as to protect one another and their reputations. It is therefore extremely risky to keep them at the table."

A survey by the *McKinsey Quarterly* in February 2009 found that nearly half the boards surveyed felt their chairman had been ineffective in implementing strategies to deal with the crisis.[17] It is likely directors assumed the crisis was just part of an economic cycle and no one took the initiative to challenge that thought.

PITFALL #2: Distraction and Overcommitment

VCs may serve on too many boards to be productive, or they may have written down their investment in the company and lost interest. The CEO faces a dilemma if that board member has priorities ahead of his particular company. The CEO is best served by asking the VC to consider appointing a less-burdened colleague to the role, or to free up more time for the effort. Entrepreneurs should always try to find out current deals VCs on their board are participating in. It is likely that VCs distracted by other ongoing deals will have less time to focus on the entrepreneur's company.[18]

Board members with operating experience in the company's domain may become overinvolved and advance personal ideas without support from the rest of the board and without trying to generate consensus. This approach often leads to interpersonal conflict and accentuates board divisiveness. Another VC says, "Frankly, this is an area where many boards overstep their bounds. They try to second-guess the management they hired by injecting themselves in daily decision making. It is important for the CEO to have the management authority to run the business (and provide the necessary return for the shareholders). The CEO should have the courage and personality to stand up to board members who overstep their mandate in this area."[19]

PITFALL #3: Lack of Alignment Among Board Members and Investors

Strain at the board-VC level has evolved into a major problem in Silicon Valley as a result of the technology capital market downturn. For example, many VCs and others, including passive angel investors, invested in seed and "A" rounds expecting to see their investments appreciate. Instead, since mid-2000 these early-round investors have experienced significant dilution of their ownership stakes because of subsequent financings completed at lower valuations, often with special liquidation preferences attached to the most recent investment capital. This misalignment of financial concerns often leads to an erosion of trust between the VCs and the entrepreneur. A case of a divided board can be observed in Yahoo with regard to its decision to get acquired by Microsoft in 2008. The board was split into two factions, one led by Chairman Roy Bostock and another by then CEO Jerry Yang. Despite Yang's responsibility to preserve shareholders' value, he resisted the deal based on sentimental reasons, which was thought to be irrational by the Bostock faction.[20] Unsurprisingly, this was followed by his resignation as Yahoo's CEO.

CASE STUDY: Pets.com

Pets.com, an online portal that sold pet items online, was an icon of the dot-com bubble, going from IPO to liquidation in just nine months. Pets.com was backed with US$50 million by Hummer Winblad Venture Partners, Bowman Capital, and Amazon.com. Pets.com overinvested in infrastructure such as warehousing and even took out US$1.2 million Super Bowl prime time ads. It soon became clear that the company needed a critical mass of customers to break even in four to five years. However, the dot-com bubble burst and the company undertook actions to sell itself without avail.

Pets.com's VCs failed to provide advice and monitor the business in their haste to see returns during the dot-com boom. The entrepreneur built an overly aggressive marketing campaign in the hope of boosting the sales of its products and services quickly. Unfortunately, the plan backfired and the revenues generated were never enough to cover the high marketing cost. In retrospect, the potential benefits of marketing campaigns like Super Bowl advertisements were over-hyped in the Internet buying culture of the time. IT-focused VCs such as Hummer Winblad, Bowman, and experienced player Amazon should have known better. What developed was an agency problem be-tween short-term-oriented VCs and longer-term-oriented owners. The company focused on increasing market share at the expense of bottom line, making a rush to IPO during the lucrative bubble period where stock prices were soaring even without concrete earnings. While taking a fast track to IPO isn't necessarily wrong, VCs could have kept an eye on the massive burn rates that Pets.com was facing. However, they focused too much on increasing the user base to maximize their valuation (following in the footsteps of earlier start-ups Yahoo, Google, and Amazon) for IPO. Therefore, a refocus on the fundamentals of the company—cost, efficiency, and profitability—should have been the order.

Another reason Pets.com failed can be attributed to not employ-ing the right communication tools. Despite the massive popularity of the sock puppet icon, it failed to communicate effectively to the public about the company's capabilities and products. This is reflec-tive of the expertise of its executives. A VC's main role is to as far as possible install the best management team. This would include mar-keting experts for Pets.com. This never happened, even as Pets.com engaged in the most elaborate A&P campaigns during the dot-com boom. Conversion rates were low. Today, the sock puppet icon is still well known, however, the products associated with it are still hazy. VCs could have gotten experts, knowing the kind of marketing cam-paign Pets.com was going to launch. This would apply to logistics management as Pets.com fared terribly in its logistics organization, losing many customers in the process. It often took too long for pet food to arrive, and pet owners usually require the food fast. As a key process and core competitive advantage over physical stores, disruption of this raises serious red flags. Again, VCs failed to see this and install proper operational processes and expertise before its Pets.com customer base departed. Pets.com would have been for better off if it had found VCs with expertise in warehousing and distribution instead of software- and IT-focused VCs. Matching capa-bilities from the start is crucial to the success of the business.[21]

PITFALL #4: Temptation to Make Excessive Capital Investments in the Initial Phases of a Business

Increase your capital investments *only* if you have the revenue to back them up. Larger boards may have misaligned investors who take a stance of excessive complacency and self-satisfaction. Complacent boards may be too enthusiastic about expanding and underestimate the potential risks. This attitude has been deadly to some public companies (such as Tyco, HealthSouth, and Adelphia). In the case of Tyco, the board did not make any real attempts to remove the CEO even when he authorized improper payments amounting to US$20 million to the lead director without the knowledge of any other directors.

PITFALL #5: Failure to Focus on Market and Industry Analysis

Proper market and industry analysis is the key to success for any business. Always have a conservative forecast of future earnings and demand estimates. The board should be asking: What are top three toughest issues facing our company? Is the board actively monitoring and focusing on those issues? Always have a *contingency fund* and a *Plan B*.

Endnotes

1. Christopher Rider and Philip Tetlock, "Venture Capitalist Decision Making: Designing Organizations to Check Cognitive Biases," 2006; retrieved from www.babson.edu/entrep/fer/2005FER/chapter_i/summary_i8.html, June 25, 2009.
2. James Freeman, "Who's Going to Fund the Next Steve Jobs?" *Wall Street Journal*, July 18, 2008; retrieved from http://online.wsj.com/article/SB121633667123063791.html, June 25, 2009.
3. Scott Kirsner, "Why Facebook Went West," September 9, 2007; retrieved from www.boston.com/business/technology/articles/2007/09/09/why_facebook_went_west/?page=full, June 25, 2009.
4. Erick Schonfeld and Peter Thiel, "Best Predictor of Startup Success Is Low CEO Pay," TechCrunch, 8 September 2008; retrieved from www.techcrunch.com/2008/09/08/peter-thiel-best-predictor-of-startup-success-is-low-ceo-pay/, June 25, 2009.
5. Arthur Rock, "Strategy vs Tactics from a Venture Capitalist," *Harvard Business Review*, November 1987, pp 63–67.
6. John Doerr quote retrieved from www.mbadepot.com/search/keyword/John+Doerr/quote/, July 6, 2009.

7. Paul Gompers and Josh Lerner, "The Venture Capital Revolution," *Journal of Economic Perspectives* 15, no. 2 (Spring 2001): 145–168. Kleiner Perkins Caufield & Byers, "Profile of John Doerr," n.d.; retrieved from www.kpcb.com/team/index.php?John%20Doerr, June 25, 2009. Kleiner Perkins Caufield & Byers, "Profile of Heidi Roizen," www.heidi.roizen.com/, June 25, 2009. Heather Connon, "Gags-to-Riches Tale of the Welsh Wizard Who Bet on YouTube," *Guardian,* October 15, 2006; retrieved from www.guardian.co.uk/media/2006/oct/15/business.newmedia, June 25, 2009. Alorie Gilbert, "Legendary Venture Capitalist Looks Ahead," CNET News, November 27, 2004; retrieved from http://news.cnet.com/Legendary-venture-capitalist-looks-ahead/2008-1082_3-5466478.html, June 25, 2009. Asap staff, "The Best VCs," *Forbes,* May 29, 2000; retrieved from www.forbes.com/venturecapital/asap/2000/0529/098.html, June 25, 2009.

8. Morten Sorensen, "How Smart Is Smart Money? A Two-Sided Matching Model of Venture Capital," *Journal Of Finance* 62, no. 1 (February 2007): 2725–2762.

9. Julia Hanna, "The Money Connection—Understanding VC Networks," Harvard Business School Working Knowledge, December 4, 2006; retrieved from http://hbswk.hbs.edu/item/5506.html, July 6, 2009.

10. Qianqian Du and Ilan Vertinsky, "Risk Mitigation Strategies of Foreign Venture Capitalists in China," University of British Columbia—Sauder School of Business, working paper, July 2008; retrieved from http://ssrn.com/abstract= 1154809, July 6, 2009.

11. Yahoo Small Business, "What Do Venture Capitalists Look For?" Yahoo Small Business Website, retrieved from http://smallbusiness.yahoo.com/r-article-a-1296-m-2-sc-58-what_do_venture_capitalists_look_for-i, June 25, 2009. Gary Fowler, "What Do Venture Capitalists Look for in Entrepreneurs?" Planet Analog, June 29, 2007; retrieved from www.planetanalog.com/showArticle.jhtml?articleID=200001707, June 25, 2009. Anjana Vivek, "What Factors Do Venture Capitalists Consider Before Funding Projects?" *Financial Express,* May 27, 2005; retrieved from www.financialexpress.com/old/fe_archive_full_ story.php?content_id=92022, June 25, 2009. Allen Stern, "6 Tips for Hiring Top Talent at Startups," Center Networks, March 18, 2008; retrieved from www.centernetworks.com/startup-hiring-tips, June 25, 2009. Dave Lefkow, "A Recruiting Guide for Start-Ups," Ere.net, April 18, 2007; retrieved from www.ere.net/2007/04/18/a-recruiting-guide-for-startups/, June 25, 2009. Dharmesh Shah, "5 Quick Pointers on Startup Hiring," March 9, 2007; retrieved from http://onstartups.com/home/tabid/3339/bid/1278/5-Quick-Pointers-On-Startup-Hiring.aspx, June 25, 2009. Laura Lorber, "How to attract Talent to a Small Company," Wall Street Journal Online, September 12, 2008; retrieved from http://guides.wsj.com/small-business/hiring-and-managing-employees/how-to-attract-talent-to-a-small-company/, June 25, 2009.

12. Business Link, "Common Mistakes When Starting Up—and How to Avoid Them," n.d.; retrieved from www.businesslink.gov.uk/bdotg/action/detail?type=RESOURCES&itemId=1075219871, February 9, 2009. Ctrip, "Ctrip Reports Fourth Quarter and Full Year 2008 Financial Results" (news release), February 8, 2009; retrieved from http://ir.ctrip.com/phoenix.zhtml?c=148903& p=irol-newsArticle&ID=1254111&highlight=, June 26, 2009. A.

Muse, "Should Your Startup Release Financial Data?" Texas Startup Blog, May 28, 2008; retrieved from www.texasstartupblog.com/2008/05/28/should-your-startup-release-financial-data/, June 26, 2009. Reuters, "Ctrip Awarded Famous Chinese Trademark Honor," April 3, 2008; retrieved from www.reuters.com/article/pressRelease/idUS104339+03-Apr-2008+PRN20080403, June 26, 2009. Reuters, "Equitas to Raise 10 Bln Rupees Via Debt, Equity," October 3, 2008; retrieved from http://in.reuters.com/article/indiaDeals/idIN-BOM5506720081003, June 26, 2009.

13. Alan B. Eisner and Zur Shapira, "Attention Allocation and Managerial Decision Making," July 1997, Information Systems Working Papers Series, 1997. Available at SSRN: http://ssrn.com/abstract=1284291.

14. The calculation works like this: $1.00 - (.95 \times .95) = 0.0975$, or 9.75 percent.

15. Peter Rip, "Fail Fast, Fail Often," EarlyStageVC, January 28, 2007; retrieved from http://earlystagevc.typepad.com/earlystagevc/2007/01/fail_fast_fail_.html, June 26, 2009.

16. Aaron K. Chatterji and Michael W. Chatterji, "Shamed and Able: How Firms Respond to Being Rated" (revised May 2008), Harvard Business School Working Paper, 9-807-093.

17. Andrew Campbell and Stuart Sinclair, "The Crisis: Mobilizing Boards for a Change," *McKinsey Quarterly*, February 2009; retrieved from www.mckinsey-quarterly.com/Governance/Boards/the_crisis_Mobilizing_boards_for_change_2300?pagenum=2, June 26, 2009.

18. Jacob Webb, "Board Meeting Etiquette, Part 1 (The Purpose)," January 12, 2009; retrieved from http://everydayentrepreneurship.com/2009/01/12/board-meeting-etiquette-pt-1-the-purpose/, June 26, 2009.

19. Ibid.

20. Ina Fried, "Report: Yahoo Board Divided Over Microsoft Bid," CNET News, February 15, 2008; retrieved from http://news.cnet.com/8301-13860_3-9873041-56.html, July 6, 2009.

21. Jeff Fischer, "Why Pets.com Died," November 14, 2000; retrieved from www.fool.com/portfolios/rulebreaker/2000/rulebreaker001114.htm, March 22, 2009. Troy Wolverton, "Pets.com Latest High-Profile Dot-Com Disaster," November 7, 2000; retrieved from http://news.cnet.com/2100-1017-248230.html#, March 22, 2009. Brad Stone, "Amazon's Pet Projects," *Newsweek* 123, no. 25 (1999): 56. Leslie Kaufman with Saul Hansell, "Holiday Lessons in Online Retailing," *New York Times,* January 2, 2000, Sect. 3, p. 3. Mara Reinstein and Steve McClellan, "Super Bowl Spots Don't Score," *Broadcasting & Cable* 130, no. 6 (2000): 28. Inside CRM Editors, "The 20 Worst Venture Capital Investments of All Time," n.d.; retrieved from www.insidecrm.com/features/20-worst-vc-investments-111907/, June 26, 2009.

4

Growing Together

The growth phase of a company is exciting and exhilarating for both the investors and the entrepreneur. This chapter outlines the growth journey that VCs take alongside the entrepreneur.

Led by Hian Goh and Maria Brown, the Asian Food Channel was launched in mid-2005 into multiple territories across the Asia-Pacific region. The Asian Food Channel went beyond just pictures, with the creation of a new and unique lifestyle brand that crossed countries, races, and religions, bringing the highest quality of television to its viewers.

A relatively young media company in an industry dominated by well-established corporate giants, this five-year-old firm has created waves in Asia with new ideas and trends in the branding of programming. Its independence allows it to take bigger programming risks, select from a wider range of content, and tailor-make a pay TV channel specifically for the Asian audience to international broadcasting standards.

Both founders possess a combination of expertise in traditional media and finance, and it is the synthesis of these strengths that has helped them in realizing their entrepreneurial ambitions. Coming from the investment banking industry, Goh has a background that provides the company a sound understanding of raising capital, structuring a durable business model, and exploiting new revenue streams. In contrast, Brown's strength from her tenure at the BBC has been pivotal in her ability to drive, develop, build, and implement a locally produced TV brand with a strong Asian look-and-feel that is able to compete with and beat long-established players, and attract an ever-growing audience of both viewers and advertisers.

This unique combination of personality and skills has provided a perfect complement to each other, and helped to create a well-balanced team that is successful in navigating the challenges of this rapidly changing media industry.

Goh and Brown represent the entrepreneurs' dream in the new economy, individuals who leave established careers and paychecks to risk it all to create something new. AFC has attracted the likes of institutional investors Symphony Capital, a private equity firm helmed by Anil Thadani, whose previous investments include Aman Resorts, Apollo Hotels in India, and Parkway Hospital in Singapore. Today, Symphony counts AFC as its key media asset; a pay TV channel that broadcasts to more than 20 million viewers in seven countries, and continues to mature and develop into a major player in the Asian media industry.

As Dr. Finian Tan, chairman of Vickers Venture and an AFC investor, recalls, "When two young entrepreneurs came to see me three years ago to start a Food Channel, Hian was still in school at INSEAD and Maria on leave from the BBC. I liked them a lot, funded them, and became their chairman. Today, the Asia Food Channel is in Singapore, Philippines, Indonesia, Hong Kong, and Malaysia. And the two young visionaries, now experienced media managing directors, are in their element, steering AFC to greater and greater heights."

Jeff Chi adds, "We liked the idea and followed these two students to StarHub. StarHub would agree to their idea only if they could go overseas and get the content they wanted to have on their channel. So we gave them the money to go overseas to get the content. Now they are doing well and have about 4 million customers. The management team of AFC was attractive because both founders had relevant experience in media. One was an investment banker and the other used to work at the BBC and could understand the operations of a channel."

CASE IN POINT: Asian Food Channel

With investments from Symphony International Holdings Limited (SIHL) significantly strengthening the financial backing of the company, the Asian Food Channel continues its fast expansion as a trailblazer brand across the Asia-Pacific Region.

The Asian Food Channel (AFC) is the region's only 24-hour food channel dedicated to airing the best food and lifestyle programming from around the region and around the world.

Based in Singapore, AFC's wide Asian distribution footprint currently covers seven territories and growing with 20 million viewers, on basic tiers of all the major pay TV platforms across Southeast Asia.

The channel leads the ratings in its territories, regularly showing up as the #1 lifestyle channel in terms of popularity and loyalty against comparable international pay TV channels. Broadcast platforms include

- AFC StarHub Channel 69 (Singapore)
- Astro Channel 703 (Malaysia)
- First Media Digital 1 Channel 76 (Indonesia), Prime Indovision Channel 22 (Indonesia)
- Now TV Channel 527 (Hong Kong)
- Skycable Channel 58 (Philippines)

AFC is essentially a broadcaster. Its business model is based on producing and licensing top-quality lifestyle content and shows from all over the world and selling them into international markets.

Like most pay TV channels, it derives its revenues from a healthy mix of subscriber fees and channel advertising revenue (the Internet platform is provided free.) The company is also aggressive in pursuing alternative revenue streams including an e-commerce store, mobile strategies, and VOD. AFC executes 360-degree advertising and marketing campaigns and solutions for leading FMCG, Financial, and Travel brands.

AFC targets high-flyers (professionals, executives, and managers), the modern woman, as well as the discerning foodie. Its online presence supports the channel with program information, recipes, content, and e-commerce.

AFC attracts advertising dollars from top brands in Asia. Today, the company has expanded its portfolio of advertisers from food companies to autos, financial services, kitchenware, white goods manufacturers, and tourism agencies that now utilize the channel's ratings and demographics to reach out to their target audience. AFC successfully engages advertisers and viewers with a host of marketing communication activities, events with PR support, and media coverage.

Features

24-hour food channel. Comprehensive website with daily updates on programs, recipes, and e-commerce.

Benefits

Viewers can watch at any time of the day and receive a wide range of culinary programs. Viewers are driven by the Channel to go online to download relevant information, subscribe to AFC's newsletter, and interact further with its advertisers.

Probable Segments

Housewives, adults with an interest in food and cuisine, and aspiring yuppies.

Threats

Other channels broadcasting occasional culinary shows
   Websites offering free recipes with good reviews (for example, www.allrecipes.com)
   Online download versions of the same cooking programs broadcast on AFC

Customer Loyalty

Yes, if a customer enjoys the programs, there will be follow-ups. They can also sign up online as members to receive AFC news, recipes, and so on.

Gateway or Dead End

Gateway. There is potential for collaborations with regional production houses to include other genres of programming. If AFC's brand equity builds up, it can expand its retail line to include more kitchenware or culinary items. AFC can also aim to spread its network to non-Asian countries.

Sensitivity to Price

Not applicable. AFC is a channel on cable service providers. Its website does not include membership fees either.

Identifying Platinum Customers

AFC can track membership usage (customer specific) and viewership rates (country or area specific).

Symphony International Holdings Limited is the lead investor in the Asian Food Channel. The strategic investment company focuses on long-term direct investment opportunities and its investment in AFC reflects a strategy of investing in consumer-focused lifestyle businesses in Asia. In line with its expansion plans and future growth, the Asian Food Channel has moved into larger premises at the new media hub Fusionopolis at One North. Here are some exchanges from an interview with Maria Brown on the success of AFC.

> *Q:* Why did VCs invest in your company? (Or how did you get funding?)
>
> *Brown:* We went to our VCs and told them our story, what we wanted to do and why we believed it would be a success. Our VCs tell us they were impressed with that story, our passion, but mostly with the management team. Indeed, what they said to us was they liked the management team enough to invest in them whatever business idea they had brought before them. This is very key because it is about the trust, if your VCs trust you, and that you are working as hard as you can and that you are obsessed enough to never stop driving the business, they will trust you enough to support you during good and bad times.
>
> *Q:* How did you get your first seed money?
>
> *Brown:* First, by building a management team that were expert in their respective fields. It included individuals who had stellar experience in the media industry, so they knew the game that we were about to enter very well, and also individuals from the finance industry who knew VCs and the funding process. The business plan, presentation, and other items were highly researched and well-presented. The team had already started to execute the business before the series A funding by using their own money. By the time series A was closed, the team had already had indications for contracts, options for supplies, and had started preliminary hiring. The fact that the team started to execute it is in our opinion the key reason why any VC would invest, because it demonstrated that here was a group of people who were going to

start their company whether they got funding from this source or not.

Stages of Development

When AFC was first launched in mid-2005, it had operations only in three countries: Singapore, Hong Kong, and Malaysia. Today, after five years, it has operations in a total of seven countries including the major ones in Southeast Asia, broadcasting to an audience in excess of 20 million. One of AFC's hallmark achievements was to broadcast on Malaysia's Cable-TV provider Astro as a basic-tier channel, meaning that consumers who subscribe to Astro automatically get AFC. It took AFC three years to successfully negotiate this outcome.

Stages of Financing

AFC's seed capital came from personal funding from both its founders Hian Goh and Maria Brown. Concurrently, they managed to obtain equity financing from Finian Tan, founder of the Vickers Financial Group, a private equity and venture capital firm. In May 2008, AFC managed to secure financing from Symphony International Holdings Limited to support its growth phase.

Jeff Chi summarizes, "What VCs look at before investing are market size, competitive advantage, and great team. The market size has to be big and growing fast. The competitive advantage should be one that would make the company one of the top three players in the field, and there must be a plan on how to defend it. The team is the most important because it is not easy to build a successful business. The team must have guts to change path if things go wrong. Also there must be integrity and experience. A team with experience is important as a lot of risks are involved. A key figure in a team will be able to close deals and add credibility."

What Star VCS Do: Winning Techniques

When it comes to the growth phase, top VCs have another set of techniques they bring into play, as shown in Figure 4.1.

Entrepreneurs

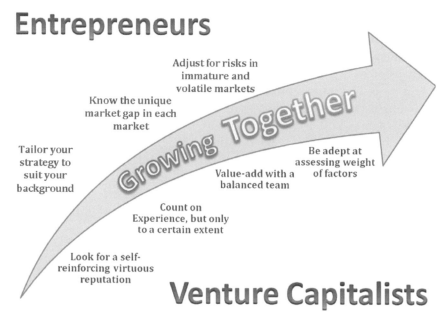

Adjust for risks in
immature and
volatile markets

Know the unique
market gap in each
market

Tailor your
strategy to
suit your
background

Be adept at
assessing weight
of factors

Value-add with a
balanced team

Count on
Experience, but only
to a certain extent

Look for a self-
reinforcing virtuous
reputation

Venture Capitalists

Figure 4.1 Contributions to Growth

- Look for a self-reinforcing virtuous reputation.
- Count on experience, but only to a certain extent.
- Value-add with a balanced team.
- Be adept at assessing weight of factors.

WINNING TECHNIQUE #1: Look for a Self-Reinforcing Virtuous Reputation

Like will draw like. A sterling reputation has a virtuous effect that leads to better dealflow. Once tarnished, a reputation is difficult to salvage. As Aesop's fuller (a specialist in bleaching and finishing cloth) told the charcoal burner who wanted to move in with him, "The arrangement is impossible; whatever I should whiten, you would immediately blacken again with your charcoal."

Andy Tang explains, "Try not to focus on immediate advantage such as getting into a hot deal. It is more important to show people that you can value-add. With a reputation, people (entrepreneurs and LPs) come to you. In the initial stages, product development is more important than marketing. VCs should focus on the best product development to add value to a company. In turn, this will improve dealflow and the brand of being a value-add investor will improve dramatically over time. In the long run, this will create the most return for LP."

This is a common phenomenon in the venture capitalist-entrepreneur relationship—what goes around does come around. The circle is a tight-knit one. "The odds are significantly against you when you're starting out," says Sean Dalton, general partner at Highland Capital. Even if you have a great deal of money, the best entrepreneurs won't care—they'll just want a good partner. And that comes by building a reputation over time: "It's all about performance—it's easy for an entrepreneur to make a few phone calls and find out what value you added to your last venture and how you behaved when things didn't go well."

WINNING TECHNIQUE #2: Count on Experience, but Only to a Certain Extent

Venture capitalists typically must wait a long time, often up to several years, for outcome feedback on their investment decisions, and interpretations of such outcomes may vary due to unknown causal variables, inaccurate feedback, and random error.[1] Shepherd, Zacharakis, and Baron found that experience exhibits a curvilinear (inverted U-shaped) relationship with decision reliability and accuracy.[2] The venture capitalists in the study scored higher on decision accuracy and reliability with increasing experience but, after 13 years of investment experience, the effects of additional experience were detrimental.

Moreover, reliance upon matching past successful or failed funded ventures, the authors claim, leaves venture capitalists susceptible to availability biases that render them more overconfident for failure predictions than for predictions of success. Such overconfidence is not necessarily likely to cause poor decision making but is likely to inhibit learning and decision improvement.[3] Many standard economic models assume that people, being rational economic agents, would not make decisions that violate their preferences. However, this is not necessarily so; as long ago as the 1950s, political scientist Herbert Simon suggested that people make irrational and suboptimal choices, despite available information, because there is a natural limit to the human ability to process data and handle complex computations.[4]

For Dixon Doll, co-founder of DCM, operating experience counts, yet it must be complemented by other key attributes: a strong work ethic, personal integrity, high energy, strategic IQ, and the willingness to work with people of all types (often called emotional intelligence, or EQ).

The traits he looks for seem to be found in successful VCs in other geographies. Neil Shen, now managing director at Sequoia Capital China, was instrumental in the product creation and customer acqisition at Ctrip, where he was CFO and raised venture capital funding. Ctrip.com now has 19 million registered members, and launched several innovative products, including Major Natural Disaster Travel Security Fund to help deliver worry-free travel experiences, and Ctrip PASS, a voucher booklet designed to change the way people travel. These Ctrip innovations have made Ctrip China's most successful online travel service company, with net revenues of US$217 million in 2008.

Joichi Ito, a venture capitalist and an early angel investor in Six Apart, Technorati, Flickr, SocialText, and Last.fm believes that the key value that he provides is networks and advice (when the entrepreneurs need it). Conventional incubators tend to focus on low-value infrastructure. Good entrepreneurs get these really cheap and do not want to give up equity or cash for infrastructure. "Successful entrepreneurs didn't want to come to my incubator. They only wanted specific advice and didn't want the whole package. Those entrepreneurs who went into incubator needed spoon-feeding." Besides funding, Ito helps the entrepreneurs with their business plans, provides board advice, and introduces them to networks:

> I use the product and I know all of the first-tier VCs in the U.S. and connect them on a trip to SV and Europe. I figure out which VC will be most likely to meet them, set up the meetings and prepare them. For Last.fm, I brought in the COO and the VCs (Index ventures). These three entrepreneurs grew to have 100,000 users in three or four years, and became angel invested, VC-backed, and eventually a US$100 million exit.

> In the consumer Internet space that I invest in, it is faster to do a Web site and iterate than to do a business plan.

Our investment criteria are narrow. The product must minimally have 10,000 (usually 30,000 to 50,000) users and have not raised any money yet. They are typically in beta, growing 30 percent to 50 percent a month and only require US$100,000 to US$200,000 of seed investments (majority into the servers).

He helps guide the company into the next phase: hiring people and fine-tuning the product, and he invests US$50,000 to US$100,000 with five other people in return for stock options.

WINNING TECHNIQUE #3: Value-Add with a Balanced Team

In *Romance of the Three Kingdoms*, the founders of the Han dynasty have a balanced team. Zhang Fei is a go-getter with the courage and resources, Liu Bei has the pedigree, charisma, and managerial skills, and Guan Yu has the strategy and experience in warfare.

"I have the means," said Zhang Fei. "Suppose you and I raised some troops and tried what we could do."

"The peach trees in the orchard behind the house are just in full flower. Tomorrow, we will institute a sacrifice there and solemnly declare our intention before Heaven and Earth, and we three will swear brotherhood and unity of aims and sentiments: Thus, will we enter upon our great task," Liu Bei replied, "I am of the Imperial Family, Liu Bei is my name. And I wish I could destroy these Yellow Scarves and restore peace to the land, but alas! I am helpless."

And Guan Yu said, "Though not born on the same day, month, and year, we hope to die so. Our first move should be to fight the rebels in Northern China."

Lin Hong Wong says that lack of unity in a team is a common cause of downfall of a start-up. This tends to occur when the company is faced with serious problems, and disagreements arise over future directions. VC firms therefore like to see a start-up team where two or more of the key founders have worked together before, or a CEO that has the skill to forge teamwork.

Wong adds,

When hiring VC investment staff, I look for individuals with several years' work experience and one of the following backgrounds:

- An engineer (with working experience) with an MBA.
- A start-up entrepreneur with an MBA. (Note: This could also be a corporate intrapreneur who had spun off from an MNC.)
- An accountant (preferably with manufacturing experience) with an MBA.
- An engineer or accountant with management consulting experience.

While business knowledge and industrial experience are essentials, experience in starting companies or working in a start-up would be an added advantage in an investment staff. However, this does not necessarily mean that the start-up must have been successful. Experience in failed start-ups would be of tremendous value, provided the staff has learned their lessons well. This is also true for entrepreneurs in investee companies.

Wong says that the investment staff must have skillsets relevant to the investment focus of the fund. For a life science venture capital firm, for example, a Ph.D. in life sciences is often a threshold criterion. Early-stage life sciences require a high degree of technical knowledge to assess the viability of the scientific application, process, or business model. However, for a fund in the energy, electronics, or clean technology sector, a Ph.D. is not a necessity, but work experience in the relevant industries would be particularly helpful.

He also says that the staff must have the skills required for their responsibilities. Some VCs separate deal-making and deal-monitoring responsibilities. Thus, a staff member with accounting or management consulting experience would be more suited for monitoring of portfolio companies.

And you have to judge the particular person. There is no ideal profile and there are certainly trade-offs to be made.

However, there are certain deal breakers. These are the three largest ones:

- Apprehension about or even lack of appreciation of technology
- Neither an MBA nor actual business experience, especially no experience with starting a business
- Lack of accounting and financial savvy

The top-quartile VCs interviewed for this book did not differentiate among MBAs. Someone who has gone through a relatively low-ranked school but has gleaned the essence of looking at issues through a business lens and forged a useful network would be more valued than someone who has gone through a prestige program and done nothing except attend a lot of classes. An NUS MBA can be better than a Harvard MBA in the right context.

Other key principles for putting together a team:

Develop a structured process of hiring. Soo Boon Koh of iGlobe Partners says, "Even if you are a general partner with a strong track record, it is not easy to recruit another general partner to repeat your track record." That is, even a good investor may recruit someone who is not good at investing. It is better to have a process for recruiting, one that takes into account not just job skills but ability to cooperate with others. The common fallacy is that the more team members, the lighter the workload and the better the performance. In reality, each team has to find a sweet spot, with enough of the right people to get the job done without getting in each other's way. Team members can be competitive and yet cooperative. Respect and harmony among team members are crucial. For a VC fund, there is an optimum size to operate effectively. The lead partners of the VC firm must build a culture for their firms.

Soft skills matter. Recruiting is about the probability of hires. The recruits of a top sovereign wealth fund include both Ph.D.'s and those who haven't finished school. For their venture capital and private equity (VC/PE) positions, they recruit people who are adept at making deals and wheeling and dealing. With more MBAs gravitating to PE, there are plenty of smart candidates to pick from. A recruiter at a the sovereign wealth fund explains that he looks for "negotiators and relationship-builders; someone who can appreciate the give-and-take in a deal and get a sense of people and what's there to offer on the table. Analytical skills are a threshold quality. Risk aversion and one-track thinking are shunned."

According to one leading VC, judging an individual is based on "gut feel." She adds, "To encourage an entrepreneur requires constant persuasion. VC is a people business. People must be willing to listen to you. A VC must have the judgment to bet on the trustworthy guy."

Analytical talent. "In recruiting junior investment associates, many of their résumés will have strong analytical capacity. What I look for is to find people with common sense, which is just not so common," Soo Boon Koh says. Good VCs are logical thinkers who can see what's around the corner sooner. For Hans Tung, a partner at Qiming Venture Partners (formerly a Vice President at Bessemer), an apprenticeship at Bessemer provided the finishing touch to becoming a VC. "Bessemer is really a smart shop, full of dynamic personalities and sharp investors. At their core, they are very analytical thinkers." According to Tung, the partners at Bessemer frequently work with junior professionals to develop investment roadmaps. Tung believes this helps them to increase the odds of anticipating the "Next Big Thing." "It is both a top-down, AND bottom-up approach." Tung explains, "At Bessemer, we would first analyze industry trends, growth drivers, and identify potential inflection points across sectors and sub-segments. We would then seek out companies in each sub-segment from bottom-up, and pick out those who we think are poised to take advantage of the rising tide." Tung has noticed the same practice at Qiming. "At Qiming, we have 4 industry teams: consumer/Internet, healthcare, cleantech, and IT. We develop investment roadmaps for our respective sectors and follow through in our execution. I have noticed good VC firms are those who have consistently done this well."

Financial background. As Soo Boon Koh points out, "Investment professionals with relevant financial banking background are valuable in the VC business. It would be better if these professionals have strong domain knowledge and operating experience in a specific industry, too."

Curiosity. Being able to ask relevant questions is a critical skill in the industry. Tung has seen first-hand how this elicits entrepreneurs and other industry players to share more information, and also help them to step back and rethink their own experiences more clearly. Tung says, "All these have led to better insights." After consolidating inputs up and down the value chain—from a start-up's suppliers and partners to their customers—the venture capitalist can then make a more informed judgment on a potential investment.

Tung highlights the importance of mentorship. "I had the benefit of working with three senior partners at Bessemer on China deals. Rob Chandra, David Cowan, and Ron Elwell were all experienced investors and operators in their own right. Working with them forced me to examine and reexamine strategic and operational issues faced by entrepreneurs, and weigh the associated risks and rewards more systematically." Tung elaborates, "Being able to spot potential winners at an early stage is a trained art. After some practice, it is not as hard for smart VCs to list all the risks associated with an early stage deal. After all, these companies are young, small, compete in emerging and unproven markets, and thus have lots of areas to improve. But the difficulty lies in developing the ability to identify that one or two key success factors, which would ultimately determine whether these bets become winners."

Tung values how an effective partnership can lead to clearer thinking and better decisions. At both Bessemer and Qiming, CEOs of portfolio companies need to present to the entire firm. Tung marveled, "It's amazing how after a 90-minute session, the presenting CEO would often comment that we have collectively left no issues uncovered." Tung has continued this approach at Qiming. "At Qiming, we push ourselves to think ahead," said Tung. "We often ask ourselves, 'what would China look like three to five years from now' and 'what does that mean for industries A, B, or C, and categories X, Y, or Z?'"

Commitment to geography. Bessemer Venture Partners, a venture fund consistently ranked as top-quartile and backed successes such as Skype, Staples, Blue Nile, Hotjobs, Verisign, Ciena, and Gartner, spotted the expanding Asian market. Bessemer entered India in 2003–2004, and China in 2005. According to Tung, the fund intended to tackle two emerging markets at the same time. "It was a valiant effort. But at the end, it was too difficult. China and India are so different from the US that each required at least one senior partner to spend material time on the ground, and firm support to build up a sufficiently large local investment team, to make impact and adjust existing practices to suit the local environment." Bessemer has since decided to pull out of China for now and focus on opportunities in the US, India, and Israel."

WINNING TECHNIQUE #4: Be Adept at Assessing Weight of Factors

Professor Josh Lerner of Harvard Business School explains that VCs take into consideration positive and negative factors that result in the decision to go ahead or pass on a deal. In certain cases, the VC might say "In spite of ABC, X is so attractive that we go ahead." It is critical for a venture capitalist to circumvent the focusing effect (or prediction bias)—the process whereby people place too much importance on one aspect of an event, which causes error in predicting the future outcome. Aggregating facts is not sufficient. The VC has to be good at making judgments and scratching off options. This cannot be encapsulated in a market-based system, which is probably better at aggregating the information than at decision making. For example, a study by Tsvi G. Vinig and Maartan De Haan on the criteria used for screening business plans found that both Dutch and U.S. VCs consider the entrepreneur as the most important criterion in evaluating business plans, but in second place, Dutch VCs rank innovative products or services, whereas U.S. VCs look at proprietary, protected products.[5]

A top VC interviewed for this book recounted a boardroom discussion where the debate was whether the company should be in a leading market position or whether it was going too fast. Both perspectives are right, and the debate can't solve which is a good move. What distinguishes good VCs use to from the run-of-the-mill is their ability to assign the right weight to the factors. The weight depends on the lens through which VCs look at the issue and how they reverse-engineer the priorities to view the issues.

What Entrepreneurs Should Do: Commandments to Follow

Working for growth, entrepreneurs do best when they apply certain techniques:

- Tailor your strategy to suit your background.
- Know the unique market gap in each market.
- Adjust for risk in immature and volatile markets.

COMMANDMENT #1: Tailor Your Strategy to Suit Your Background

Opinions differ as to whether the broader scope of investments by VCs in Asia will persist. Andy Tang, managing director of DFJ Dragon, says, "DFJ does not invest in traditional industries for two reasons: due to the tech background of its team, and because they are not too sure how long this sector will last. The market segmentation is clear in the United States—there is a clear distinction between early-stage VC and late-stage PE who invests in cash flow businesses. A VC/PE hybrid is forming in China because every VC firm is growing so quickly. PEs do not take deals in traditional businesses due to their larger fund size, hence this segment is filled by VCs. However, the investment skillsets are totally different." Tang predicts that the traditional segment in China probably will last long enough for a couple of funds, but VCs might face constraints in dealflow after that. "DFJ Dragon was designed to build a platform built to last more than 10 funds."

COMMANDMENT #2: Know the Unique Market Gap in Each Market

One of the leading VCs we interviewed watches out for the supply and demand of late-stage investors and early-stage investors. She subscribes to the Silicon Valley model and laments, "We have too many PE houses with ex-investment bankers dealing with SMEs [small-medium enterprises], mostly revenue-positive late-stage deals and little deals coming from IT. For companies of this stage, an IPO is not too difficult. The most difficult time is behind them. PE firms expressed that they can add value, but some can and some can't. For these companies, the next step is to expand regionally. Companies in Singapore can already do that. At late stage, companies do not need a lot of help."

Eric Tao, vice president of Keytone Ventures (formerly an associate at KPCB China), concurs. "The investment strategy for China is very different. Companies like Google with 100X returns don't come to China. VCs tend to do later-stage deals and invest in the later rounds. For example, U.S. Kleiner Perkins offices invest in over 30 pre-revenue companies. The KP office in China is completely the opposite; our China team never invests in companies without revenue, unless the company has a extremely convincing model and clear customer absorption rate. One Facebook in the U.S. will spawn 20 copycats in China overnight."

COMMANDMENT #3: Adjust for Risk in Immature and Volatile Markets

Although some investors are leery about the picture in the short term, the long-term view among top-quartile VCs is that market demand in Asia is still growing. Nonetheless, the China markets are still immature and volatile, according to Ken Xu, a general partner at

Gobi VC, a China-based early-stage venture capital firm focusing on digital media. The cycles of entrepreneurship and high-tech innovation have been relatively short, resulting in a lack of infrastructure for entrepreneurs, whether legal, financial, or cultural. Additionally, this has resulted in a smaller pool of experienced entrepreneurs and managers from larger corporations entering the venture capital industry, creating a distinction with U.S. firms. Fledging entrepreneurs in Asia do not have easily accessible role models or guidance in creating new businesses due to the small pool of venture capitalists or entrepreneurs working on their second or third venture they can draw from. Another resource that is not readily available to all entrepreneurs is a strong personal network. In Asia, family, educational, and other personal relationships are essential for doing business.[6] Asian firms have not much experience and in particular they are not experienced with term sheets. They have no background or track record, so VCs have to be more hands-on and use their own networks to do due diligence.

Pitfalls to Avoid

The growth stage has dangers of its own:

- Assuming an emergent market will behave like a settled one
- Ignoring unique characteristics in markets
- Believing people are the same everywhere
- Trusting the regulatory framework to work smoothly
- Doing what the Romans do

Asian VC versus Silicon Valley

Is Asian VC just like Silicon Valley VC? If not, are the differences a reflection of immaturity (Some day, China VC will be just like SV VC) or factors unique to China that will persist?

Insights
- Long-term convergence, but Asia will have its unique flavors due to inherent differences in infrastructure, law, and culture.
- Investment in a broad range of sectors in Asia may only be a transient phenomenon.

PITFALL #1: Assuming an Emergent Market Will Behave Like a Settled One

According to Paul Vega, a researcher at INSEAD who has done innovative work regarding foreign and local venture firms in China, "Venture capital is an established industry and business model in the West, with finely tuned and tested investment processes, especially with reference to the Silicon Valley example."[7]

Asia is an example of an emerging model undergoing a teething process. Lin Hong Wong says that the Asian model for VC firms is in the process of evolving:

> There is no clear, distinct model. Given the dominance of U.S. VCs, and specifically because a large proportion of Asian VCs are subsidiaries based on U.S. practice, it is natural that the structure and practices are closely aligned to those of U.S. VCs. Even in Europe, the VC industry is slanted toward the U.S. model. However, many European VCs differ from U.S. VCs in areas such as portfolio valuation. In Asia, many may call themselves VC firms, and may adopt VC structures, but may actually invest mostly in late-stage companies, in view of the lack of start-ups and the poor performance of start-ups in general.

There is consensus among our interviewees that the U.S. model is more refined. U.S. VCs have gone through decades of development and it is widely predicted that China and the rest of Asia will have to go through similar refinements in their VC model. Differences in corporate and tax laws between the United States and other geographies may lead to divergence in practice. However, as corporate and tax laws are merging worldwide, Lin Hong Wong predicts the convergence of practices.

When asked what were the differences between Western VC and Asian VC, Lip Bu Tan replied that there are similarities and differences in the West and East. The similarities are in investment structure, with exit vehicles primarily in IPO or M&A. Similarly, in their early days, U.S. VCs did not invest in tech only, but also into airlines, railroads, and retail. (Currently most U.S. VC investments are in technology while investments in China are in a broader range of sectors.) China is going though the growing pains that the U.S. VC business went through in its early days. Eventually, VCs in Asia will be more specialized and the value of domain knowledge will be more appreciated. With low-hanging-fruit deals gone, companies and VCs will be called to solve hard problems.

PITFALL #2: Ignoring Unique Characteristics in Markets

In China, Jeff Chi predicts, some of the current practices will persist. "In the context of RMB funds becoming popular and more investments exiting on the domestic market," he says, agencies will be providing a variety of services, including "domestic listing and merger and acquisition services for both investors and enterprises."

York Chen adds that there are unique peculiarities in China. The principles may follow those of Silicon Valley but Chinese characteristics will persist. VCs in China have more branch offices, and more supporting staff with a diversified investment focus. Companies divest—that is, go to IPO or arrange to be acquired—in various places, not just in New York.

He elaborates,

> China is different [from the United States]. In U.S. VC firms, the partners lead the entire deal cycle, from finding dealflow to networking to operational value-add. [The partner] is the main instigator. The value-chain is well-established. In Asia, the biggest difference is the reduction in labor cost. The phenomenon of a partner being supported by a larger supporting team is a norm. For example, Legend Capital has five or six partners such as Wang Neng Guang, and they are supported by 40 professionals who assist with industry study, investments, legal, and due diligence. For iD Tech-Ventures, we have six (growing to be eight in the new fund) partners, six vice presidents of investment, and support staff (human resources and accounting). In China, the ratio of one partner to two supporting staff is normal.

> The second is distance and need for branch offices. In Silicon Valley, most of the traveling by a VC is done by driving from Palo Alto to San Francisco. In China, it is unrealistic for a partner based in Beijing to understand operations in provinces like Gansu or Xinjiang. A VC in the U.S. may have two offices, one on Sand Hill Road, another in Boston. A VC in

China would need to have operations in Beijing, Shanghai, Shenzhen, and Guangzhou to fully cover the dealflow. Currently, IDG has offices in Taipei, Beijing, and Shanghai.

The need for proximity is further explained by another top-tier venture capitalist that we interviewed, who says, "We have three offices in China (Beijing, Shanghai, and Hong Kong). Particularly in early-stage ventures, we have to have a presence (within two hours' drive). In China, we know the deans, the faculty, and the brightest students."

York Chen continues,

Third, there is a difference in industry sector focus. In the United States, the focus is on TMT, biotech, and clean technology. In China, there are broader sectors that VCs invest in.

Fourth, divestment is another complexity. U.S. venture-backed start-ups typically exit in Wall Street. Exits are more complex in China as firms can exit in Tokyo, London, New York, Singapore, and even China itself.

Venture capitalists in the United States more often assert contingent control rights, indicated both by the use of convertibles and decisions to replace the entrepreneur. And U.S. VCs have a better capacity to screen projects and to ensure success in the early stages than European VCs.

Lip Bu Tan from Walden cited more differences. A key difference is that in the United States, the founding entrepreneurs take a smaller ownership stake, and in most cases, the founding entrepreneurs are replaceable. In Asia, the founding entrepreneurs take a larger ownership stake, and instead of the VC firing them, the entrepreneurs fire the VC preemptively. In Asia, the VC has to be more humble and bring more value-adding partnerships to the table.

In Asia, the due diligence is not as simple as in the United States. The U.S. VC makes a few calls to check on the management with customers. In Asia, people are more reticent (Asians typically do not badmouth each other) and feedback is more subtle—this makes the due diligence process harder.

In Asia, especially in media-related sectors, government regulation changes rapidly. Asian VCs cannot operate blindly without checking the current status of regulations. For example, Youku.com, Tudou.com, and 56.com may be the most popular video-sharing sites in China, but within the last few months, they've all suffered from downtime. The likely reason? Online videos are a great medium for sharing things like porn or political dissent, two things the Chinese government sometimes censors. This past winter, the Chinese government introduced new regulations that require any new video site to have a license showing that it is majority-owned by a government-controlled business.

Monitoring in the United States is relatively straightforward. In Asia, the situation is less transparent and monitoring is more intense. Walden's Asian team is bigger and the monitoring process is more rigorous and labor-intensive. Entrepreneurs do not reveal everything voluntarily. Usually, Asian entrepreneurs act first before they inform the VC. The environment is not as legalistic, and the standards of governance are not up to scratch. Integrity and trust become important. It is usually not sufficient to take a story told by accounts at face value.

PITFALL #3: Believing People Are the Same Everywhere

Wayne Dai was a tenured professor at U.C. Santa Cruz who before he started a company with one of his Ph.D. students. Now VeriSilicon Holdings Co., Ltd. ("VeriSilicon") is a fast-growing venture-backed silicon solutions company that was ranked one of the Red Herring's 100 Private Companies of Asia and also one of the EE Times 60 Emerging Start-ups. He witnessed firsthand the difference in the entrepreneurial scene between the West and the East. "[In China], there is conflict between returnees and locals. 3i funded my competitor with $37 million and they almost closed down, even though they are doing what we are doing in the same place: Shanghai. Returnees from the U.S. are quite different, even if they have lived in China a long time before leaving. You can be a good technologist, but local people welcome them to transfer technology, bring ideas or conference proceedings or tapes of lectures at Berkeley or Stanford."

Dai adds: "Locals need career paths; you have to give them room to grow. You can import returnees at the top level but not at the middle. Returnees fail because they think it's easy. They are techies who don't know how much manufacturing and sales are behind the success of the chips they designed."

On picking a partner in China, one of the top-tier VCs interviewed for this book offers the following advice. "We were interested in China for a long time. Choosing a partner was always a difficult decision. We didn't have the luxury of someone whom we know very well in California. We like the fact that our founding managing director in China has worked in mainland China for a number of years and was associated with a successful company which had started from nothing. He also had corporate experience in several large global banks. He is also a smart individual."

Information asymmetry in early stage. Ken Xu elaborates, "When the company is in an early stage, the form of the company is still amorphous. Why would an investor want to invest in this company? How do you structure a deal in China? There is a need to learn new IT skills to understand the technology and for a VC to make an informed judgment."

PITFALL #4: Trusting the Regulatory Framework to Work Smoothly

The absence of a clear regulatory framework for private equity in emerging markets in Asia may also slow the pace of investment. Jeff Chi predicts that the practice is drifting toward a hybrid. The Asian model is becoming slightly different. A lot of people think they are drifting toward the U.S. model, but there is a consensus among senior VCs that the model is inherently Asian. Key drivers include differing government regulation on restructuring. (China is establishing RMB funds.) If onshore investing is practiced in Singapore, you cannot allow the issue of preferred shares. There is no legal infrastructure and the concept of options is not practiced, only pseudo options. Legally, there is no such thing as options in China, either. The Chinese model may morph toward a new form, and it is likely that the Chinese system will adapt due to different infrastructure.

In the United States, the government generally adopts a laissez-faire policy toward venture capital activities, says Ken Xu. The Chinese government, in contrast, heavily regulates the industry, adopting draconian policies toward venture capital. For example, it imposes very strict regulations on media, which have affected companies like Tudou, one of the top-rated media-sharing Web sites in China. "Venture capitalists have to be very careful in China," says Xu.

PITFALL #5: Doing What the Romans Do

The risky nature of emerging markets like China characterizes the industry there, a leading VC interviewed for this book. "There are insufficient pure technology companies for VCs in China. Hence, investment for VCs is arbitrary—like playing in a casino. No corporate transparency, investment is tarnished by corruption, GPs and entrepreneurs will get away with corruption with no one questioning them. LPs do not know the details and often end up looking for big-name GPs instead of conducting due diligence." She cites an incident where a GP callously liquidated the venture of a successful entrepreneur for a quick return, as the entrepreneur was held helpless by term sheet clauses. Returns are arbitrary in China. Integrity is the differentiating factor. It is important to be wary of outcome bias—if you judge past experience by outcome rather than by processes, you may find yourself in a very difficult position.

Endnotes

1. D. A. Shepherd and A. L. Zacharakis, "Venture Capitalists' Expertise: A Call for Research into Decision Aids and Cognitive Feedback," *Journal of Business Venturing* 17, no. 1 (2002): 1–20.
2. D. A. Shepherd and A. L. Zacharakis, "The Nature of Information and Over-confidence on Venture Capitalists' Decision Making," in *Venture Capital* (Vol. 2), edited by M. Wright, H. Sapienza, and L. Busenitz (London: Edward Elgar, 2003), pp. 124–144.
3. Michael D. Ensley, "Institutional Isomorphism in Venture Capital Investment Decision Making: Industry Characteristics and Investment Preferences," Rensselaer Polytechnic Institute (RPI)—Lally School of Management & Technology, January 15, 2006.
4. Herbert A. Simon, "A Behavioral Model of Rational Choice," *Quarterly Journal of Economics* 69, no. 1 (February 1955): 99–118.
5. Tsvi G. Vinig and Maarten De Haan, "How do Venture Capitalists Screen Business Plans? Evidence from The Netherlands and the US," December 16, 2002; available at SSRN: http://ssrn.com/abstract=321860 or DOI: 10.2139/ssrn.321860.
6. Silicon Moon, "Immature Venture Capital Industry in Asia," September 29, 2003; retrieved from http://bernardmoon.blogspot.com/2003/09/immature-venture-capital-industry-in.html, June 26, 2009.
7. Paul Vega and Li Choy Chong, "Venture Capital in China: Strategy and Decision Making," *European Business Forum* 18 (Summer 2004) 63–65; retrieved from www.ebfonline.com/Article.aspx?ArticleID=257, July 3, 2009.

5

Smart Money

THE TOP VC ON YOUR BOARD

The best venture capitalists are not passive investors. They make a difference in company building with their advising, recruiting, and partnering.

—Bing Gordon,
Partner at Kleiner Perkins Caufield & Byers

To return to a favorite analogy, venture capitalists really are like skilled chefs, producing special dishes (successful companies) individually. As in the kitchen, scaling up by mass production is often counterproductive and leads to a sharp deterioration in quality and value. Our panel of top-tier venture capitalists agreed that smaller groups of people tend to make better decisions on the board of a company. (Too many cooks do spoil the broth.)

VCs also need the top chefs' ability to use the items at hand to create a feast. When VCs make an investment, they should be looking for what you have, not for what you might wish you have. The best chef makes the best chicken dish with limited ingredients. However, having a few fresh ingredients helps.

This chapter outlines what the best VC chefs do to turn what is available into a winning chef's special. Figure 5.1 provides an overview.

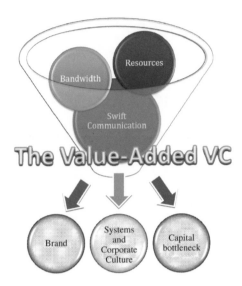

Figure 5.1 How VCs Add Value

If I invest, I am prone to think like an investor, favoring my return over what's best for the team and often its long-term business.

[Angels] pay for the privilege of helping the company.

Tom Alberg, managing director of Madrona Venture Group, walks out of the Computer Science Lab in the University of Washington, delighted at the progress of the research in the university. At this rate, there is a realistic possibility of a spin-out. Alberg and his partners (Paul Goodrich, Greg Gottesman, and Matt McIlwain) have helped to spin out more than 10 companies from the University of Washington's Computer Science and Engineering Department, including Farecast, Impinj, Netbot, Performant, Physware, and Skytap. University commercialization is a core strategy for Madrona. It has been investing in early-stage technology companies in the Pacific Northwest since 1995, and recently announced the closing of Madrona Venture Fund IV in 2008. The fund was oversubscribed at US$250 million, exceeding the target of US$225 million.

Madrona invests in early-stage companies in sectors such as consumer Internet, commercial software and services, digital media and advertising, networking and infrastructure, and wireless—however, it has delivered consistent top-quartile returns from successful investments such as ShareBuilder, Isilon Systems, World Wide Packets, and iConclude. The secret of this success?

"Madrona is entrepreneur-focused. They are not afraid to get a little bit dirty and really roll up their sleeves to help build successful businesses," says Sunny Gupta, CEO of Apptio, a Madrona portfolio company. "This is my third Madrona-backed company. They have a winning strategy that works well for entrepreneurs as well as their fund investors."

Madrona has always believed that early-stage venture capital is a local business," says Matt McIlwain, a managing director at Madrona. "The Pacific Northwest is a leading center of technology-driven innovation, and we expect its influence to grow in the years ahead. We know the region and its entrepreneurs well and think something special is happening here."

VCs all provide financing, but the money isn't always the same: there is smart money, plain-vanilla money, and dumb money. At the top of the list is smart money. This comes with wisdom, not just intelligence and energy. The best VCs unbundle control, advice, and money. Passive investors provide just plain money, leaving the entrepreneurs to figure things out for themselves. Dumb money is the most unhelpful of all, and can even be destructive. Providers of dumb money are most likely to trumpet their value-add. Typically, the more money there is, the smarter it becomes. Bobby Chao summarizes the situation in these terms: "An effective VC brings significant value to the table of a start-up. Such VCs, either one individual or a team of talents, should always bring real battle experience to the entrepreneurs of the start-up. Top choice for such a VC is one who has started and succeeded with a company."

The most tangible value that VC firms add to businesses is capital to meet business expenses, especially before the business breaks even. This "patient" capital, as described by Manju Puri and Rebecca Zarutskie, gives the entrepreneur more time to succeed.[1] On the contrary, they point out, taking on debt would subject the entrepreneur to more immediate pressure as installments on loans need to be repaid immediately along with the incurred interest expense.

In October 2008, Sequoia Capital hosted a mandatory CEO meeting on Sand Hill Road. About 100 CEOs gathered, and the mood was somber. A slide filled the huge conference room screen as people assembled inside the conference center to take their seats: a gravestone inscribed with "R.I.P., Good Times." The only time Sequoia had assembled all CEOs like this was during the dot-com crash.

The assistance of a venture capitalist is most valuable in bad times. The archetypical venture capitalist is selective. When considering an investment, venture capitalists carefully screen the technical and business merits of the proposed company. They pick minority ownership, invest in only a small percentage of the businesses they review, and take a long-term perspective. The bulk of them actively work with the company's management by contributing their experience and the business savvy they have gained from helping other companies with similar growth challenges.

The investment by venture funds into portfolio companies is called *disbursements*. A company will receive capital in one or more rounds of financing. A venture firm may make these disbursements by itself or it may draw in other venture firms (a process called *co-investment* or *syndication*). This syndication provides more capital resources for the company. Firms co-invest because the company investment is congruent with the investment strategies of various venture firms and each firm will bring some competitive advantage to the investment.

The lead venture firm will provide capital and management expertise and will usually also take a seat on the board of the company to ensure that the investment has the best chance of being successful. A portfolio company may receive one round, or in many cases, several rounds of venture financing in its life as needed. A venture firm may not invest all of its committed capital, but will reserve some capital for later investment in some of its successful companies with additional capital needs.

What Star VCs Do: Winning Techniques

What top VCs do to develop smart money boils down to the following techniques:

- If possible, win preemptive acceptance.
- Match the increasing sophistication of the new breed of entrepreneurs.
- Diversify risk and minimize mistakes.

WINNING TECHNIQUE #1: If Possible, Win Preemptive Acceptance

The work begins early in the game. Noubar Afeyan of Flagship Ventures coins the term "preemptive acceptance." He elaborates,

"If we do our job right, the entrepreneur will take our term sheet preemptively. We will proactively engage the entrepreneur to work with us so entrepreneurs will not need to shop for a higher term sheet. Generally, when we work with a group of entrepreneurs, we will say 'If you really want to find out what your valuation is, I would be happy to wait and find out. However, if they want me to evaluate and when I issue the term sheet and there is agreement that term sheet is reasonable, they will accept it.' In most cases, we preempt the competition and when there is a competitive situation, we demonstrate to entrepreneurs that the overall value proposition of our involvement is higher than what others may offer—it is not atypical that entrepreneurs will take our term sheet even though we might have offered a lower price." The best VCs generally do not compete on price or terms; instead, they focus on building a trusting relationship with the entrepreneur, taking part in the entrepreneur's hopes and dreams, and explaining how the VC is motivated to help them achieve their goals. In a deal that is highly competitive, the best VCs can make rare exceptions and agree to modify the price or terms in the entrepreneur's favor, but this is not the norm.

WINNING TECHNIQUE #2: Match the Increasing Sophistication of the New Breed of Entrepreneurs

Geographies like China are seeing a new breed of entrepreneurs who are increasingly Western educated. Many ambitious young Asian entrepreneurs are returning to China to make it big. When Bo Shao got an MBA from Harvard Business School in 1999, he then returned to China to launch EachNet, an eBay-style consumer auction site. At that time, his move was unusual. "Of the 11 people originally from mainland China in my Harvard class, I was the only one in China," says Shao. "Everyone else wanted a green card." After launching EachNet in 1999, he sold the company to eBay (EBAY), which bought a minority stake for US$30 million in 2002 and then paid US$150 million for the rest of the company in 2003.

With top Silicon Valley venture capital firms on the prowl in China, India, and other parts of Asia, all of them eager to fund the entrepreneurial dreams of young Asians, now it's unusual to find people who don't want to return to the region. Fortunately for young people starting up new businesses, there's a growing familiarity with entrepreneurship, especially among Chinese and Indians. Avnish Bajaj last year started Matrix Partners, a Mumbai-based firm focusing on early-stage investments. He himself is a former entrepreneur, having started consumer auction site Baazee in 1999. (Like EachNet's Shao, Bajaj also sold his company to eBay, in 2004.) "Since 1999, there's been a sea change," says Bajaj. "The entrepreneurial ecosystem has changed." He recalls starting Baazee and trying to negotiate office space with a landlord who wanted to see four years of the start-up's balance sheet. "So we didn't have an office for a year," says Bajaj. "Today, people know what start-ups are and don't ask those kinds of questions!"

South Korean tech start-ups used to get three times the amount of VC investment their Chinese counterparts received. "Now it's the reverse," says a Korean venture capitalist, who estimates tech-related companies in China got between US$600 million and US$700 million in VC money in 2007, compared with just US$290 million for Korean companies.

WINNING TECHNIQUE #3: Diversify Risk and Minimize Mistakes

Jeffrey Khoo and Kim Seng Tan, managing directors at 3VS1, also learned to hedge their investments in different emerging technology sectors to improve their chance of success. In the early days of Bluetooth and Wi-Fi, they bet on both Bluetooth and Wi-Fi by investing in a leading Bluetooth SOHO Gateway company in the Silicon Valley and also into a fabless semiconductor company focusing on Wi-Fi and wireless communications.

Top investors, in addition to having ample capital to invest (it's true that "you need money to make money"), understand, manage, and minimize their (and their capital's) exposure to various types of risk (political and country, economic, currency, and so on). They also understand the importance of diversity in allocating resources for investment, whether that entails equities, bonds, derivatives, or funds of funds. A single entrepreneur should not be a heavyweight in the portfolio of the venture capital provider, nor should the portfolio company be an insignificant member whose success or failure will have no direct impact. An entrepreneur would expect to be between 5 percent and 25 percent of the VC's total portfolio, including of the portfolio of the finance provider on whose behalf the VC is doing the investment. Entrepreneurs are also looking for the VC to provide an accurate valuation of their company as reflected in the percentage of equity an entrepreneur would need to part with for each million dollars of investment.

What Entrepreneurs Should Do: Commandments to Follow

We know that it takes more than solid financial support to get a company off the ground.[2]

—Kleiner Perkins Caufield & Byers

When it comes to assessing the value of money, entrepreneurs have a full set of 10 commandments:

- Do not expect VCs to have all the answers.
- Look for the deal with the highest probability of closing.
- Find the entrepreneurial passion.
- Pay attention to VC brand name.
- Seek ruth.
- Follow personal chemistry.
- Do your due diligence on the VC.
- Find VCs who can add complementary value on your multi-faceted challenges.
- Remember that nothing replaces actual operating experience.
- Watch the track record of your board.

COMMANDMENT #1: Do Not Expect VCs to Have All the Answers

VCs are not gods. Entrepreneurs cannot expect to be told what to do by VCs. This bit of wisdom goes back thousands of years. As Aesop has the demigod Hercules tell the carter who prayed to him for help when his wagon was stuck in the mud, "Put your shoulders to the wheels, my man. Goad on your bullocks, and don't ask me for help until you have done your best to help yourself. If not, you'll ask in vain from now on."

If you look to your VC for the elixir of business life, you are likely to be disappointed. Research by KPMG shows that late-stage venture capitalists recognize the importance of identifying and solving problems with portfolio companies but acknowledge that their reaction to issues is often too little too late.[3] Intervention tends not to involve a heavy commitment on the part of the private equity house and predominantly involves the replacement of underperforming management teams, so the one looking for rescue is the least likely to benefit from it. Private equity houses rarely have the people with the right skills or resources to regularly respond more proactively. They are sometimes able to supplement deal skills with appropriate management expertise, allowing proactive assistance to be given to portfolio companies to add or protect value, but it is unwise to count on them to do so.

COMMANDMENT #2: Look for the Deal with the Highest Probability of Closing

Securing VC funding is not just a numbers game. Entrepreneurs face a trade-off between choosing the offer with the highest valuation and one that will close the investments. It is best to turn down term sheets with high valuations that seem unlikely to materialize. Although valuation is still important, the process is akin to an auction. Even when the term sheet is offered, things may go wrong at the last moment.

Andy Tang adds, "From my M&A experience in selling, you do not pick the offer with highest price, but rather, the offer with the highest probability of closing a deal. Given a sophisticated investor, the price has to be within range but what's more important is the credibility of closing a deal." He points out that entrepreneurs risk the fate of Aesop's dog—the one who lost his bone while trying to steal another from his shadow in the stream. Even though most VCs abide by an honor code and regard a handshake as a promise, some will offer a term sheet and then refuse to close the deal.

COMMANDMENT #3: Find the Entrepreneurial Passion

Entrepreneurs like entrepreneurial investors. "Entrepreneurs tend to fall in love with people who fall in love with their idea," says Noubar Afeyan of Flagship Ventures. Entrepreneurs tend to be passionate about what they do about changing the world and the successful ones have antennae that detect that. They can intuitively figure out that VCs who are passionate are likely to last with them over the bumps on the road, bringing resilience and staying power.

Tim Draper of Draper Fisher Jurvetson adds, "I had lots of ideas for different businesses and wanted to pursue all of them, but I knew there was not enough time in the day to do it all. Venture capital allowed me that flexibility. I don't run any of the companies, but I get to work with them and create with them. Also, my father was a VC, and so was my grandfather. I am 'son of VC' model." Lip Bu Tan, founder of Walden International, advises that it is important to ensure that the VC firm shares the entrepreneur's vision and is willing to commit the passion, time, and bandwidth to help the entrepreneur build the company.

COMMANDMENT #4: Pay Attention to VC Brand Name

Reputation plays a critical role in determining who entrepreneurs should look for when choosing their partnering VC firms. A consistent dealflow can be attributed to good reputation. The top VC firms always get the opportunity to screen the best deals. Hence, they have the chance to invest in the best deals, leaving only the second tier or nothing for the rest. In addition, these top-tier venture capital firms are able to choose companies with sound management teams that are capable of both strategizing and executing their plans. Hence, less involvement is required from the venture capital firm in terms of management, allowing the start-ups to focus on milestones.[4] This creates a virtuous circle—if you can line up a top-tier VC, that tells the world you are one of the top prospects, and that makes everything easier.

Among other advantages, the franchise power of a top firm with brand-name partners brings with it a monopoly on the best entrepreneurs. The best headhunters want to work with top-tier names, which helps their companies attract the best teams. The best law firms will be engaged. Portfolio companies get more publicity due to higher press attention. The *keiretsu* effect—networking between portfolio companies and the moral suasion for companies to buy from one another—helps portfolio companies secure recognizable anchor customers. A top name also attracts the best investment bank, usually resulting in a more successful IPO.

When asked what is the winning formula, a top-tier VC we interviewed said, "I wish I knew. It sounds simple but a big part is showing up for work every day. Having invested in a successful venture, you are automatically excused from working hard. Being associated with successful ventures helps. The venture industry is a service business. It is not always about the valuation; a smart entrepreneur would choose the VC which would give him the best service.''

COMMANDMENT #5: Seek Ruth

Are you familiar with the word *ruth*? You've probably heard the related word *ruthless*, but few know that its root is the basis of a compelling and important virtue. The dictionary will tell you that *ruth* is a noun (pronounced to rhyme with *tooth*) that refers to pity or compassion, and to some related emotions.

Compassion is a most important notion in the capital formation process. If financial acumen and adequate intellect are constants among those who survive in the field, then it is compassion that separates one VC from another. For top-quartile VCs, the defining combination has been a trio of financial acumen, intellect, and compassion.

One top-quartile venture capitalist interviewed for this book elaborates: ''My partner and I were the largest individual share-holders of realtor.com (Homestore) at the time of the IPO. We beat out most large VCs. By the time of the IPO, we were joined by Kleiner Perkins, GE Capital, and most of the top VC firms. We ''won'' the initial capital opportunity because of our attributes. This brought our initial US$500,000 investment to a liquid value of over US$100 million in less than five years.''

Dick Kramich of NEA has been cited by CEOs of his portfolio companies to be positive without being arrogant.[5] He is confident yet open to ideas of others, and still ''amazingly quick when replying to board decisions and action items.'' Meetings are discussions, not dictated one-way sessions. From the entrepreneur's perspective, Hian Goh of Asian Food Channel believes that the best VCs are those who are committed to a cooperative relationship, not an adversarial one, and have enough faith in the entrepreneurs to let them run their business.

COMMANDMENT #6: Follow Personal Chemistry

There is also need for personal comfort between the CEO and the VC. Andy Tang says, ''I tell my portfolio CEOs that I am the fourth founder of the company. I am passionate, roll up my sleeves, and take pride in the company. I let them feel the same way and show that my addition would result in a stronger team. For a CEO, [signing with a VC] is frightening and a VC can be perceived to do a lot of damage. Some VCs do not do deals with people they do not know, but this severely restricts the dealflow. I take a moderate approach but with someone familiar and where there is personal comfort, it is easier to add value. If you chase the hottest deals, you are bound to do deals with people you do not know. If we do indeed do a deal with someone we do not know, we do a lot of reference checks.''

Noubar Afeyan says, ''There is massive heterogeneity in personality and character types in venture people they deal with. Although entrepreneurs, in general, like people who give them money, there has to be chemistry. A strong relationship will develop if they sense the person has integrity and is trustworthy.'' This is of particular salience if the entrepreneurs have a choice. ''The entrepreneurs are stuck talking to these people three or four times a week and if you don't like this person, it can be quite painful.''

In a hot deal, entrepreneurs choose who will be allowed to invest, says York Chen. VCs have to compete for deals. The shrewd entrepreneur will look beyond the financials. The VC will be the shareholder and take a board seat. The VC will also be seen as a core joint entrepreneur and a co-founder and will stay with the entrepreneurs throughout good and bad times for four or five years. Key questions asked: Can the VC and entrepreneur coexist? Can they get along with each other? Can they communicate intelligently with each other? The VCs and the entrepreneur have to agree on the big direction. A good fit of complementary skillsets is a win-win for the portfolio company.

In some Asian countries, many cultural obstacles still remain for entrepreneurs. Ta-Lin Hsu, chairman of H&Q Asia Pacific, says that Japanese entrepreneurs bemoan the fact that Japanese culture still is not supportive enough to young people keen on launching their own businesses rather than going to work for big corporations. ''Entrepreneurs are rare species in Japan. The government have tried to promote entrepreneurship in Japan, but they understand that it's a very, very difficult thing for Japanese.''

CASE IN POINT: PART

Chaming Zhang was an entrepreneur from Taiwan who had just started PART, a social networking service providing netizen blogs, photo albums, friendship and dating services, and wireless value-added functions. In the existing business model, the unique and exclusively owned chameleon advertisement on its home page is welcomed by many famous brands, such as Lancome, Sony, Estee Lauder, Dior, Oral-B, Pepsi, and China Merchant Bank's credit card.

York Chen, general partner of iD TechVentures, had known Zhang well. Both of them came from Taiwan. When iDT VC made the investment, the company was fundraising Series A and about to expand to China. Due to the formative nature of the company, iDT VC was not only a passive financial investor but was actively involved in the entrepreneurial process. Chen says that the start-up's expansion was more like a joint effort between the founders and iDT VC.

Zhang's PART, based in Taipei, Taiwan, was just entering China. iDT VC already had four years behind it and had experience to advise. iDT VC was perceived as a co-founder and joint entrepreneur and injected money and experience into the start-up.

As a new investor into PART, iDT VC was in a position to know less but better appreciate what was happening, Chen explains. The firm was able to stand beside the entrepreneur and jointly chart new directions for growth. This kind of long-term development can benefit shareholders as well as the entrepreneur, even though receiving a capital injection means that entrepreneurs have to share ownership with others. If different stakeholders pursue different ideas about moving the start-up, there can be immense friction. Chen adds, "When a high-handed investor is involved, this can be messy." In mainland China, PART has received funding from Taiwan-based iDT and from Japanese firms JAIC and Cyber Agent within two years of its founding. In its third round, it was joined by Vickers Financial.

It is not the answer that enlightens, but the question.

—Decouvertes

You can tell whether a man is clever by his answers. You can tell whether a man is wise by his questions.

—Naguib Mahfouz

A prudent question is one-half of wisdom.

—Francis bacon

COMMANDMENT #7: Do Your Due Diligence on the VC

Due diligence matters. VCs won't put money into start-ups until they know who and what they're dealing with. Smart entrepreneurs play by the same rules. Entrepreneurs tend to be so thrilled to be under consideration that they pay little attention to the track records of the VCs who seem willing to provide funds. But no matter how warm and friendly they seem, venture capitalists are big believers in due diligence, the process whereby they investigate the track records of the entrepreneurs under serious consideration for receiving investment funds. Understandably, they want to do everything possible to reduce their investment risks. Entrepreneurs would do well to perform their own due diligence. Basic principles:

- Ask smart questions.
- Remember the maxim: He who shares the danger ought to share the prize.
- Discuss corporate governance.
- Find out what resources the VC can bring.
- Assess bandwidth.
- Look for swift communication.

Ask Smart Questions   Once they invest, VCs have a huge amount of power. They can force changes in management and determine whether follow-up investment funds will available to keep a start-up going. To reduce the risk of getting in with the wrong crowd, entrepreneurs should ask some pointed questions of their own, including How much value-added is the VC firm likely to provide? VCs are fond of arguing that entrepreneurs gain all kinds of intangibles in exchange for selling stock to the professional investors— business advice, networking opportunities, key contacts—and that these actors help justify a lower valuation vis-à-vis what an entrepreneur might have obtained from family or angel investors. Speak with other entrepreneurs who have received funding from the VCs you are investigating. Make it a point to speak with entrepreneurs who have gone through some kind of crisis. How did the venture capitalists react? What actions did they take?

Sudhir Sethi's first advice to entrepreneurs is to choose their investor based on track record and value-add. It is important for the entrepreneur to find out if the VC is worthy of sitting on the board and being a "first-stop mentor." The VC-entrepreneur relationship in early venture funding lasts for years; entrepreneurs must use trust as a significant criterion in addition to capital and valuations. Tim Draper of Draper Fisher Jurvetson predicts that the venture capitalist who is most likely to succeed is "the one who is the most determined to fight for the entrepreneur."

Remember: "He who shares the danger ought to share the prize"
VCs are often susceptible to loss aversion—the tendency to strongly prefer avoiding losses over acquiring gains. A good VC shares both the joys and woes of start-ups. VCs can improve the quality of the team. VCs and entrepreneurs (or founding teams) must build smart teams who can scale up the business and also keep the flock together. Good teams can weather business down-cycles; bad teams find it difficult to grow even in good cycles. In addition, entrepreneurs must focus on building value and valuation from an exit point of view. In a tough IPO market, scale, differentiation, and plain old profits are critical to a successful exit for investors and founders.

Discuss Corporate Governance   A venture firm may also bring in corporate governance. Studies have shown that venture capital firms help establish better corporate governance, which results in higher-quality financial reporting. This will aid the entrepreneur by increasing the likelihood of IPO or trade sale. Studies have also shown that publicly listed companies backed by high-quality VCs have lower abnormal accruals and lower likelihood of financial restatement. Hence, they have a 5 percent lower chance of getting liquidated or delisted as compared to those not backed by venture firm.[6]

Find Out What Resources the VC Can Bring   The nonfinancial contributions from a VC may be intangible, but they can be very real:

- *Strategic counseling:* The VC is able to assist in areas in management consulting, accounting, and finance decisions if the entrepreneur lacks people with skillsets in these areas.
- *Introductions to key organizations and individuals:* Well-networked VCs are able to build on their relationships with the financial, media, research, and corporate communities that can assist the entrepreneur in creating a successful, sustainable, and market-innovating business.[7]
- *Assistance with operations and process improvements:* VCs able to tap their experiences handling a large portfolio of companies can assist in improve the operations and processes of the entrepreneur's venture, making it more efficient and competitive.
- *Assistance with recruitment:* VCs can recommend certain individuals for key positions on the management team such as the CEO or the CFO, providing candidates who are experienced and able to add value to the venture.
- *Building credibility and reputation:* Reputable VCs who have consistent records with their portfolio of companies can improve the reputation of the entrepreneur's business.[8]

The top-tier VCs we interviewed have money, networks of contacts, ethics, and ideas about how to increase the chances of success of a start-up. When an entrepreneur needs access to businesspeople, investors, or partners, good VCs typically do not hesitate to suggest possibilities, and they will also arrange for the contact to be made quickly, further helping drive the business. (For example, Dick Kramich of NEA looks for outstanding people to be part of his global brain trust constantly and invites young people to join gatherings, events, and meetings so they can learn.)

Lip Bu Tan encourages portfolio companies to do due diligence in which the VCs value-add. Do they value-add in terms of access to customers, product ideas, and management recruitment? Are there synergies with the rest of the VC's portfolio? (That is, Are the other portfolio companies complementary or competitors?) Can the VC help hire people whose strengths would complement the team's weaknesses? In certain cases, VCs can help a business attract the best talent by supporting generous incentives through stock options for long-term motivation.

Lip Bu Tan quotes an example of a smart entrepreneur (Telegence) that received eight competing term sheets from different VCs and eventually chose Walden and NEA (New Enterprise Associates). The prudent entrepreneur did the necessary reference checks, and went through in detail on the 34 proposed points on how Walden could value-add, asking questions like "How many boards are you on? How much resources can you spare to help my company?" An example he quotes is Wong Hoo Sim, founder of Creative Technology, who initially told Tan that he hates VC. However, due to Walden's reputation and Tan's willingness and commitment to roll up his sleeves to help build the company, Creative chose Walden. Currently, Tan is still helping Creative.

Entrepreneurs like VCs they think can expand potential for their project. Noubar Afeyan adds, "They tend to prefer true partners to mere investors and overweight the connectedness of VC to industry (not academia). For example, a VC who sits on the board of Microsoft is more useful to entrepreneurs than someone who may be a great investor but cannot open these doors." Srikanth Ramachandran, an entrepreneur at At Life Pte. Ltd., a computer software company, adds, "Money being equal, there would be four major criteria—investment contract (devil is in the details), operations support (business development help in selected markets as Asia is diverse), ability to lead in subsequent rounds, and exit support (likely to be M&A network)."

Eddy Shalev, managing partner of Genesis Partners, addresses big market needs and value-adds by expanding the horizon of markets and sectors for his portfolio companies. Increasingly, he is finding that his venture-backed companies are fulfilling these big needs in the consumer market:

> In recent years, we have seen a new generation of Israeli entrepreneurs ready to build truly global businesses that are based in Israel and not necessarily U.S.-oriented. Many consumer-electronics start-ups in our portfolio, such as Oree, PrimeSense, or Modu, are highly focused on key decision makers based in Asia or in Europe, as well as in the U.S. These companies are establishing a presence in whatever markets they need to; they are hiring talent from around the world and they are building a robust ecosystem

that can support their market penetration efforts. We are also seeing a willingness on the part of VCs and entrepreneurs to build businesses outside of the traditional areas of high technology. This includes consumer electronics, but it also includes some areas of environment, energy, and industrial applications where Israeli technology is also world-leading.

Assess bandwidth A portfolio company CEO of NEA explains, "When you are in meetings with Dick [Kramich], you feel as if you and your company are the most important to him. You get undivided attention. The quality of time spent thus becomes very high and so do the quality of decisions." Similarly, Zac Boon of McLean Watson tells his companies, "I am available," but he also communicates clearly that the entrepreneurs should have done their homework before consulting him. However, he adds, "When you have a hard problem, I will do my very best to help you."

Look for Swift Communication The ability to communicate with the VC firm is an important criterion. Entrepreneurs typically prefer those VCs who are friendly, personable, and sympathetic, and who employ simple, uncomplicated evaluation processes. Start-ups gain competitive momentum because of swift decision making. A founder of one of the portfolio companies mentored by Dick Kramich of NEA says, "As fast as the decision approval is needed, I find e-mails from Dick from NEA among the first to arrive. VCs are terribly busy and travel a great portion of their time. Dick responds swiftly in spite of the intense demands on his time." Great VCs respond, fast. Pick investors who give you what feels like an unfairly large share of time and mind. For example, Pierre Hennes of Upstream Ventures is located in close proximity to his start-ups. One is one floor above him and the others are a few minutes' drive away, allowing him to interact with them frequently across multiple levels, both formal and informal. Being in constant communication with his portfolio companies, he can turn stone into gold. Pushing the portfolio's management to think bigger, faster, and stronger is one of the cornerstones of his success. He also actively surfaces opportunities for the companies to market themselves at national and international platforms.

COMMANDMENT #8: Find VCs Who Can Add Complementary Value on Your Multifaceted Challenges

Kathy Xu, managing director of Capital Today, has spent a lot of time with entrepreneurs and grown together with them. She sees three areas where VCs can contribute a great deal to the success of their portfolio companies:

- Brand
- Systems and corporate culture
- Capital bottlenecks

Brand   What is the difference between Wahaha mineral water and other types of mineral water? There is no difference in taste; water is the same. Why do they have higher volume of sales? Evian water is so expensive, why do people still consume it? The difference is brand. Customers perceive a venture-backed company as having a better brand.

Systems and Corporate Culture   Soft and vague though it may seem, culture is essential to install at the start of the company. How powerful is a corporate culture? Huawei, Legend, and Haier all depend heavily on the culture to manage people. Initially, companies tend to try for management by system, but eventually management by culture makes things go much more smoothly. When Kathy Xu invested in 51Job, the company had only five employees. The CEO did a lot of things himself. When the company grew to 100 people, its revenue growth hit a plateau with only 30–40 percent annual growth. The CEO had not taken a single day of leave for five or six years. We then hired four senior management team members from Huawei to instill corporate culture and the annual company growth increased to 120 percent. The company still sold the same product with the same brand and employed same business model. What changed was systems and corporate culture. Why the big difference? Everyone was dedicated and hard-working. To them, it was not just a job, it was a chance to carve out a career.

Culture is an amazing force. You can't poach anyone from Alibaba even though they could afford to leave whenever they wished. Jack Ma, CEO of Alibaba, has motivated his employees to build a US$1 billion enterprise. Systems and performance reviews are indispensable, and rewards are pegged to performance review.

Without the proper incentives and culture, retail purchasing employees often succumb to offers of kickbacks. But once you spend some time to fine-tune the system and understand the employees' mind-set, you can inspire them to find customers even after work—without kickbacks or other improper payments in either direction. It is the CEO's duty to instill the cultural mind-set and emphasize the importance of the team. The company will not collapse because a particular individual leaves. There can be a team of A players when everyone feels what they are doing is noble and there is dynamism in the culture.

Capital Bottlenecks VCs can solve quite a lot of problems; the solution is straightforward when a company has no money to put out advertisements or no resources to hire people. But just how much does the CEO need? Despite the need for money, the founder generally wants to remain the majority shareholder. How do you solve the problem? For an e-commerce firm, VCs typically prefer to invest at least US$2.5 million each tranche for two tranches, predicting that US$5 million would bring RMB500 million in annual sales.

Another company Kathy Xu has served as a director was Netease.com, first founded by William Ding (Ding Lei) in June 1997 in Guangzhou. With a team of software engineers led by Ding Lei, they created the coding of a bilingual Web-based distributed message system similar to hotmail. This system became very popular; it was able to attract major players and gained significant market share in the Internet messaging industry in China. This attracted investors such as Barings Private Equity Partner Asia to invest. Kathy Xu, as China head of Barings Private Equity Partner Asia, invested on behalf of Barings a total sum of US$5 million and even held on to the stake after the IPO. Eventually, Barings exited in 2004, gaining an IRR of 40 percent from its initial funding. Similarly, News Corporation invested in Netease in 2000 and exited with a total sum of US$4.6 million and an agreement with Netease. com that they can use their advertising holdings in Asia, worth US$2 million.[9]

Small businesses and start-ups often face the problem of lacking track records and core competencies compared to other competitors who are more well-established. With a well-established VC–for example, 3i–investing in the business, they send a signal that the management is credible and worthy of confidence. This will greatly facilitate the process of building relationships with various customers and suppliers.

CASE IN POINT: Amazon.com

One entrepreneur that clearly benefited from the value-add of a VC was Jeff Bezos of Amazon.com.[10] When pursuing VC financing for his venture, Bezos rejected offers from two funds that offered him more money than the VC he finally chose: Kleiner Perkins Caufield & Byers (KPCB).

When asked why he had accepted the lower bid from KPCB, Bezos responded, "If we'd thought all this was purely about money, we'd have gone with another firm. But KPCB is the gravitational center of a huge piece of the Internet world. Being with them is like being on prime real estate." As a result, KPCB was able to value-add to Amazon.com by improving its credibility and reputation, which were considered key criteria for Internet start-ups during the dot-com boom.

In addition to investing US$8 million and improving Amazon.com's reputation, KPCB also persuaded Scott Cook, chairman of Intuit, to join Amazon.com's board of directors. Furthermore, KPCB also recruited two vice presidents for the company. Finally in May 2007, KPCB assisted Amazon.com in going public.

Thus, this example illustrates how choosing a VC goes beyond the financing benefits, as the right VC for the entrepreneur can contribute much more in ensuring that the business is successful. However, it is also important to note that caution is in order: VCs may promise value-added assistance without being able to pull through on their promises.

COMMANDMENT #9: Remember That Nothing Replaces Actual Operating Experience

Entrepreneurs appreciate a VC's background as a practitioner. Kim Seng Tan of 3VS1 began his career with Texas Instruments (TI) Singapore as a systems engineer before moving on to Nortel (Northern Telecom Asia). He then moved on to the banking industry and was involved in the retail banking, electronic banking, trade banking, and commercial banking operations at the United Overseas Bank in Singapore. His partner, Jeffrey Khoo, started his career as an engineer at HP before moving to Government of Singapore Investment Corporation (Real Estate Division) in Redwood City, where he managed the property investment portfolio in Silicon Valley and the Greater Seattle area. In the early 1990s, he returned to Singapore for family reasons and started different businesses, including a real-estate business involved in the Financial Square in Shanghai, China, and Tasek Plaza & Tasek Office Complex in Johor Bahru, Malaysia, and a regional travel business with annual sales in excess of US$100 million.

Jeffrey Khoo and Kim Seng Tan felt that their operational and entrepreneurial experience helped them understand the needs of entrepreneurs. They could see concerns from an entrepreneur's viewpoint and be more effective coaches, warning against blind spots. Tan places a premium on working with talents and teamwork, and would "rather hire the top brains than claim to be top brain that will do wonders by himself." Their experiences also allowed them to motivate entrepreneurs to move toward success rather than away from failure.

For example, 3VS1 invested in a company that develops custom-engineered high-performance fabrics. It has worked closely with the CEO, an outstanding scientist, to focus on early revenue generation by addressing the ready markets in order to fund its further research and development of new generation products. Jeffrey Khoo and Kim Seng Tan had seen a lot of technology companies and their conscious focus on product and market risks helps their portfolio companies to improve their chances of success and reduce financing risk. Today, the high-performance fabric company has developed a full range of special fabrics with substantial market applications and currently enjoys a healthy cash flow.

Mike Hirshland, general partner at Polaris Ventures, advises, "At Polaris, we as partners will not be the smartest individuals in any given field." He instead urged budding venture capitalists to develop the ability to identify opportunities and judge character; over time, to focus on various specialties and sub-specialties and hone their knowledge of these areas. In addition, a lot of opportunities in the tech sector are about execution, not technical expertise, says Raj Kapoor, managing director at Mayfield, a venture capital firm based in Menlo Park, California. A sense of timing and a good marketing instinct are two qualities at a premium in today's market. "It's not about specialization," says Stan Reiss, a general partner at Matrix Ventures. "It's about quickly figuring out new trends within your general area of expertise. The people who hop around a lot will be successful."

People Risk The people behind the money need to be a major factor in the choice of VC. The technical contribution is a given, but it's the soft skill attributes that are key to any relationship of this nature—and they have a significant impact on the business's progress. The VCs' intentions and motives, how they handle challenges, what their people skills are, whether they inspire and add value, and a number of other attributes make successful business relationships. It's the invisible and unspoken agreements that often cause the trouble. The key is seeing these before entering into an agreement and making them visible. Mitigating the people risk on both sides will improve likelihood of a mutually satisfactory conclusion.

Recruiting The top venture firms, for the most part, play the role of a business partner.[11] With the top firms having a good reputation, they are able to hire the best people within the industry and provide the company with a wide range of human capital from various industries.

Intuitive Wisdom Dick Kramich of NEA knows when the hard decisions must be made. It may be management stepping aside, or a need for refinancing in times of trouble. He understands the competitive maneuvers of start-ups, faces reality with clarity, and has the will to make the best of difficult situations. A portfolio CEO says, "I recall how he gave his opinion about what to do after the analysis was completed. It is there that he seems to know the best move among the many, with uncanny intuition. Years of learning, from mistakes as well as winners, has given him much wisdom and perspective."

In Singapore, one of the VCs we interviewed explains, companies cannot grow big because of the Singaporean ecosystem. At late stage, companies do not need a lot of help. The tough part is already over. The key is how a VC can help the entrepreneurs at the right time; how to go overseas to Europe and the United States and how to bring technology to the United States. VCs need to prove their worth by handholding entrepreneurs and motivating them.

COMMANDMENT #10: Watch the Track Record of Your Board

Shrewd entrepreneurs tend to pick their board members carefully, as they get more than money with a venture capitalist. Learn the exit policy of the VCs you are considering and observe their track record. Do they stick on beyond requirement and want to become the entrepreneur themselves? Or do they abandon a portfolio company when the business environment gets hot? Can you expect support if the funds requirement shoots up, and will that support come at a cost? By "come at a cost" I mean: Will the VC revaluate and change the ratio of millions invested per percentage of equity?

When asked why an entrepreneur would pick one VC over another, Lip Bu Tan advises his entrepreneurs to look at the following characteristics:

- What is the VCs' track record? A smart entrepreneur would make reference checks to see how the VCs have acted in the past. How do VCs behave on a board? Are they helpful? Do they have sector expertise? Are they egocentric? Do they have integrity?
- What is the VCs' fund lifetime? For example, if they only have five years in their fund life, and this is the last deal they invest in, they might not have the eight years you will probably need to build a great company (which would exceed the timetable of their fund life) and end up selling the company prematurely.

In general a shrewd entrepreneur would ask the following questions before choosing a VC:

1. Are my goals aligned with the VC's? (Quick exit, play for the long haul, and so on.)

2. Is there chemistry between me and the specific partner who will be working with my company, so we can work together, trust each other?
3. What is the history and track record of the VC firm and the partner?
4. How well connected is the VC? The partner? Can they open doors, bring in customers, relationships with strategic partners, and so on? How wide is their network?
5. How have they treated founders in the past? Do they tend to respect the entrepreneur or bring in "general management" and replace the founders soon?
6. Is the VC willing to be satisfied in working where the entrepreneur or founder still has sufficient control stake in the company?
7. How deep are the VC's pockets? Is the firm likely to be willing to participate in future rounds of financing?

In addition, many VCs have an option to fund the venture through more than one institution, and if VCs opt to finance from one of the funds where their interest is higher, the entrepreneur would take that as a signal of commitment, but would also be wary of the funder not exiting as planned.

The experienced entrepreneur looks for the following:

- Someone who truly believes in the business and shares in the vision, and is willing to properly fund the business, knowing there will be unforeseen hurdles that will need to be overcome.
- A track record of successful exits within similar markets.
- Someone it is possible to trust and have good rapport with.
- The best valuation and deal. Any entrepreneur would want to protect the upside. An entrepreneur would rather retain sufficient control and realize the returns for the risks being taken.

There is no one-size-fits-all solution. The decision would differ because of the type of entrepreneur (goals, level of risk taking, domain, and so on) and the situation (the round, maturity of idea or product, capital needed, and the like). Generally, entrepreneurs interviewed for this book believe in self-financing as long as possible and bringing the company to a reasonable valuation before approaching VCs.

Pitfalls to Avoid

When recruiting VCs, watch for the following pitfalls:

- Bringing in outside investors despite a difference in interests
- Mismatching expectations between entrepreneur and VC
- Becoming meat in a sandwich
- Training your replacement

PITFALL #1: Bringing in Outside Investors Despite a Difference in Interests

Entrepreneurs often see their venture as personal property—not without justification. The emotional and physical effort and financial resources they invest into the venture makes it as dear as a child. As the venture reaches the growth stage, some of the entrepreneur's formal control over the venture may have to be sacrificed to attract funding. This often takes the form of an equity stake sale to outside investors not involved in the creation of the venture and not part of the VC firm itself. The primary interests of these investors are financial. These investors will naturally do what they think appropriate to harvest or increase the financial return on their investment.

Arthur Rock, a pre-IPO investor in Apple, had no qualms about getting Steve Jobs out of Apple when he felt that the founder's behavior would damage the company. Steve Jobs at this point (in 1985) was very much in charge of high-tech product development within Apple. (It was the era of the Lisa and the first Macintosh.) He insisted on devoting a lot of resources to developing higher-end products that were visionary but failed to deliver commercially. His abrasive nature also alienated a lot of engineers and members of Apple's management team, and the poor sales of the products he developed and his attempt to try to regain control of the company through getting then-CEO John Sculley removed from the board did not help his position. The board (which included Mark Markkula, Apple's initial angel investor) decided instead that Steve Jobs was the reason for the company's poor financial performance and voted him out. Markkula had a hefty financial stake in Apple and at this point in Apple's life most probably decided that Apple's financial performance was more important than the individual insights and ambitions of one eccentric founder.

Markkula and Rock were necessary to Apple when they came in (1977 and 1978 respectively). Their investments were needed for prototype development. However, the balance of power and interests shifted after the IPO. Apple as a listed company needed to be accountable to shareholders (including Markkula and Rock) with shorter-term financial interests. It also had a formal organizational structure that Steve Jobs was reluctant to operate within. He was now an impediment to Apple's functioning as a normal company with a more conservative risk appetite in terms of strategy and product development. Steve Jobs still needed the VCs. However, Mark Markkula and Arthur Rock did not need Steve Jobs anymore.

PITFALL #2: Mismatching Expectations Between Entrepreneur and VC

When an entrepreneur seeks an investment of about US$1.5 million and says that's about all the capital the firm will ever need, VCs might feel that the investment or the idea isn't big enough for an institutional investor. Typical venture funds are in the US$50 million to US$500 million range and have five to 10 partners. Each partner can only invest in a handful of companies, so that dictates they have to put US$5–US$10 million into a company over its lifetime—making a US$1.5 million investment look too small (one VC can't keep track of as many companies as that would involve). The statement can also indicate that the opportunity is just too small. VCs want to fish in the "10x back on their money" pond, and if the company can be self-sustaining on that little money, there is probably not much barrier to others who want to do the same thing. It can also mean the entrepreneur isn't focused on the right thing (for a venture deal): making a valuable thing using cash as the rocket fuel.

PITFALL #3: Becoming Meat in a Sandwich

In emerging markets such as China, the *sandwich model* often catches investors. That is, a foreign business leaps at the chance to cooperate with a venture investor in China, only to find itself in a situation in which the supplier is a partner and the end customer is also a partner. The profit margins of the foreign business are squeezed because its books are open to both the supplier and end customer members on its board. Meanwhile, the foreign investor does not have similar access to what is going on with the supplier and the customer.

PITFALL #4: Training Your Replacement

The *training school model* is another risk of investing in China. A foreign firm is likely to have the opportunity to work with a domestic Chinese company producing "good enough" product for the domestic market. The foreign investor has a state-of-the-art technology and agrees to a joint venture with the domestic company because of strategic advantages (while the domestic company still keeps producing its "good enough" product). On the surface, the two companies do not compete since they are attacking different market segments and have different business expansion goals. Most likely, however, the domestic company with the "good enough" product will learn from state-of-the-art operation and its product quality is going to improve. Nothing is likely to happen on the joint venture end. The domestic company might even take over the whole market and the joint venture would be an abysmal failure. The foreign investor provides a good training school for the whole improvement of the domestic company but takes very little away from the deal.

Endnotes

1. Manju Puri and Rebecca Zarutskie, "On the Lifecycle Dynamics of Venture-Capital and Non-Venture-Capital-Financed Firms," Center for Economic Studies Working Paper, CES08–13, 2008.
2. Kleiner Perkins Caufield & Byers, "About Us," n.d.; retrieved from www.kpcb .com/, June 27, 2009.
3. KPMG. "Insight into Portfolio Management: Private Equity Research Programme," Manchester Business School, February 2002; retrieved from www .venturecapital.gov.br/pdf/insight.pdf, July 5, 2009.
4. Brian L. King, "Strategizing at Leading Venture Capital Firms: Of Planning, Opportunism and Deliberate Emergence," *Long Range Planning* 41, no. 3 (June 2008): 345–366.
5. John King, "Great VCs Respond, Fast: Pick Investors Who Give You Unfair Share of Time and Mind," August 7, 2008; retrieved from http://nesheimgroup .typepad.com/my_weblog/2008/08/great-vcs-respond-fast-pick-investors-who-give-you-unfair-share-of-time-and-mind.html, July 1, 2009.
6. Wongsunwai Wan, "Does Venture Capitalist Quality Affect Corporate Governance?" Unpublished working paper, doctoral candidate, Harvard Business School, 2007.
7. Gaebler.com. "About Us: Our Value Add," n.d.; retrieved from http://www .gaebler.com/Gaebler_ValueAdd.htm, July 5, 2009.
8. Steve Rogers, *Entrepreneurial Finance: Finance and Business Strategies for the serious Entrepreneur* (New York: McGraw-Hill Professional, 2009).

9. Wang Chaoyong, "Venture Capital Drives the New Generation of China Rich," February 2007; retrieved from www.21i.net/print.html?page_id=211&l=1&r_id=, July 2, 2009.

10. S. Rogers and R. Makonen, *The Entrepreneur's Guide to Finance and Business: Wealth Creation Techniques for Growing a Business* (New York: McGraw-Hill Professional, 2002).

11. "Money Is Just the Starting Point; Good Venture Capital Firms Often Play the Role of Business Partner," Tech Capital Partners, October 26, 2000; retrieved from www.techcapitalpartners.com/news/001026rec.asp, July 1, 2009.

6

If You Need to Woo a
Turkey Buzzard

This business must be learned from the bottom up. Anyone who has not lost a company and not fired friends is not a venture capitalist.
—Stanley Pratt

This chapter differs from the rest of the book because it's all about VCs and what they do to succeed. That makes it required reading for entrepreneurs! When you're planning to work with a VC, you need to know how venture capital firms are judged and how they raise their funds. After all, as the saying goes, if you need to woo a turkey buzzard, you have to play the buzzard game. It is naive to walk into that game blind.

Limited Partners Make the Game Work

Limited partners (LPs) are investors in venture capital funds. VCs raise money from LPs, just as companies raise money from VCs. VCs convince LPs of their credentials and, to a lesser extent, their business plan.

LPs usually have to make stronger commitments than VCs with even less data. A VC who loses confidence or interest in a company can choose to stop pouring money into that company. The result is often that its investment gets diluted, perhaps massively, but it still has an investment there without taking on further risk. LPs who lose confidence in a VC fund technically still face a legal obligation to continue meeting their capital calls. At best, they have no choice but to throw good money after (perceived) bad. At worst, they face losing all their capital.

The process that venture firms go through in seeking investment commitments from investors is typically called *fundraising*. (The same term tends to be used for the investment in portfolio companies by venture capital firms, but the process is quite different.) In the investment commitment process, a venture firm prospects for investors with a view to amassing a fund of a target size. It will distribute a prospectus to potential investors and may take from several weeks to several months to raise the requisite capital. The fund will seek commitments of capital from institutional investors, endowments, foundations, and individuals who seek to invest part of their portfolio in opportunities with a higher risk factor and commensurate opportunity for higher returns.

Because of the risk, length of investment, and illiquidity involved in venture investing, and because the minimum commitment requirements are so high, venture capital fund investing is generally out of reach of the average individual. The venture fund will have from a few to almost 100 limited partners, depending on the target size of the fund. Once the VC firm has raised enough commitments, it will start making investments in portfolio companies.

A limited partner interviewed for this book (an institution currently managing more than US$3 billion placed with various VCs) has a few criteria for selecting a VC to work with:

- Historical performance.
- Level of adventurousness of the fund: the more conventional it is, the more competition there is in the field.
- Depth of team: it is preferable to join current partners who have been through a full investment cycle, to confirm that the partnership is working. Typically, institutional investors do not place capital in funds raising their first dollar, nor the first

close (the first series of LP commitments, typically a fraction of the total fund size).

- Macroeconomic conditions: it is best to go into a market with a "tailwind"–a set of general conditions that promote success for ventures of this type. Going to a market with a "headwind" blowing can be detrimental to fund's returns.

For each fund, this LP would construct a balanced scorecard for

- Country risk
- Current assets under management
- Visibility for first close
- Expected return on investment
- Scope of investment

Returns of Venture Capital

Over the long run, averaged over multiple funds and vintage years, venture capital has a higher rate of return than most other asset classes. This higher average return is the market's quid pro quo for the investors' acceptance of the drastic ups and downs in this highly variable asset class. Although the typical venture investment generates a negative rate of return, the outliers like Google, Microsoft, Cisco, and Apple have given venture capital its superior rate of return. Public markets have played an important role in the process, providing both the public appetite for new issues, as well as currency for acquisitions of venture-backed companies by public technology companies.

Individuals and Institutions

Tim Draper explains simply, "For individuals, it is generally by convincing them that you will be successful, you will help create great businesses, you will build great value, employ large numbers of people, and make them a lot of money."

Draper adds, "For institutions, it is all about the track record. You have to have invested successfully before. You need to look like an institution before institutions will want to invest with you. They are fiduciaries and have responsibilities to their beneficiaries, not to mention potential liability."

Capital Calls

Making investments in portfolio companies requires the venture firm to start "calling" its limited partners' commitments. The firm will collect or "call" the needed investment capital from the limited partners in a series of tranches commonly known as "capital calls." These capital calls from the limited partners to the venture fund are sometimes called "takedowns" or "paid-in capital." Some years ago, the venture firm would "call" this capital down in three equal installments over a three-year period. More recently, venture firms have synchronized their funding cycles and call their capital on an as-needed basis for investment.

Illiquidity

Limited partners make these investments in venture funds knowing that the investment will be for the long term. It may take several years before the first investments start to return proceeds; in many cases the invested capital may be tied up in an investment for seven to 10 years. Limited partners understand that this illiquidity must be factored into their investment decision.

Other Types of Funds   Since venture firms are private firms, there is typically no way to exit before the partnership matures or expires. In recent years, a new form of venture firm has evolved: so-called secondary partnerships that specialize in purchasing the portfolios of an existing venture firm. This type of partnership provides some liquidity for the original investors. These secondary partnerships, expecting a large return, invest in what they consider to be under-valued companies.

Advisers and Funds of Funds   Evaluating which funds to invest in is akin to choosing a good stock manager or mutual fund, except the decision to invest is a long-term commitment. This decision takes considerable investment knowledge and time on the part of the limited partner investor. The larger institutions have investments in excess of 100 different venture capital and buyout funds and continually invest in new funds as they are formed.

Some limited partner investors may have neither the resources nor the expertise to manage and invest in many funds, and thus may seek to delegate this decision to an investment adviser or so-called gatekeeper. This adviser will pool the assets of its various clients and invest these proceeds as a limited partner into a venture or buyout fund currently raising capital. Alternatively, an investor may invest in a "fund of funds," which is a partnership organized to invest in other partnerships, thus providing the limited partner investor with added diversification and the ability to invest smaller amounts into a variety of funds.

Side Dish: The VC Fundraising Process

The VC fundraising process involves a number of reliable techniques:

- Deal with information asymmetry and the LP conundrum.
- Understand the hidden markers.
- Mind the Pareto principle.
- Welcome competition; it begets quality.
- Control the built-in moral hazard in the LP-VC relationship.
- Look for companies funded by more experienced VCs; they are more likely to go public.
- Stake claims in emerging markets.
- Understand the LP dilemma.
- Note that excess capital is the enemy of returns.

WINNING TECHNIQUE #1: Deal with Information Asymmetry and the LP Conundrum

Data-driven predictive models are close to impossible in the LP business. Even with an intuitive model, an LP often tends to be optimizing multiple goals, not just pure IRR. As interviewees, one from a major corporate LP (with more than 25 VC relationships) and the other a pension fund manager for one of the largest public employee pension funds in the United States, explained:

> Corporate: We have no idea anymore what makes a top-tier venture fund.
> Public: I think I should invest in smaller VC funds to get a high IRR, but I (1) have no staff, (2) can't be more than 10 percent of any fund, and (3) get measured in the short term by how much money I put to work. With US$X billion to invest, I can't write a check smaller than US$50 million and would prefer US$100 million.

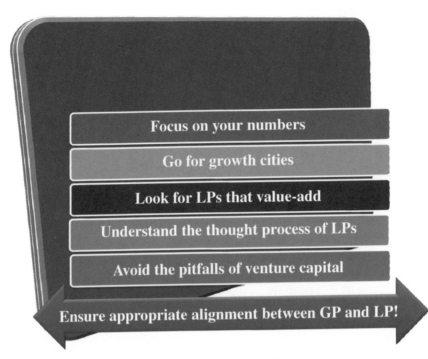

Figure 6.1 What It Takes for a VC to Raise Money

Most LPs are driven to partnership longevity as a proxy indicator for predicted success. Why are predictive models about relative manager performance so difficult? I think it is the interaction of several factors: First, there is a lot of noise in the causal modeling of financial outcomes (public market, business cycle, technology cycles, small sample sizes, and so on). In addition, the lack of transparency is a serious problem for anyone trying to assess fund manager performance. And few VC firms have institutional business strategies that transcend the immediate principals. The net result is that the prevailing model for venture investments appears to be driven by two selection criteria:

- Longevity as proxy for performance
- Current top-quartile performance as a predictor of next fund top-quartile performance

Alignment Capital published an analysis of fund managers that speaks to these two criteria. After analyzing 645 separate venture funds, its researchers found that longevity weakly correlates with IRR, showing continuous improvement between funds I and III, but leveling off thereafter. Top-quartile funds were a fairly decent bet, but second-quartile funds were nearly as likely to have a top-quartile follow-on fund as the current top-quartile funds.

So the two criteria of longevity and current performance are directionally accurate, but don't predict future performance with any meaningful precision. This is probably why so much capital continues to flow into the business—half the firms are in the top half.

Historical performance can only take you so far. One needs a theory of future drivers of returns to select among venture capital managers. Being yet another top-half IT fund is not enough to be considered seriously by anyone. LPs construct portfolios of all private equity and venture capital investments based on their strategies, applying sound financial principles of predicting correlations of returns to maximize risk-adjusted return. The typical VC fund attributes are size, industry, stage, and geography. These attributes pass for strategies in most fundraising conversations.

WINNING TECHNIQUE #2: Understand the Hidden Markers

Venture capital firms' remuneration is typically based on an annual management fee plus some percentage of the realized profits from the fund. Professor William Sahlman from Harvard Business School points out that good venture capital firms, by accepting a finite funding life and performance-dependent compensation, are signaling their quality in relation to weak ones, but that the funds provider has to invest in intensive screening to guard against false signals.[1] Sahlman's study addressed the actions of funds providers very much as "stylized facts," without a detailed examination of the nature of targets set and the monitoring process. More recently, an empirical study by professor Paul Gompers and Josh Lerner finds evidence that the use of covenants in the contracts between funds providers and venture capital firms is not only a means of dealing with agency problems but also a reflection of supply and demand conditions in the industry.[2]

WINNING TECHNIQUE #3: Mind the Pareto Principle

A persistently true phenomenon is that 80 percent of the returns are generated by the top 20 percent of funds. Limited Partners who invest in venture funds always say that they want to back top-quartile managers (that is, funds that deliver in the top 25 percent of returns.) This makes sense because the venture capital business is very much an asset class where past successes are a strong indicator of future successes. However, even this stratagem has its flaws: if the bottom 80 percent of funds yield only 20 percent of the returns, at least 20 percent of the top quartile (the ones between 75 percent and 80 percent) are not worth investing in. Fred Wilson, managing partner of Union Square Partners, examined the returns of a particular vintage of funds started in the dot-com bust, focusing on the returns of the different quartiles.

He found that the top quartile as a group is not close to distributing the paid-in capital for 1999 and 2000 and the total value over paid-in capital for the entire period hovers around 1x. That means that if LPs had followed conventional wisdom and were able to get access to the top funds, they would be looking at a get-your-money-back scenario. This is the reason venture as an asset class has been questioned of late (especially in the dot-com vintage). Chin Chao of Sirius Ventures explains the quantitative markers of a top-quartile fund is to return 2x cash on cash (for every dollar that the LP puts in, US$2 come out). However, these funds are few and far between.

WINNING TECHNIQUE #4: Welcome Competition; It Begets Quality

Dr. Helmut Schühsler, managing partner of TVM Capital, observed that in the United States, early-stage businesses are still going strong, especially in Boston, Silicon Valley, and San Diego. The U.S. VC business is healthy to the point of being overfunded in many areas. There are a lot of VCs and many with substantial amounts of newly raised money. Competition is a dominant force that drives prices up.

"In Europe, on the other hand," he says, "I think there is a different problem. The industry is not high on the list of the LPs at all, and it's difficult to defend your existence as a European venture capitalist in general. This is based not only on perception but also on actual performance numbers. It always takes longer in Europe, and European valuations have been following the U.S. market in a peculiar way: in buoyant markets, it takes a year for Europe to follow the way up. In down markets, Europe follows practically in sync with the United States. This leaves often only months or weeks to sell at a good price, in a positive and optimistic environment. I still believe that the interest in Europe is coming back with some investors as they realize that this is an underserved market with a small group of people who actually made money in the past and low levels of competition.

"I believe that there is a group of U.S. firms that are superstars: they are the Sequoias or Accels or Kleiner Perkins of the world. They have proven able to make outsized returns in most of their funds from their involvement in companies like Google and Amazon. Below that very small group, the next-best U.S. VCs and the top European VCs have comparable performance."

WINNING TECHNIQUE #5: Control the Built-In Moral Hazard in the LP-VC Relationship

An agency theory perspective has been used to examine the issues in a pioneering study by William Sahlman, which analyzed the nature of the relationship between funds providers and venture capital firms and identified the mechanisms used to help minimize these agency problems.[3] These mechanisms included incentives for mutual gain, the specific prohibition of certain acts on the part of the venture capital firm that would cause conflicts of interest, limited life agreements, mechanisms to ensure gains are distributed to investors, expenditure of resources on monitoring the venture capital firm, and the regular distribution of specific information to the funds providers by the venture capital firm.

WINNING TECHNIQUE #6: Look for Companies Funded by More Experienced VCs; They Are More Likely to Go Public

This technique follows both from the direct influence of more experienced VCs and from sorting in the market, which leads better companies to approach more experienced VCs successfully.[4] Sorting creates an endogeneity problem, but a structural model based on two-sided matching is able to exploit the characteristics of the other agents in the market to separately identify and estimate influence and sorting. Both effects are found to be significant, with sorting almost twice as important as influence for the difference in IPO rates.

WINNING TECHNIQUE #7: Stake Claims in Emerging Markets

Many Western LPs appear to be following a herd mentality of not wanting to lose out on the next Baidu (the Chinese search engine that became a major success story for its venture capital backers after a NASDAQ IPO in September 2005). For a fund of funds to gain access to top-quartile GPs, it takes more than just money, according to a representative of a top Asian sovereign wealth fund that preferred to remain unnamed. "There are many funds with a few hundred million. Good ones don't necessarily want to talk to you. What would tilt the odds in your favor are unique connections and the ability to make funds come around."

As Andy Tang of DFJ Dragon told us,

> We focus more on LPs who can provide tangible help. I constantly tap into LPs for introductions and due diligence. (The LP might know someone who works in the company we are interested in investing in.) Of course we have financial LPs. So we have a good mix. We leverage on former CEOs, and strategic individuals come in.

> Due to their global deployment, LPs have a wider range of selection. Fund-seekers are also more open. According to a partner at an Asia-focused fund of funds who has been investing in private equity in China for more than 20 years, mainland business owners now have a better appreciation of the private equity industry and are more receptive to accepting capital from professional fund managers. In addition, banks have increased the utilization of leverage, and the supporting infrastructure for the banking industry has evolved. High-profile exits by IPOs have whetted the appetite further.

LPs are flocking to Asia. Kelvin Chan of Partners Group adds, "There are more funds of funds coming to Asia. LPs which come to Asia would usually choose two countries, either Hong Kong or Singapore. However, in the past, most FoF just have investment offices in Asia, managing just frontline operations. Sourcing of deals is managed out of the head office. We see more funds of funds expand to provide fund administration."

Noubar Afeyan, managing partner and CEO of Flagship Ventures, elaborates,

My impression is that first of all, LPs in the U.S. rarely invest in new funds—80–90 percent have only invested in one or two new funds in the past five years. Fund managers like to play safe. When top-quartile VC funds do poorly, they are excused, because of poor macroeconomic environment. When they do well, it is naturally because they are top-quartile funds.

The venture mind-set has recently favored specialization; instead of going into generalist new funds, they are going into new relationships to diversify into new approaches. For example, rather than finding the next generalist like Kleiner Perkins, LPs are increasingly investing in geographies like the Midwestern United States or the Far East, or in specialties such as cleantech or nanotech. There is no such thing as a top-quartile fund in a specialized segment. A Russia or a China fund is more likely to get U.S. interest than a fund in Boston and San Francisco. (An LP would already have 15 of these funds.)

He cautions that funds of funds would invest in Asia for geographic diversification but due to the emerging nature of these funds, expectations need to be managed.

WINNING TECHNIQUE #8: Understand the LP Dilemma

Andy Tang points out that VC markets are inefficient. LPs have prior commitment to a fund, so it is tough emotionally for them to switch decisions. A lot of decisions are long-term decisions—they commit a fund and are not thinking about switching. In a public market, there is no commitment—I can buy Coke and sell Pepsi tomorrow.

A decision by an LP has to be subjected to the company process and it depends on the investment horizon. Once you have invested in a company, it takes awhile to figure out whether it is good and bad, before you can present to the investment committee. It is hard to change quickly and that motivates LPs not to keep an active eye, as decisions are hard to change quickly. It is rational for LPs to keep to their decisions and change slowly.

Andy Tang's description of the relationship strikes me as symptomatic of endowment effect, the tendency for people to value something more as soon as they own it, as applied to LPs.

For Gobi VC, raising the first fund was tough as it had to fundraise amid the financial crisis. "We raised our second fund based on our encouraging results in the first fund. We were also clearly focused on digital media early-stage deals in China. LPs look for discipline and frown at investors that herd," says Ken Xu, partner with Gobi VC, pointing out that financial and technology background matters in his field.

WINNING TECHNIQUE #9: Remember That Excess Capital Is the Enemy of Returns

Venture capital faces a classic Prisoner's Dilemma. Excess returns (the pursuit of the top quartile) are a zero-sum game. Each new entry increases rivalry and more deals get done in every sector at higher and higher prices. Entrepreneurs are able to raise money from a broad range of sources other than venture capitalists, including angels and corporations.

It is impossible for everyone to be in the top quartile, and the presence of more firms competing for the same finite set of top deals leads to the lose-lose quadrant for all players. Each player faces the choice of staying or exiting and if everyone chooses to stay, everyone loses. Based on the theoretical scenario illustrated in Figure 6.2, your firm will experience a 10 percent loss and everyone else a 20 percent loss in this situation. Exiting the market marginally increases the staying party's expected returns, that is, a 20 percent return for the firm still in the market. This applies if your firm stays and everyone exits; capital is scarce and returns will be excessive for your firm. The capital exodus begins to change the dynamics of the industry, reducing rivalry for deals and dropping prices to more reasonable levels. If everyone in the market exits including your firm,

		Everyone Else	
		Exit	Stay
Your Firm	Exit	0 %, 0 %	0 %, 20 %
	Stay	20 %, 0 %	−10 %, −20 %

Figure 6.2 Risk Capital Prisoner's Dilemma

capital invested in new ventures would be zero and returns consequently will be zero.

Not for the Faint of Heart   Venture capital is considered a game for the sophisticated investors.[5] By definition, there is no ready market for the shares of the private companies in which venture funds invest. Investors hang onto them until the wished-for liquidity event (exit) of going public, or being bought out by another company. Setting a value on these assets in the meantime is more an art than a science, but you can be assured that the valuations are both related to the NASDAQ averages and even more volatile. The investors' shares in the fund itself are likewise illiquid. If they are saleable at all, it will be at a deep discount to another qualified investor. Once you are in a fund, all you can do is grit your teeth and hope it's one of the funds that win.

You may also be assured that you will take losses the first few years. The annualized percentage returns for maturing funds (five-plus years from inception) are a sort of polite fiction. This isn't a Certificate of Deposit (CD) or T-bill that quietly and evenly accrues interest over time. In venture, bad news arrives first, hopefully followed by good news in the long run. Some call this the law of the J-curve, as sketched in Figure 6.3. The reasons for this phenomenon are fairly simple.

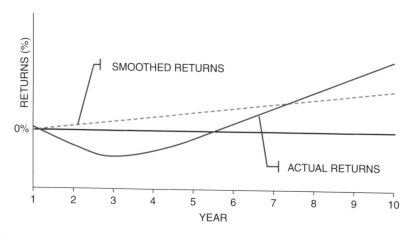

Figure 6.3 Graph of J-Curve Effect

Source: CalPERS On-Line, www.calpers.ca.gov.

The J-Curve is highlighted by the solid curve. In the initial years, investment returns are negative as the GPs will make capital drawdowns to cover management fees, and underperforming investments are written down. Over time, ventures invested in by the fund will build value as revenues generated will be large enough to offset expenses in the company, resulting in cash flow to the fund. As the fund matures, this incoming cash flow will counter the initial drop and pull up the value of the fund making it profitable in the long run. An investor must thus be able to weather the initial years of negative returns and wait a long time before seeing tangible returns.

Brand new start-up companies are by definition risky, and some fraction of investments in them will turn out to be bad choices. The wise fund manager will kill and write off the bad ones as soon as the trouble is apparent. Meanwhile, the good companies take time to build their products, reach their markets, grow, and exit at a profit. Management fees, the largest part of the overhead costs of a fund, are charged evenly through its life based on its total size (committed capital), so that expense is also front-loaded compared to the eventual profits as good investments mature. So not only do you get to grit your teeth, you're on a roller coaster ride that almost always starts out with a swoop toward the ground.

Why do public institutions invest in venture capital funds, if it's such a risky business? The answer is quite simple. Over the long run, averaged over multiple funds and years, venture capital has historically produced returns superior to any other legitimate asset class. According to the recent survey of Thompson Reuters, venture capital continues to exceed NASDAQ and S&P returns across all time horizons, despite the closed IPO window and the so-called "fair value accounting" standards that oftentimes artificially depress portfolio values. (See Table 6.1.)

This higher average return is the market's quid pro quo for the investors' acceptance of the drastic ups and downs in this high-variance asset class. A prudent manager of a long-term portfolio such as a pension fund or endowment won't put a high percentage of the portfolio into venture capital, because the valuation and returns are too volatile year to year, and the asset is illiquid. But a good manager will have some fraction, often 10–15 percent, spread among multiple VC funds to enhance the long-term return on assets. Institutional managers may drink Maalox during the down years, but they can

Table 6.1   Thomson Reuters' U.S. Private Equity Performance Index (PEPI)

Fund Type	Investment Horizon Performance through 9/30/2008				
	1 Yr	**3 Yr**	**5 Yr**	**10 Yr**	**20 Yr**
Early/Seed VC	0.2	3.8	5.1	37.2	21.6
Balanced VC	−6.4	7.4	11.5	14.9	14.7
Later-Stage VC	8.6	12.0	10.5	8.9	14.7
All Venture	−1.6	6.6	8.6	17.3	17.1
NASDAQ	−21.4	−1.1	3.1	2.1	8.7
S&P 500	−22.0	−1.7	3.2	1.4	7.5
All Venture (through 6/30/2008)	5.3	8.5	8.8	16.5	16.9
All Venture (through 9/30/2007)	26.6	11.0	6.8	17.8	16.4

Source: Thomson Reuters/National Venture Capital Association

console themselves at that time and the law of averages are on their side.

Unintended Consequences   A good investor in venture capital funds should understand this proposition and be ready to withstand bad years in order to participate in the good ones. By contrast, corporate investors are notorious for their inability to invest through the whole cycle. They tend to enter the VC markets when they are already buoyant. Since dropping valuations and low returns can make things too hot politically for their in-house management sponsors, they often drop out at the bottom of a market, either ceasing investment or liquidating their portfolio entirely. This makes the average corporate source less desirable to fund managers, and pretty much guarantees that they miss the rewards of market upturns, which are supposed to be their compensation for being in a volatile asset.

Hence, the first unintended consequence of disclosure of VC returns by public entities: They will start to act more like corporate investors. The newspapers are, after all, going to need to get a return on their investment of time by running more stories, and there is the public interest to be served.

The next unintended consequence is that public entities will have more trouble placing their money into venture capital funds.

Venture capital management firms prize investors who are loyal when times are bad. They dislike investors who create extra burdens of reporting and entanglements with regulations and politics. Compared to private institutional investors, public entities will become a denigrated class. This is not speculation. Managers from firms such as Crescendo, Storm Ventures, Charles River, and Sequoia have publicly stated that they will be less likely to take money from public entities, or will avoid them entirely. The upshot is that public entities will end up in funds whose managers have had lower performance in the past, since these funds have less choice in investors. Another bias toward lower performance.

A venture fund subject to this type of reporting will become the victim of understandable discrimination by entrepreneurs. The start-up executive with a good track record and a choice of investors is not going to accept exposure to this risk and will simply avoid such funds. Since fund managers cannot accept the downward bias on performance this implies, at this point public entities will be kicked out of the venture asset class entirely. They then lose access to the greater returns over time that have been provided to their overall portfolios.

And the final unintended consequence is of course the loss of the portfolio yield that it was said to be in the public interest to protect against undue influence in the first place. The first-order losers? The retirees, students, and universities that are the beneficiaries of the public entity portfolios.

What Star VCs Do: Commandments to Follow

How do LPs identify high-potential VCs? That is, what does it take for a VC (or PE firm) to raise money? Here are some of the principles they follow:

- Focus on the numbers.
- Go for growth cities.
- Look for LPs who value-add.
- Understand the thought process of LPs.
- Use track record as the litmus test.
- Exercise people judgment.
- Ensure an appropriate alignment between GP and LP.
- Promote capital efficiency.

COMMANDMENT #1: *Focus on the Numbers*

Zero2IPO, a research center on venture funds in China, has carried out comprehensive investigations into venture capital firms covering investment, management, financing, and exit. It assesses capital under management, total amount of capital raised, total number of deals closed, total amount of capital invested, total number of exit cases, exit amount, and return level as major indexes for ranking and adjust them annually to best match the development of this industry.[6]

Venture Fund Economics: Gross and Net Returns   The returns venture firms get on their investments are termed "gross returns."[7] The industry norm is that 2x "net" returns to the LPs is the lowest attractive return on a venture fund. This means that for a dollar invested in the fund, LPs receive two dollars back. The differences between gross returns and net returns are large in the venture and private equity business and it's important to understand them and be clear about what numbers you are using when you talk about returns.

Venture capital insiders know that the fund has to get a lot more than US$2 back on its investments to be able to give its investors US$2. That's because before the investors get their money, the fund takes a management fee. And if there are profits, the managers of the fund take a carried interest on the profits. Most funds charge a carried interest of 20 percent. However, there are funds that charge 25 percent or even 30 percent carried interest fees. Market theory suggests that the best funds charge the highest carried interest fees (the higher the capital gains, the higher the funds' carried interest fees). The management fees don't go directly to the fund managers but help to pay the costs of running the business. For small funds, administrative costs take up the bulk of the management fee. For larger funds, fund managers may get a significantly large salary. Management fees typically range from 1.5 percent per year (for large funds) to 2.5 percent per year (for smaller funds), typically tailing off after the first five years to much lower percentages to reflect that the work of putting the fund to work (in actively soliciting for investments and value-adding to portfolio companies) is largely over. An appropriate balance should be made between management fees and carried interest fees to provide incentives for fund managers to make winning investments. Since the carried interest is only paid on gains, a fund that is not profitable need not pay a carried interest.

Using a US$100 million fund to model the fund economics, assuming a $1/3$ hit rate ($1/3$ home runs, $1/3$ break even, and $1/3$ losers), a two percent management fee, and 20 percent carry, the VC charges US$2 million in management fee per annum and would need to achieve almost four times gross returns to return about two and a half times net returns.

Generally speaking, the difference between net and gross returns show the fees charged by the venture firm. Understanding venture firm economics will help a company determine how much equity to give up when negotiating a deal. For a simple tool to calculate the IRR of a VC fund, please refer to http://wayofthevc-irr.easyurl.net.

Human Resource Cost An associate or analyst who joins a VC firm under a LP/GP structure without becoming a partner is fundamentally a cost center. Rationally, partners will only hire someone like this for one of two reasons—either the associate or analyst is making life significantly easier for the partners, in a way that makes the trade-off worthwhile (the associate or analyst costs less than the marginal life benefit the partners get from having a partner around), or the analyst or associate helps create more "carry" (that is, by managing more deals with an additional staff and therefore deploying more capital; possessing a skill set that will help build the portfolio, or the like). Hiring an analyst who fails to do at least one of these things is not an effective use of management fees. The area is gray for principals, VPs, and junior partners who are managing their own deals as well as supporting partners' deals.

For example, a US$50 million fund operating on a 2 percent management fee and 20 percent carry would incur costs of about US$1 million for its fund management partners. If the fund hires three associates to source and close deals, paying them on average US$5,000 apiece per month, it incurs US$180,000 per annum on expenses.

What LPs Want: Returns The single most important criterion for LPs when deciding which venture fund to invest in is the amount of returns they expect to receive. LPs look out for "returns, returns, and more returns." VCs competing against other asset classes for cash will find it hard to attract LPs when returns have been poor. LPs will be very hesitant to hire new fund managers or invest more capital into that asset class. As venture capital investing is tough, LPs would rather stick to the 20 to 30 top-quartile venture funds in the world with a solid track record in making above-average returns.

So which matters more, relative performance or absolute performance? LPs want the highest possible returns but whether they look for absolute or relative performance depends a lot on their risk profiling. Absolute market risk estimates a potential total loss expressed in currency terms, while relative market risk measures the potential for underperformance.[8] In a relative return fund, LPs have the choice to judge the risks they are undertaking, paying the GPs to take risks to capture the premium in that asset class. However, for an absolute return fund, the investment is capital and it is possible that every dollar will be wiped out in the venture and there will be nothing left for the LPs in the end. Absolute return funds are definitely considered more risky, and LPs will also know that more leverage strategies are employed. Therefore, when considering relative or absolute performance, LPs must understand the risk they wish to undertake.[9]

Barry Drayson of Nanoholdings says, "Our LPs were initially high-net-worth individuals investing US$200,000 to US$500,000 each to make up US$15 million; our Series B was comprised of two companies in the energy industry seeking a window on how their core markets might change and IP that might address that change; the two invested US$10 million and US$5 million. If I were to persuade a U.S. LP to invest in 'our Asian VC' today, I would emphasize the inexorable knowledge growth and available skills to bring science to market at a highly competitive price; that is, VCs with access to Asian technology, Asian engineering of that technology, VCs with access to Asian subsidies and collaboration, VCs with the ability to manage Asian assets."

Long-term liabilities or short-term investments? In a recession, the capital markets are more conservative and funding opportunities may be limited. However, in a boom, VC funds typically expand and there is an overflow of capital but limited quality deals, thereby reducing their returns. LPs with short-term horizons would expand and move into long-term asset allocation decisions.

CASE STUDY: Panorama Capital LLC

Panorama Capital LLC (www.panoramacapital.com) is a venture capital firm focused on life sciences and technology companies. Based in Menlo Park, California, Panorama Capital was founded in 2005 by Srinivas Akkaraju (M.D., Ph.D.), Christopher J. Albinson, Rodney A. Ferguson (J.D., Ph.D.), Shahan D. Soghikian, and Damion E. Wicker (M.D.), along with a core team of investment professionals who worked together for many years.

Value-Adding

''Panorama Capital works attentively with us day after day supporting our vision for an innovative media enterprise,'' says John Battelle, CEO of Federated Media. ''From finding key members of the team, helping to shape the model and technology, and even acting as our corporate development team in key situations, my experience working with Panorama has been nothing short of excellent.''

Track Record

Since 1990, the Panorama team, which previously managed the venture business at JP Morgan, has consistently produced top-quartile returns, including successful exits from more than 50 IPOs and M&A transactions. Recent exits include Corus Pharmaceuticals, Piramed Limited, Portal Player, Renovo Limited, Seattle Genetics, Sierra Logic, Tacit Networks, Valere Power, and Yipes Holdings.

Experienced Advisory Boards

Panorama's investment professionals have extensive experience investing with entrepreneurs in companies at all stages of development. Four advisory boards augment the team's investment network and comprise 80 members from industry-leading companies including AT&T, Agilent, Cisco, Facebook, Genentech, GigaOm, Google, Johnson & Johnson, Microsoft, Priceline, Rambus, Red Hat, Roche, Schering-Plough, TechCrunch, Texas Instruments, and Yahoo.

COMMANDMENT #2: Go for Growth Cities

In China, there were 21 IPO exits in 2007 and 18 IPO exits in 2008. On average, trade sales have a higher multiple than IPOs in China.

Investments stem from the purely public sector, transitionary sector (such as hog farms and sheep farms), and private sector (privatization of the Chinese economy). Some of these will stay mixed. VCs have indicated that it is the best interest for a founder to have 30–35 percent of control of the company to have a true direction. The government can retain a majority shareholding if it takes a passive, hands-off policy.

A former general partner at Catalyst who is raising a fund in China is getting introductions and meeting governors of China. He tells the governors, "I am raising a fund 500 million: what do you have to offer me?" He then takes these conversations and the dealflow he gets from the government to LPs, saying essentially, look at the dealflow and the commitments from the government that I have. These cities compete and they have cash and are striving to attract VCs in the cities.

COMMANDMENT #3: Look for LPs Who Value-Add

For Lin Hong Wong, the litmus test of a successful VC firm is one with a good track record of successful investments. How does an LP evaluate this? "It depends whether the LPs are Asian or U.S.-based. Asian LPs are usually less involved, less sophisticated, and have less experience in evaluating VC firms and partners. U.S. LPs are more sophisticated and thorough. In their due diligence, they ask a lot of questions and even go as far as visiting portfolio companies and questioning them on their relationships with the VC firms." U.S. LPs typically go through several rounds of grilling of the VC partners in their due diligence. In one instance, Wong's team had to answer a 300-page questionnaire, and even then the LP did not invest in the end.

Wong adds, "There are LPs and there are LPs. Good LPs help by asking the right questions, and thus help the VC team to focus on important issues. Good LPs will also bring in other LPs. On the other hand, good VC firms are those that have investment strategies that are appropriate based on the industrial and economic development of their investment territories. Good VC firms will also have teams with the requisite skillsets to source and evaluate the types of investment opportunities that can be found in their territories. LPs will assess these qualities in their due diligence of the VC firms."

He further points out, "It is also important for VC firms to value their LPs and be forthcoming with providing information promptly and openly and also frequently keep in mind co-investment and direct investment opportunities for LPs. By cultivating a mutually beneficial relationship with several high-value-add LPs and of course by achieving good returns, we incentivize them to continually participate in our new funds."

HRJ Capital, a fund of funds that invests in venture capital, private equity, and real estate, has a large percentage allocation (guaranteed access) to top-tier venture funds in the United States (Sequoia Capital, Kleiner Perkins, and the like). This in turn creates demand from global LPs for access to the HRJ fund of funds as many of these top VCs are closed to new investors. What is intriguing is that the founders include Harris Barton, an offensive lineman who played for the San Francisco 49ers, and other former professional American football players, and they originally got to know and secure these allocations in these funds due to their football stardom and access. As an unnamed source confides, "Story goes that they would invite VC GPs to the Super Bowl. The GPs would ask if they can bring their sons. They provide prime football tickets and introductions to football stars." Today, they manage US$3 billion in a fund of funds that is growing globally.

Brian Hampton, principal of Oak Street Capital LLC and director of business development at Exccess LLC, says, "It all starts with an idea. The best entrepreneurs create the best ideas. The best ideas and best entrepreneurs attract the best venture capitalists." The following figures frame his statements perfectly. Nine hundred VC firms backed 91 percent of NASDAQ companies, yet only five VC firms were partners with 52 percent of them. These five (KPCB, Khosla Ventures, Benchmark Capital, NEA, and Accel) were the firms behind reputable brands such as Amazon, eBay, PayPal, and Yahoo.

As noted, in terms of performance, the VC asset class consistently surpasses bonds, real estate, private equity, and equity indexes such as S&P 500 and NASDAQ 100. Despite VCs' favorable returns, however, not all are the equivalent of Michael Jordan in basketball. There remains a stark 43 percent return spread between the top-quartile and third-quartile managers' performance over the past decade. As Jack Meyer, former CEO of Harvard Endowment, puts it, "Everyone would like to get into a Kleiner Perkins fund, but you can't." "The only thing harder than getting money from Kleiner Perkins is trying to give it to them. In fact, you don't ask, you wait to be asked," says David Kaplan, author of *The Silicon Valley Boys* and *Their Valley of Dreams.* Eagles don't flock. *Forbes* and *Fortune* magazine hailed the co-founder of Sun Microsystems as the number one VC, adding, "There are venture capitalists, and there's Vinod Khosla." Very much, indeed, VC is not just an asset class but an access class.

COMMANDMENT #4 Understand the Thought Process of LPs

A significant proportion of LPs are funds of funds, which are popular vehicles for many small and mid-sized institutional investors primarily because they provide access to top-tier managers, professional selection expertise, and diversification across multiple managers to mitigate risk. One such fund of funds is HarbourVest, named North American Fund of Funds of the Year by Private Equity International in 2007. HarbourVest also received this recognition for 2006, 2004, and 2003.

In the United States, LPs such as CalPERS (the California Public Employees' Retirement System) publish GP returns, and this creates considerable pressure for all the rest of the LPs to disclose financial data as well. This is not true in Asia, where information is still hard to obtain throughout the private equity industry. Scholarly attempts have been made recently to quantify the third factor-diversification benefits. One recent noteworthy study was done by Bjoern Born, Tom Weidig, and Andreas Kemmerer based on Monte Carlo simulations.[10] The results illustrated the diversification benefits of a fund of funds, more specifically, the study showed that investing in a fund of funds will produce higher returns per unit of risk than selecting an individual fund.

This data also suggests that by randomly picking 20 U.S. venture funds over a five-year period, there is a negligible chance of generating a negative return. Diversification in this same random manner provides similar results for a buyout fund of funds—approximately a 2 percent probability of a negative return. This is a powerful conclusion when compared to the wide dispersion of returns that might result from selecting an individual fund manager (which the same data indicate will provide a negative return 22 percent of the time). The collective conclusion is that a fund of funds manager who selects a diversified group of top-tier fund managers should be able to do even better than the random simulated fund of funds results in this study.

Given how hard it is to access top-quartile funds, how do LPs identify high-potential VCs? The best LPs use both quantitative and qualitative means. Reports such as those produced by Cambridge Associates track the quantitative returns of funds and benchmarks this against funds of other vintages and industries.[11] LPs further supplement this with interviews with the VC funds, funds they have syndicated with, and their portfolio companies.

When it comes to getting in, LPs have a widely networked relationship to size up VCs they see coming over the horizon. It is an averaging phenomenon. An LP frequently asks for the names of three top VCs. The answers from various sources will typically include two different names out of the three, but the LP will see one name being mentioned repeatedly, and that is an indication that the one fund is performing above the sigma.

A good way to get in (for a VC) is to get a VC fund (preferably one funding the company in question) to contact the LP that you want to meet with. If the VC says good things about you—say, "We are currently not fundraising now, but can I send them over?"—the new fund has one foot into the door. Once they meet the LP, they have to differentiate themselves from the pack with their approach and network.

Another approach is for the venture fund to do some direct investing with the fund that it wants for an LP, so as to begin to build a relationship. By building increasing trust, the VC thereby develops further interaction.

Noubar Afeyan, managing director of Flagship Ventures, adds,

> An LP will find it easier to get into a fund with a history of less than 20 years—a Flagship Ventures rather than a Sequoia Capital. This is just our third fund. Even though our first two funds are top-quartile, I would say that the best way is to pick top quartile funds while they are reasonably young. When these funds are fairly old, this is a different prospect. Folklore associated with how hard to get into are 20–30 years old. It might be better to look at third, fourth, and fifth funds, building a long-term relationship (say for 10 years). Most existing LPs in these funds have the "right of first refusal,"

which enables them to buy into a new fund before new LPs get a chance to. LPs may even pay money for unfunded commitments, just to get into the funds. The idea is to prove to be a stable source of capital, and hopefully get into their next fund. I am not sure if it is worth the effort. Beta is not tested across a generational change but rather, tested across the same set of partners. If the fund has the same set of partners, beta correlation is high. However, we are seeing funds which are undergoing a transition, where everyone in the team, including the senior partners, are changed.

A study by Alignment Capital, on 645 venture funds, found that IRR weakly correlates with funds' longevity.[12] Signs of transition also do not stop a lot of funds from investing.

A deeper look into the psychology of LPs helps understand why this is the case. Most decision makers working for LPs are not really getting a profit share, so they are not motivated by making a strictly right decision. Instead, they are motivated by the desire to make a *right-looking* decision. If you buy an established name such as IBM and it doesn't do well, it's easy to blame it on portfolio theory. The portfolio has to appear well balanced. It seems likely that only the most skilled and personally involved investors use all available information to adjust their capital allocation to funds and, as a result, eliminate reliance on performance predictability.

It's useful to pay attention to personal transitions and strategy. Ideally, LPs want to catch young VCs who are on the rise with early success. For example, CalPERS gets to know GPs through many years of initial co-investment. This allows LPs to assess the consistency of the GPs. One of the biggest Achilles heels for LPs is to overfocus on specific hits. If the returns have not been there at the fund level, even though it includes some specific companies that have generated compelling returns, it may not be a good investment.

COMMANDMENT #5: Use Track Record as the Litmus Test

"Funds are the people," a top sovereign fund representative explains. "When you look at a fund with a 10–15 percent IRR, you spotlight on whatever he has done in the past. Their skills and network ideally should be complementary."

LPs also look for teams whose members know each other well and have complementary skillsets. Ken Xu, partner with Gobi VC, says, "We have a lawyer, and a former banker, and I am a Chinese local. We are focused on data and have a long-term objective in China. A good FoF manager should have prior experience in direct investment to know how to value-add. Otherwise, he is merely allocating assets."

First-Time Funds Are Risky   The lack of a proven track record disadvantages first-time funds. Ideally, an LP would need to observe two or three cycles of track record of the GP. By this time, the investment window might have passed. Inexperience also disadvantages first-time funds. "For a first-time fund, the partners have no experience of a bubble. They have no financial experience," one of the VCs we interviewed adds.

Kelvin Chan of Partners Group goes so far as to warn against first-time funds. First-time fund managers entail extra risks due to team dynamics. Sometimes, it turns out the team cannot work together. In a big group, this can be even more challenging. When you look at a team, you look for the right background in each individual. The GP has to be independent and be able to make accurate decisions, as that's the one who is rewarded with most of the carry. LPs prefer independent GPs.

When asked how his first fund was raised, Andy Tang from DFJ Dragon explains, "Our first fund was a much smaller fund. LPs prefer track record. Bobby Chao raised the first fund based on his network with a lot of investors and his personal track record. We raised the second fund based on the track record of our first fund. In our third fund, we looked at the processes. LPs dug deeper and asked why we did well."

Capabilities Required for VC   When experienced LPs look for VCs to place their funds with, they look for a number of specific qualities:

- Experience
- Passion
- Integrity
- Pattern-recognition skills

Pattern-recognition in VC requires incredible instincts honed by experience and combined with the ability to quickly and accurately size up situations and draw effective conclusions. In addition, several qualities separate the most desirable VCs from the rest of the pack.

Good Deals Sourcing   What can one VC bring to dealflow that others cannot? Jeff Chi captures it in one sentence: "If my current team comprises two MIT graduates, and I have two candidates I am considering hiring, one from MIT and a second one from Stanford, I would choose the Stanford person to expand the network."

More leads do not necessarily lead to more good deals. One critical success factor in sourcing for good deals is access to networks and people that matter. Hence, VCs that situate themselves in better-quality networks gain an edge over others by exposing themselves to superior investment opportunities and information. It has been observed that VCs with quality networks not only gained access to better dealflow but also enjoyed notably better fund performance as measured by the rate of successful portfolio exits. On top of sourcing better deals, well-networked VCs had considerable leverage in providing more value-add to their portfolio companies, and this further enhanced fund performance.[13]

Screening and Evaluation   Knowledge is key in filtering good deals from bad ones. However, a venture capitalist cannot possibly be well-versed in everything under the sun. Therefore, the VC needs to be well-equipped to tap into the knowledge base of others. Being well-acquainted with people who know the answers and understanding enough about the industry to ask the right questions will enable the VC to obtain critical information much needed in screening and evaluating deals. The VC's network thus comes into play as its contacts can provide information that may be private or not easily obtainable. For example, the investor can approach people in a social network to seek private information like the competency or track record of the management of a company that is looking into expansion. Also, many popular VC targets—especially the high-growth start-ups in the technology, medical, or biotechnology industries—reveal promising products with technicalities that may be too sophisticated for the layman to understand. VCs should therefore first gain enough knowledge about such industries to ask the right questions in their assessment. This is also why many VCs tend to specialize in investments in certain industries, allowing them to create niche focus and accumulate industry-specific experience.

Value Creation   In addition to the injection of capital, VCs also provide other forms of value-add to portfolio companies. VCs create value via their role as active investors that drive a rapid process of change. They provide specialist expertise with a wealth of industry experience and business knowledge. VCs also catalyze high growth with a hands-on advisory approach in directing management in strategic decisions. Moreover, VCs are able to tap into their extensive networks and link their portfolio companies with resources like legal and regulatory expertise. Strategic alliances are also forged with other companies in their portfolio to create synergy. Finally, VCs add value by sourcing for divestment targets in a trade sale when exiting the venture. The reputation of a VC can be helpful in negotiating favorable terms for its portfolio companies as it sends a signal about the capabilities and credibility of the management and company.

Andy Tang, managing director of DFJ Dragon, elaborates,

> Most LPs want to be in the region and establish a foothold first. They are in Asia to make money in the long run and to establish a strategic foothold to make money in fund four and five. The bigger investment funds and pension and mutual funds invest in a team who have done it before in China or at least outside of China. In China, they are limited by people with good sustainable track record, hence LPs will gravitate toward people with track record outside China. They look beyond performance and book value into internal processes. They dig deep into processes such as dealflow tracking mechanism, network of deal sources, and the investment committee.

LPs assess whether a VC is adding value to the portfolio—both monitoring and managing it. Predominantly, the best VCs are focusing on value-add to their portfolio companies, which confers sustainable advantage. Even though VCs are credited for getting into hot deals and often can get a return by getting into hot deals, such incidents may be flukes rather than indicators of probable future success.

Sustainable advantage is a VC's core competency to add value. What you do to increase the value of company contributes to your brand. The litmus test LPs apply: would you work with this VC again?

An LP will ask you: How did you get into such a deal? If the answer is *I knew this guy; he introduced me to the deal,* the advantage is not sustainable. A person can be nice only one time. If a VC has the reputation as knowing all the customers, knowing the space thoroughly, having a good reputation, that's a VC to deal with.

Adding value is one of the most overused and overworked phrases in the industry. This phrase is often disguised as *Company-building expertise.* In the best case, you see a partnership like Google, where the relationship between the entrepreneurs (Larry Page and Sergey Brin) and venture capitalists was the key to success. The value added by the venture capitalists (apart from just funding) in terms of bringing in CEO Eric Schmidt, who minded the store and helped Google function in the business world while Brin made deals and Page handled technology, is what brought the company to where it is at present. This worked out well due to the clear understanding between the three parties from the beginning. By bringing in two VCs as opposed to the conventional one VC, Page and Brin made it very clear that they wanted to keep majority control over the business and have the power to decide on its overall direction.

Zac Boon from McLean Watson adds another perspective. "Which are the deals you originate? Syndication is good, but can [the VCs] look you in the eye and say, they originated the deal? The dealflow has to be proprietary. For my case, most angel investments I make (although I do not exclusively make angel investments) are with friends or acquaintances who are unlikely to squander away the venture capital. If they fail, it is usually because of market failure. I am fine with market failure. The other question is, what are the exits and what is the performance of the companies?" Yan Huang, partner at CDH Ventures, elaborates, "CDH is known for working with other VCs. However, we usually lead or co-lead the deal and seldom follow other VCs."

Consistency also matters. Sutter Hill partner Don Valentine missed out on the dot-com boom, but he doesn't regret it. He recommends VCs pursue laser precision on sectors they understand and do well. That is why he has consistently performed above average. A fund with see-saw returns is not a top-tier fund (this refers to returns compared to the industry). Even for legendary Lip Bu Tan, the last Walden fund did not do so well—Stanford Endowment pulled as one of the LPs.

Corporate Governance Asian investors sometimes get into private equity thinking that they are likely to hit the jackpot. Often they end up disappointed after the market crests, and they find their funds are among the outliers and underperformers. That's often enough to put off their investment committees from future private equity investment.[14]

When asked what he is looking for in an Asian manager, Kelvin Liu of Invesco's fund of private equity funds unit, whose firm currently manages US$4 billion within a series of global funds of funds, replied, "To be profitable, that they have a good track record and make money and understand the local environment. We want them to adhere to high ethical standards. On top of what we look for in the U.S., we look for them to be foreign-educated outside of Asia as by proxy that exposes them to corporate governance issues."

The experience from brand name funds has been gravitating toward Asia, and given the credit crunch in the United States that trend might increase. Venture capital is remaining resilient due to the lower leverage and the continuing demand for new technology.

Post-Deal Support   Private equity funds can also get access to funds with capacity issues. Individual funds and partners often respect experienced investors and accept their money because they know that they won't panic when the market corrects by 30 percent. Sometimes individual investors do. Also all the relationships are already in place between the manager and the fund of funds.

The Market Need for Funds of Funds   A top fund-of-funds manager confides, "Because it is a complicated job, that's why funds of funds exist. The histories are short, private equity managers seldom have been out there more than 10 years, so they may have done just a handful of funds, and that means only a couple of reference points."

He elaborates, "It would not be economical for a small institutional investor to build its own allocation team, because private equity allocation is usually small, approximately 10–15 percent. Diversification is minimal for an investor with US$100 million, whereas institutional investors range from say US$1 billion up to the big players like CalPERS or the government of Singapore. CalPERS might have US$25 billion to spend on private equity. To fill that, it might have to write out checks for US$500 million. There aren't many managers who can swallow that much, either. Yet investors don't want to write US$50 million checks and have hundreds of investments. That turns them almost into a benchmark fund, simply buying across the board, exposing them to the entire asset class, rather than being able to be selective."

Asia Alternatives, affectionately nicknamed "The Charlie's Angels of Private Equity" (an Asia-focused private equity fund of funds founded by three ladies, Melissa Ma, Laure Wang, and Rebecca Xu) is one such fund that is closing the gap. It closed its first fund after raising US$515 million in 2008. The fund's original target of US$350 million was significantly oversubscribed, reflecting the strong demand from institutional investors seeking to pour money into Asian private equity.

"Asia Alternatives brings a unique perspective to manager selection, deep regional knowledge, and investment acumen," says legendary venture capitalist Arthur Rock, who is an investor in the fund. He is joined by Warren Hellman, founder of San Francisco private equity firm Hellman & Friedman.

Warren Buffett says that you can't invest just looking at the macro situation and betting everything on one sector. It is essential to match the skillsets; otherwise, you wind up like the monkey Aesop immortalized for trying to imitate a fisherman: picking up a net, he stepped on it as he threw it into the river, so it pulled him in and drowned him.

COMMANDMENT #6: Exercise People Judgment

Lin Hong Wong explains that a large part of a VC's job is interacting with and sizing up people. Accurately judging people and their intentions is an indispensable skill. An entrepreneur's C.V. does not say everything about the person, particularly character and personality. Also, an entrepreneur will put up a good front to convince the VC to invest. A VC would have to see through the front and be able to judge the entrepreneur through proper interview techniques and observation of body language as well as from thorough reference checks. "Open-ended and provocative questions, acting dumb or confused, and intentional moments of silence often elicit more information than intended to be given by the entrepreneur. Sometimes, what is not said can reveal more than what is said," says Wong.

A VC should also consult another person about the entrepreneur and form a holistic picture by triangulating views and reference checks. A top-quartile VC would have already built up a database of reference checks, along with a mental list of red flags to watch out for. For example, friction among the management team would ring alarm bells. It is also useful to scan the entrepreneur's record and look for gaps, and whether anything seems to be hidden.

For an LP considering investing with a VC, the fundraising stage is similar to what an entrepreneur has to go through.

First, a LP would assess the background of VCs and their past investments over the years, with particular emphasis on

- Track record
- Skillsets
- Future potential
- Number of years in profession
- Willingness to invest again

Track Record   LPs focus on the stage and returns of a VC's investments. For example, did the VC invest in seed deals? What was the IRR on these deals? What is the overall performance of the fund. What are the kind of deals invested in? Who has the VC worked with? What are some examples of specific deals?

Joe Rouse, a former general partner with Pioneer Capital Partners of New Zealand, noted that in a start-up, an entrepreneur was the player. As a VC, you are the coach. He adds,

This mostly stemmed from my desire to be involved in more companies than one. Armed with an MBA in corporate finance and marketing [and 10 years' operating experience inside venture-backed companies], I had little difficulty transitioning to venture capital. Then, it's a matter of persuading limited partners to trust your judgment. Due diligence is a subjective process. Ultimately, the collective opinion in the team made the difference. I have a desire to be involved strategically in young companies. I had [operating] roles in previous venture-backed companies that helped me in this regard. Tundra went public on the Toronto stock exchange. Wireless semiconductor company Philsar was acquired by NASDAQ-listed Conexant.

Key experience matters. Perhaps the best VCs are *near* entrepreneurs, or entrepreneurs who have mellowed. Lin Hong Wong says, "Whether it is for a VC or for an entrepreneur, having start-up experience is valuable. A successful start-up gives confidence and motivation for another round. A failed start-up gives valuable lessons on the risks and pitfalls."

Skillsets   LPs also assess VCs' relevant expertise in product commercialization, asking questions like these:

- What experiences do they have in working in start-ups and early-stage companies?
- How did the VCs help the entrepreneurs?
- What was the outcome?
- Can the deal be attributed to luck or calculated risk-taking?

In the early 19th century, David Ricardo allegedly made a million pounds (more than US$50 million in today's dollars)—roughly half of his fortune at death—on his Waterloo bonds. Although he was not a military analyst and had no basis to compute the odds, he knew that the competition was thin, the seller was eager, and the pounds if he won would be worth much more than the pounds if he lost.

Future Potential   What is the scope of the fund and does it make sense in the background of prevailing trends? What plans do the VCs have for this fund? Do they have any dealflow in the pipeline already?

Number of Years in Profession   Due to the cyclical nature of the venture capital industry, a rule of thumb for ability is the tenure of a VC. Poor performers are weeded out and only VCs with staying power remain in the profession. However, noting that a VC who has been around for many years but has not done any significant deals could also raise a red flag.

Willingness to Invest Again   Perhaps the key background check question is, Will you co-invest with these guys again?

If the answer is vague and generic with no detail, there is more to the story. Fundamentally, the value of a VC boils down to a network. What do VCs really offer? "Connected money," that is, who do the

VCs know—companies, customers, other VCs, potential team members. What's most important, what contacts will they actually make for you? Steve Jurvetson meets with Paul Allen and Jeff Bezos from time to time. Few VCs in Asia have that level of contacts—but the better firms are in a position to open a lot of doors. VC firms who syndicate expand the networks and resources available to them significantly.

COMMANDMENT #7: Ensure an Appropriate Alignment Between GP and LP

You can increase your chances of success by honing your communication skills. Language ability plays a role. As one VC explains: "There is a disconnect between Chinese and U.S. LPs. There is a difference between Chinese who can speak English and Chinese who can speak Chinese. Regardless of their ability as VC, it is more likely that an LP will fund Chinese who speak English because they can understand them."

For Gobi ventures, the LP (Hillman Company, a long-standing U.S.-based family office that had been the first LP of Kleiner Perkins) felt that it had to be in Asia. U.S. VC funds don't really have to raise money—those lines are being drawn in Asia right now. There was also a trusted intermediary, Peter Wendell, whom senior management in the LP knew and trusted. This is especially important with a new fund with young partners.

In addition, earlier-stage VC is less competitive and more attractive—especially in China. Funds giving US$5 million to start-ups are becoming overly competitive. Essentially, the LP is buying an option. Given the long lag between the first and final closings, by getting in at the end, they had the benefit of a maturing portfolio at an early-stage valuation.

COMMANDMENT #8: Promote Capital Efficiency

What distinguishes the top performers from the rest? In the United States, consistently strong funds have lower expense ratios than their peers and managers who have been at the helm longer. My colleagues and I asked our panelists whether they would you see this to be true as well in Asia or do other factors play a more important role? Here are some of the responses:

Flooding a Company Ken Xu of Gobi Ventures feels that in the long term, funds with low expense ratios thrive, especially when the markets are cyclical. It is possible to give too much to a company. On average, Gobi Ventures funds on average US$1– 2 million per company for its first round. There is also sufficient flexibility to fund companies for an additional year to a year and a half and pump in additional resources to beef up the sales and marketing.

Andy Tang adds that smaller funds charge a higher percentage of management fee. Larger funds, by virtue of their larger size, incur proportionately less management fees.

Overenthusiasm for Trading The most successful VCs also temper their enthusiasm for investing. Not every ball should be hit. Good batters realize that some balls outside the sweet spot should be left alone. Similarly, professional investors realize that sometimes it's better to just stand still than to rush into a stock. Retail investors often make the mistake of "flashing outside the sweet spot" because they cannot resist the temptation to trade in every opportunity. And, like an inexperienced batter, they suffer the same fate. Too much trading will lead to a lot of churn, extra commissions to lawyers, large tax implications, and worst of all, a lack of focus resulting in failed investments.

Timing As credit markets tighten, local venture capital firms are changing their tactics. Institutional capital sources usually allocate a small percentage of their funds to alternative investments such as venture capital. And as traditional stock investments shrink in the current market downturn, new funds for venture capital also dry up.[15]

"When we were raising money in 2001, that was a common refrain" (that institutional backers were overallocated in venture funds), says Tom Melzer, a founder and managing director of RiverVest Venture Partners in Clayton, Missouri, a firm that completed raising US$75 million in April 2008. "This is a difficult market to raise money for anything," he said.

In a downturn, the best investors tap proximity to their advantage and turn crisis into opportunity. For example, Advantage Capital, a group of venture capital partnerships founded in 1992, works with banks to back qualifying creditworthy businesses that have been unable to obtain traditional bank loans as credit markets tighten. Starbucks approached 300 VCs in the 1970s (when the United States was experiencing severe stagflation) before it was funded.

It is essential to understand the investment horizons of LPs. The universities are typically long-term investors as they have no need to overreact to volatility in the market. Harold Bradley, chief investment officer of the US$2 billion Ewing Marion Kauffman Foundation in Kansas City, said Kauffman commits 15 percent of its assets to private equity, of which venture capital receives about half. At the time of writing the Kauffman Foundation was moving more of its venture investments overseas, he said, because its U.S. venture investments were more illiquid as the market for initial public stock offerings had slowed. Some pension funds (whose boards frequently consist of people whose own pensions are covered) are more conservative, and although they have longer-term horizons, they are fiscally conservative and do not want to pay top dollar for good fund managers.

In a downturn, Mark Heeson, president of the NCVA, points out that venture capital investors are forced to hang on to their portfolio companies longer. Heeson says high-net-worth individuals are more likely to pull out of venture capital than institutional investors, who are looking for returns 10 years from now. He said he expects institutional investors will continue to fund venture-backed companies. "While venture capital is risky, it's a risk that is known, compared to other asset classes that have faltered over the last few weeks," Heeson says.

Spoilt for Choice   C. Scott Hamner, director of Credit Suisse Customized Fund Investment Group (which represents pensions and other large investors), acts as an investor-fiduciary on behalf of those clients. He says, "Quality and volume of funds is much greater now than it was in the past. We're seeing a convergence of our investor criteria. We have a much larger universe of funds in which we can invest. The bar for new manager relationships is higher than for managers we've known in the past."

Peter Rip, general partner of Crosslink Capital, suggests, "One needs a theory of *future drivers* of returns to select among venture capital managers. Being yet-another-top-half-IT fund is not enough to be considered seriously by anyone. LPs construct portfolios of all private equity and venture capital investments based on their strategies, applying sound financial principles of predicting correlations of returns to maximize risk-adjusted return. The typical VC fund attributes are size, industry, stage, and geography. These attributes pass for strategies in most fundraising conversations."[16]

A lot of LPs are unhappy with past performance of their investments. An LP we interviewed commented, "It's hard to compare an IRR with an index. I see a lot of shotgun marketing in the LP business. You should only be focusing on funds that are a fit for what you invest in at your stage. The attribution of your track record is important, that is, who in your fund did what. The devil you know is better than the devil you don't. Differentiation/knowing your customer is paramount. There is a 95 percent correlation between VC returns and NASDAQ. Capital efficiency is not a gating item, it's a differentiator."

If you examine who is delivering the majority of venture capital returns in nanotechnology, it is application-oriented life sciences companies, says analyst firm Lux Research. Jurron Bradley, who leads Lux Research's nanomaterials practice, says that start-ups that are tailored toward a small number of specific applications tend to be more successful than firms developing broader platforms with no clearly defined purpose.

Holistic Evaluation   Zero2IPO carried out all-round investigations into venture capital firms in China covering investment, management, financing and exit, and other areas. Zero2IPO looks at capital under management, total amount of capital raised, total number of deals closed, total amount of capital invested, total number of exit cases, exit amount, and return level as major indexes for ranking and adjusts them annually to best match the development of this industry. In emerging geographies like China, where data is scarce, there is a need to rely on local expert advisers (like Zero2IPO) for holistic assessment of the funds and to dig deeper into the data to uncover the complete picture.

Hurdles to U.S. Investors   "Most U.S. companies recognize the theoretical benefits of doing business in Asia, but can find the opportunities difficult to quantify and exploit. Often, senior management lacks the resources required to evaluate complex issues in evolving markets halfway around the world," says Matthew Swainson of the *Asian Venture Capital Journal.* Venture funds have had their fair share of hits and misses as they globalize in Asia. Collaboration between a U.S. fund and an Asia fund is theoretically sound, as it makes sense to have the Asia team be responsible for the day-to-day operations and investments while the U.S.-based team provides expertise and experience. However, practical complications such as delayed response and lack of mutual understanding frequently surface.

Side Dish: Principles for Entering the VC Industry

Suppose you want to be a VC, not just engage the support of one for your business. What do you need to do?

- Have realistic expectations.
- Market the skills that matter.
- Display less mercenary spirit, more passion and selflessness.
- Get close to VCs.

COMMANDMENT #1: Have Realistic Expectations

The demand for VC jobs outstrips the supply of VC jobs. If an aspiring VC waits until a VC spot actually opens up to try to apply for it, it is likely to be too late.[17] Instead, it is best to position yourself properly.

Be Humble   As a younger professional, it is often better to learn from someone with a lot more experience, someone who has seen it all before. Listen to what VCs and entrepreneurs are saying and digest the info before positioning yourself as an expert in some field. A large part of a job as a VC will be listening and asking smart questions, so see what they ask. One of our interviewees advised, "Respect experience. It is not advisable to criticize a start-up, because the entrepreneur could be affiliated with the VCs." The best course of action sometimes is to listen.

Those who aspire to enter the venture capital industry are well-advised not to embark on an active, ongoing search for a job in venture capital. In an uptime, there is usually a shortage among the most experienced VCs and the existing experienced VCs are often already on multiple boards and do not have bandwidth to take on any more investments, while their junior staff are still coming up to speed. Venture firms thus elect to bring someone in from the outside to bolster capacity right away, with the natural inclination to hire from large companies who are potential acquirers of the portfolio companies. The window of opportunity is short and VC is a career more than a job, and due to the small firm size, if you turn down an opportunity today, it could be a full five-year cycle before another opportunity presents itself.

Be realistic about your prospects of joining the industry. Tell people who are connected and that you know well, so that they might suggest you to a firm or headhunter doing a search. But don't put yourself out there too much. If you don't fit those criteria, maybe you should think about positioning yourself for the next cycle, and make sure that next time around you will fit the profile. For more tips and tricks on finding a venture capital job (as well as a live directory of jobs), please refer to http://wayofthevc-jobs.easyurl.net.

Business School?   Bing Gordon, a partner at Kleiner Perkins Caufield & Byers, who has been on the board of Amazon since 2003, shares the following:

> Kleiner Perkins values operating success.
>
> I always tell 20-somethings to think of their potential investment in an MBA as
>
> - *An expensive necessity for promotion in some fields (especially banking and consulting)*
> - *A very expensive opportunity to change industries or fields*
> - *A very stimulating vacation that you get career credit for*
>
> In general, it is not worth going to business school if you already have a fast-track career in an industry you love.

Bobby Chao, founding managing director of DFJ Dragon, adds,

> Business school teaches common sense. People go there to confirm their own common sense, to spruce up their confidence, and to build up their network that is otherwise impossible. Whoever agrees with me on these points makes his or her own decision whether to go to B-school or not. My

biased opinion about schools: Stanford is small (around 300 students or so every year) and is located right next to 40 percent of the VC money in U.S. and the innovation center of Silicon Valley. Harvard is too big (approaching 1,000 students every year); it becomes the academic heavy and is closer to financial services industry in New York. Stanford, bar none, so far has the track record of producing the most entrepreneurs and VCs. A recent graduate means a talented person who has not been tainted. While VC profession remains largely a black box operation, an untainted and talented person fresh out of B-school will be ideal to be my apprentice. He or she may not be the preferred candidate for other firms after working with me for few years.

Barry Drayson believes that business school is a sensible decision:

MBAs with whom I have worked are typically information literate; they are analytically superior; they are up to date and catch on quickly. Many are enthusiastic and leave college with a dream to do just this. VCs should nurture that. Give them two years in a VC and they will cost twice as much and want equity on day one with no proof of their concept! With a graduate, you get at least a proof of value before you give that away. Which school? MIT's VC investments make it the 22nd largest economy in the world. INSEAD at Fontainebleau? I lectured there once and they seemed to be trying to give you something for the real world; I cannot argue with Harvard. It is a bit like French food—it is defined not by how great the best restaurant is, but how good they all are. After all, it is not what they want to teach you; it is what you choose to learn.

Timothy Draper says, "Your network is important if you want to be a VC. I would choose according to the network you want to build. Maybe it is Indian School of Business (ISB) or a top Chinese business school." Norman A. Fogelsong, general partner at Institutional Venture Partners, adds, "The best background for a VC is a good education and relevant work experience, typically with a technology company. In my case, I worked at Hewlett-Packard and studied engineering, business, and law at Stanford and Harvard. Both universities have extensive networks in Silicon Valley."

Shadowing and Apprenticeship Neil Shen, founding managing partner of Sequoia Capital China, is a successful entrepreneur as well as a successful VC. His hits have included companies like Ctrip (China's largest online travel site, which he co-founded in 1999) and HomeInn (one of China's fastest-growing hotel chains, which was spun off from Ctrip in 2003), both of which are listed on NASDAQ. He grew up in Hainin, Zhejiang, and left for Shanghai when he was seven years old. Neil's mother was CEO of a state-owned enterprise and was perpetually busy, having managerial responsibility for both the work flow of the enterprise and also people working under her. He feels that his mother's work ethic rubbed off on him. When asked about his entrepreneurial instincts, he explains, "It's in the blood."[18]

Tim Draper, founder of Draper Fisher Jurvetson, further explains, "People learn by doing." Andy Tang, managing director at DFJ Dragon, started out in a corporate fund (Infineon Ventures, a subsidiary fund of a German semiconductor company) and learned from experienced veterans such as Tony Sun, the VC he did his first deal with. Tang observed Sun's finesse in company building, and how he interacted and worked with an entrepreneur. "When a company is doing well, when everything is moving like clockwork, you can't really tell the mettle of a VC. When a company is not doing very well, markets are on tenterhooks, good VCs show their true colors. A good VC is calm and composed in difficult times, and helps the entrepreneur see the bigger picture. A good VC helps the entrepreneur turn the company around from a precarious brink and work to create value for all shareholders. A good VC adds value when a company is not doing well." Tang's philosophy is to not focus on immediate advantages (such as getting into a hot deal), but to focus on more important issues like demonstrating that as a VC, he can add value to the growth of company. With a reputation, entrepreneurs and LPs can approach the VCs. A VC starting out should focus on the best product development to add value to a company, just as product development is more important than marketing a start-up early in its life cycle. In turn, this will improve dealflow and earn the VC the reputation of being a value-add investor. In the long run, this will create the most return for the VC.

Experience to Build Tacit Knowledge The myth is that a VC is either born with intuition or not; intuition is not something you can learn.

The truth is that VCs definitely do improve what looks like intuition—their tacit knowledge—because it depends on experience.

Bobby Chao of DFJ Dragon adds, "A young VC would benefit from a mentor to lead the way for the apprentice. Such an apprentice needs to have at least one of the following: family nepotism (not a bad term), an outstanding academic record, a good track record or other related trait, and lots of luck."

Bing Gordon of Kleiner Perkins Caufield & Byers says,

> There is plenty to learn about investment structures. Most operating managers, myself included, have limited exposure to financing.
>
> My "aha moment" was when I realized that it might not be hard to be a mediocre venture capitalist. After all, the investment dollars and the team sizes of the companies are usually smaller than a single video game. The hard part is exiting, because there are no rules. My sense is that it takes 10 years to hit one's stride.

COMMANDMENT #2: Market the Skills That Matter

The three most important functions of an analyst are communication, sourcing, and analysis. There are things that one can do to build those skills without joining a VC firm, such as putting forth an analysis of a new start-up or tipping VCs off to potential deals today.

Bobby Chao of DFJ Dragon says, "The prerequisites of any VC are a leader personality, management skill, analytical ability, and outstanding interpersonal skill. Based on these, a successful apprentice-turned-VC needs to rapidly build specific networks that are not easily accessible in other professions. Learn the broad base of knowledge of everything. Memorize all the people, time, and sequence of events. Learn to be yourself and be honest."

Tim Draper further explains, "It usually takes about six months for a new analyst or associate to get up to speed on our business. After that, they are quite valuable. They generate new leads, and add to our network. They allow us to leverage them to make great progress. They make for a more dynamic workplace."

The Sniff Test   Finding a good CEO running a start-up is hard. Even harder is to find someone who understands product management and marketing, who can listen to customers and synthesize exactly what the start-up has to do and how to position its product. Cultivate A-player CEOs and hone the skill of listening. Bing Gordon advises, "Learn by doing. Read a lot. Take notes so you can see how wrong you really were. And make sure to be home for dinner with the family."

A Digital Avatar   Brad Feld, Jeff Nolan, Peter Rip, and David Cowan are some examples of prolific and insightful VCs who choose to blog their thoughts. A digital presence gives people you connect with a landing page. It is the center of operations for all your online networking and a place for people to assess your background and thoughts—the equivalent of hoisting a sail on a windy day.

Be an Innovation Leader   A badge of honor as a former entrepreneur is not a prerequisite, but being entrepreneurial and innovative helps. Experiences such as chairing or starting an investment or entrepreneurship club at college or business school are quite illustrative of an entrepreneurial tendency. Bobby Chao adds, "If a person is not a managing director of a fund, be an investment staff involving a company that has a high-profile liquidity event. That can also help building up the track record. Try to organize or sponsor an event of high profile that can result in publicity."

COMMANDMENT #3: Display Less Mercenary Spirit, More Passion and Selflessness

Be passionate for the product—that is critical in the investment space. If you're doing Web services and you're not a user, you're just never going to get it. Why do people use Twitter? Why is Facebook better than MySpace? These are things you're just not going to understand if you're not a real user.

VCs often prefer to let their investments do the talking. Jenny Lee, partner at Global Granite Ventures, believes in staying out of the press (as much as she can) and would prefer that the firm stand behind its portfolio companies rather than in front. Lee and her partners Thomas Ng and Jixun Foo, all top-rated venture capitalists, believe in harnessing their team's efforts to add value and help their portfolio companies be successful. They would prefer to let the results speak for themselves in the long run and let their portfolio companies and their products speak for them. One of their portfolio investments is Chamate, a popular chain of Chinese teahouses that serve meals. There, globally recognized restaurant best practices and systems are combined with fresh, local produce and connoisseur teas. In emerging markets like China, the passion of top-tier VCs is to spot "diamonds in the rough" that have great concepts and the right motivations, but need guidance on how to execute upon them.[19]

Make Time for Start-Ups   Be selfless with your time for start-ups. One of the most valuable things a VC can do is to talk to a lot of start-ups and establish a data bank of ideas, products, and companies. This allows a VC to get a sense of quality (good teams and weak teams), preferences (what are needs of start-ups and why they would choose VC A over VC B), and best practices (the best way to hire or fire someone). Start-ups are often looking for feedback, beta testers, and ideas. The more you are available for start-ups, the more you will learn and generally be seen as a useful person for start-ups to talk to. Helping a start-up with its marketing plan is a good way to hone your intuition in developing going-to-market strategies. Time and money have karma—what goes around really does come around.

It is also important to develop creativity in seeing partnership opportunities. Johan Stael, CEO of IQUBE (a disruptive incubator and venture capital firm in Sweden), advises start-ups to ask potential partners: "Suppose we form a successful partnership, what would it look like?" Look at start-ups in unusual spaces that may not be in vogue currently. David Weiden of Khosla Ventures believes that two of the most important attributes for an aspiring VC to acquire are the willingness to bet where no one else is and the ability to sticking with tough situations.

Teach   It is easier to have a clearer understanding of the mechanics of venture capital when you attempt to teach it to someone else, which requires you to build an in-depth knowledge of the subject. Offering to teach at your local university or chamber of commerce is a valuable spur to personal growth. (As they say, if you can teach your mother, it demonstrates that you really understand the subject!) Teaching start-ups is a sobering experience and will remind you that not everyone understands the virtue of strategies such as Rich Site Summary (RSS). Teaching also allows the teacher to build networks in the entrepreneurial community, and networks are critical to start-up success. It also serves to build up the database of companies that a VC needs to be aggregating.

Volunteer   Often, the only way to get your feet wet in the industry is to offer your services for free. This can often lead to unexpected benefits, for example, one would-be VC offered to work a year for no pay; during that year, he entrenched himself within the firm so that he became a net benefit. There are obvious disadvantages to this approach—opportunity cost, if nothing else—but it demonstrates sincerity and allows the VC to assess the work of the aspiring analyst. For most, getting started as a VC involves an element of serendipity; it is seldom a carefully planned decision. Very few people start out saying, "I want to be a VC. Therefore I'm going to go through the following steps, starting with B-school."

Make Friends in Prosperity   Be helpful and generate dealflow—without trying to snatch up crumbs for yourself. Many would-be VCs have the misconception that the main responsibility of an analyst is to scan through stacks of business plans and simply separate the wheat from the chaff. In actual fact, VCs hustle hard to track down deals and expect everyone in the firm to generate dealflow and to be in touch with developments in the industry.
   Andy Tang adds,

At a bad time, it is easy for a VC to give up. If a fund has 20 or 30 companies, why doesn't the CEO just focus on the better companies? However, in the realm of VC, it is important to give every company the best shot. A company which is not performing today might be good tomorrow. If you are a good VC, you will motivate yourself and the CEO. We hire associates who will stick around to "watch the whole movie" and not those who leave after half an hour. At entry level, we look for ability to remain open-minded. In early stage, some of the business plans are far-fetched, and it's not good to be overly cynical and cautious, otherwise a brilliant idea might be shot down. But at the same time, a VC should be aware of the risk and not pursue a infeasible idea with a lot of money. We look for the ability to work with a company, communication skills, someone who can call the VP of a company and tell him tactfully such that he feels that you are helping them. With a confident CEO, giving advice is not an easy thing. Delivering advice and value itself is an art and involves the art of influence. Consultants can be good VCs because one quality of good consultants is to give good advice.

COMMANDMENT #4: Get Close to VCs

VCs tend to hire people with financial grounding. They rarely hire fresh graduates, and so a fresh college graduate who wishes to get the best possible training for an entry-level job in VC would be to get a job in an investment bank or another financial services firm. Business school students would be well-advised to look for internships that would place them in regular contact with venture capitalists (either directly or through a portfolio company of a VC). Another alternative would be to take a job at a company backed by venture capitalists and gain exposure to the venture capitalists on the company's board. Get to know VCs in the same geography in advance so that you are a known commodity when a position opens up. It is prudent to take a long-term view and keep in mind that many VCs do not follow the "Apprentice model" (investment banking to business-school to VC) but have acquired years of operating experience, had a successful entrepreneurial stint as CEO, or been involved in building and growing companies. Use your network to meet VCs. Figure out who you know who also knows VCs that you'd like to meet.

This is capitalizing on the mere-exposure effect, also nicknamed the "familiarity breeds liking" effect, a phenomenon well known to advertisers: people express liking for things merely because they are familiar with them.

Remember That 80 Percent of Success Is Showing Up Know the calendar. As a VC, you want to meet innovators, but the innovators are already getting together in meetups, co-working groups, speaking events, and user groups. They band together in close-knit networks, and these networks will be more accepting if the first time you meet them isn't when you're trying to sniff for deals and vulture around for something to shove money into. Bobby Chao of DFJ Dragon adds, "I strongly encourage each young person to start out early in making friends, helping the community, working in the fraternity, and contributing in the professional associations. These are all the best kinds of networks.''

Attending events like TiEcon, where making the right connection is streamlined to a science, is helpful. Shital Mehta, who says she had ''zero interest in being an entrepreneur,'' attended her first TiEcon as a 19-year-old college student in 2000. A panel of female entrepreneurs gave her a new calling and determination to avoid a conventional corporate career, and she started a marketing and PR firm after graduation. ''Within a year and a half, my firm grew to US$1 million in revenue,'' Mehta says. ''And three-quarters of my leads came from people involved in TiE in some way.''[20] But you can't just sit back—you need to actively keep up with what's going on.[21]

Be Social and Build Relationships with VCs   As an involved community member, it is helpful to be likable so people enjoy spending time with you. The countless hours spent in college bars should have taught you something about being nice and having a little fun. Many people succeed primarily due to their great personalities.

Having a pleasant personality, however, is not sufficient in itself. This has to be supplemented by expertise and passion. This can be demonstrated by sending VCs a report on a hot new space or a review of a product, posting insightful comments on their blogs, and showing up at key events (watering holes for VCs). VCs don't live in a bubble and their job dictates that they need to be sourcing FoF deals all the time. Sending business plans to a default e-mail address at a VC firm is tantamount to a cold call, while reaching out to VCs is more of a ''hot call'' and can be more productive. For example, Flywheel Ventures, an Albuquerque and Santa Fe venture capital firm with US$31 million under management, launched a program in which six MBAs were hand-picked from all over the country and brought to New Mexico to find out if they will sink or swim in the high-risk world of venture capital in a new internship program. The six Flywheel Fellows in the program will spend 20 hours a week with Flywheel and another 20 hours each week with one of Flywheel's venture-funded companies, such as TruTouch Technologies, MIOX Corporation, or CoMeT Solutions.

Pitfalls to Avoid

VCs are not immune from pitfalls of their own. Here are some of the common behavior mistakes VCs make:

- Overconfidence
- Whimsical recruiting
- Status quo biases
- Proximity biases
- Ignoring preexisting personal relationships
- Misreading scientific and commercial factors

PITFALL #1: Overconfidence

When a task is difficult and feedback about results is vague, it is easy to develop overconfidence. Investing in new ventures and forecasting returns are not easy tasks and often market prices of unlisted assets are affected by noise. An LP who prefers to remain unnamed observes, "Every fund manager thinks they are top-quartile." In addition, Bobby Chao of DFJ Dragon lists these common fallacies:

- You think you know the entrepreneur.
- You think you know the technology and the market.
- You think the person you will syndicate with has both the entrepreneur and the technology and market.

David Weiden of Khosla Ventures also believes that VCs often make the mistake of putting too much money into companies that are not good bets.

PITFALL #2: Whimsical Recruiting

In addition, David Weiden says, VCs tend not to focus enough on recruiting. Dixon Doll, founder of Doll Capital, agrees, pointing out that VCs fall prey to hiring people for management positions that don't work out, primarily because they do not do sufficient due diligence. Norman Fogelsong, partner at Institutional Venture Partners (IVP), believes that VCs often make the mistake of backing the wrong teams with unsuccessful technologies in markets that turn out to be too small. Another top-tier venture capitalist we interviewed commented that VCs "lose their objectivity." This, he says, is the most common mistake. He adds, "VCs make the wrong choice of individual and move too slowly to correct them."

Possible solutions: To improve recruiting, pass your acquaintance along to your partners, who do not have prior knowledge about the entrepreneur, check with your partners and recruit outside expertise for assessment of the technology and market, and understand why other people want to syndicate with you if what they have is such a good deal.

PITFALL #3: Status Quo Biases

Certain LPs are also concerned with VCs who have an inclination to keep things as they are. LPs want VCs to be receptive to changes and swift in their actions when the need arises. An LP we interviewed explained, "VCs need to be decisive when things aren't going well at a company." David Weiden of Khosla Ventures believes that VCs often do not react to problems early or decisively enough, and Dixon Doll adds, "VCs can be too passive and not really engaged and take notes during board meetings, and they do not really do anything to change the outcome."

PITFALL #4: Proximity Biases

In some cases, LPs, especially government funds, may tell VCs, "Open up an office in our province if you want an allocation on your new fund." Facing such an out-of-the-way request predicated on boosting economic development in these geographies, VCs should first consider whether such constraints align with the larger interest of their fund's scope and strategy.

As noted earlier, *herd behavior* describes how individuals in a group can act together without planned direction. This applies to VCs, too, as Dixon Doll notes. In the world of venture capital, where there is exceptionally little information, VCs fall prey to investing in me-too companies that are not really different and innovative.

Does your investment move the needle? Despite the growth in VC fund sizes over the last two decades to current billion-dollar levels, LPs feel that some VC funds are too small to be effective. These VCs need to do larger Series A and B financings for their portfolio companies to succeed. However, VCs might not have the same sentiments, because early-stage companies might be too risky for

VCs to commit a huge amount, and in the worst-case scenario, no money might be left for further rounds of financing in the most promising companies in the portfolio. Yet, from the LPs' perspective, "For us to put money into your fund, we need to commit at least US$500 million to the relationship for it to move the needle at our institution; that's why we can only fund international GPs." VC funds that are perceived to be too small will thus find it harder to raise funds from these institutional LPs.

PITFALL #5: Ignoring Preexisting Personal Relationships

Personal relationships are often part of the puzzle, and preexisting relationships between the GP and the LP prospect can make a difference when it comes down to landing that initial allocation? Bobby Chao of DFJ Dragon adds, "LPs only invest in the fund they have confidence in. Such confidence comes from familiarity and trust with the GP. How does a VC build the relationship (familiarity) and trust if it is a first-time fund? There will always be a triggering event to start it all. If it starts up right, it snowballs. Try to put yourself in the shoes of an LP. Why would they put money in your fund instead of other alternatives? The answer is rather self-explanatory."

Forming and raising a new fund isn't easy, especially for quality Limited Partners. Hans Tung of Qiming Ventures shared his experience,

> Our first fund was formed in 2005. The two founders, Gary [Rieschel] and Duane [Kuang], are experienced China VCs who were looking to build a better platform for early stage investing in China. By 2005, the Seattle-based Ignition Partners felt that China was too important to be ignored for a sizeable fund, and wanted to enter China with a trusted partner. Since Gary had backed them as an LP when he was with Softbank, and everyone has known and worked well with each other for a long time, Qiming was born as an Ignition-affiliated, but independent, China fund. Many of Ignition's LPs became Qiming's supporters too. At Qiming, we make all of our investment decisions ourselves. There is no Investment Committee in the US to report to. Several other China funds have comparable affiliations with U.S.

funds, for example, DFJ Dragon and DFJ, DT Capital and Lightspeed, IDG China and Accel, Gobi and Sierra Ventures, and GSR and Mayfield. It will take work for these funds to maintain current affiliations. Ultimately, they will last if there is synergy.

PITFALL #6: Misreading Scientific and Commercial Factors

When VCs invest in a start-up where scientists are major players, not understanding them may result in unnecessary miscommunication, which often results in loss of potential returns. Barry Drayson of Nanoholdings, an early-stage venture capital firm focusing on nano-technology, believes that the fundamental mistakes VCs make are not knowing when to cut off investments at the right time and basing investment decisions on financial models without attention to other key factors such as the go-to-market strategy.

Most of the time, VCs also do not understand that scientific people may require training in financial disciplines to align their thinking with the VC's commercial interests. The decision-making process will be fully understood and coordinated across the board if VCs are more aware of scientists' perspectives. As Barry Drayson points out, VCs must acknowledge that scientists are not engineers and communication between these parties can be fraught. Here are some of the implications of this difference:

- Unlike engineers, scientists do not suddenly start concentrating on your objectives simply because you gave them money. It is well known that scientists exhibit compulsive behavior in their work, driven more by curiosity than anything else. However illogical it may sound, money is probably the last thing on a scientist's mind.
- Notwithstanding the point about the importance of curiosity, scientists have two competencies: one is science, and the other—often the main one—is raising money. It is always wise to check on the true commercial commitment of a scientist.
- When scientists run into a problem in the lab, even facing insuperable odds, they believe they will solve it and will tell you nothing until they do. It is thus important for VCs to have constant communication with the scientists to know what they are up to.

- A scientist who discovers something valuable always wants to be the first person to stand up proudly at a conference and announce it to the whole world. This beats the purpose of the joint intellectual property agreement you had to protect the business, but it is hard to convince a passionate scientist who feels a calling to share this new knowledge with the world that protecting IP is indeed more significant.
- Scientists hate milestones. Drayson tells of one fine young man he knew who was driven to drugs by milestone stress and time pressure, and he recommends leaving the scientists to create. To the extent possible, get an engineer to handle the milestones.

Another difficulty with working with scientists is the patent system, which is broken. The best protection is market success, with all its components actively engaged. However, investors and buyers need to see patents for comfort; use patents with great forethought and a tight budget.

Endnotes

1. William A. Sahlman, "The Structure and Governance of Venture-Capital Organizations," *Journal of Financial Economics* 27, no. 2 (October 1990): 473–521.
2. Paul Gompers and Josh Lerner, "The Use of Covenants: An Empirical Analysis of Venture Partnership Agreements," *Journal of Law & Economics* 39, no. 2 (October 1996): 463–498.
3. William A. Sahlman, "The Structure and Governance of Venture-Capital Organizations." *Journal of Financial Economics* 27, no. 2 (October 1990): 473-521.
4. Morten Sorenson, "How Smart Is Smart Money? A Two-Sided Matching Model of Venture Capital," *Journal of Finance* 62, no. 6 (2007): 2725–2762.
5. Tim Oren, "Venture Capital, Public Information, and the Law of Unintended Consequences," August 13, 2003; retrieved from www.pacificafund.com/blog/2003/08/13.html, June 29, 2009.
6. "Saif Partners Is VC Fund of the Year & CDH Investments Wins PE Fund of the Year in the Event of 2007 China VC&PE Annual Ranking," report released by Zero2IPO Research Center, Shanghai, December 7, 2007; retrieved from http://research.zero2ipo.com.cn/en/n/2007-12-7/2007127215204.shtml, July 6, 2009.
7. Fred Wilson, "Venture Fund Economics: Gross and Net Returns," August 3, 2008; retrieved from www.avc.com/a_vc/2008/08/venture-fund–1.html, June 29, 2009.

8. Lisa More and J. Longerstaey, *Introduction to Risk Metrics* (New York: JP Morgan, 1995).

9. Brian Wick, "Venture Capital Financing," n.d.; retrieved from www.geocities .com/Eureka/Park/1692/vcfirms.html; June 29, 2009.

10. Tom Weidig, Andreas Kemmerer, and Bjoern Born, "The Risk Profile of Private Equity Fund-of-Funds," *Journal of Alternative Investments* 7, no. 4, (2005): 33–41.

11. Cambridge Associates LLC, "U.S. Venture Capital Index and Selected Benchmark Statistics," December 31, 2008; retrieved from www.cambridgeassociates .com/pdf/Venture%20Capital%20Index.pdf, July 5, 2009.

12. Andrew Conner, "Persistence in Venture Capital Returns," Alignment Capital Group, March 2005; www.alignmentcapital.com/pdfs/research/persistence_ pei_2005.pdf, June 29, 2009.

13. Yael V. Hochberg, Alexander Ljungqvist, and Yang Lu, "Whom You Know Matters: Venture Capital Networks and Investment Performance," *Journal of Finance* 62, no. 1 (2007); 251–301. Scott Shane and Daniel Cable, "Network Ties, Reputation and the Financing of New Ventures," *Management Science* 48, no. 3 (2002): 364–381. "How Do Private Equity Investors Create Value? A Study of 2006 Exits in the U.S. and Western Europe." Ernst & Young Transaction Advisory Services, 2007. Harry J. Sapienza, Sophie Manigart, and Wim Vermeir, "Venture Capitalist Governance and Value-added in Four Countries," *Journal of Business Venturing* 11, no. 6 (1996): 439–469. Mari Maunula, "The Perceived Value-Added of Venture Capital Investors: Evidence from Finnish Biotechno logy Industry," Helsinki: ETLA, Elinkeinoelämän tutkimuslaitos [The Research Institute of Finnish Economy], July 2006.

14. Osborne Simon, "Steering Clear of Private Equity's Bottom Quartile Funds," retrieved by subscription from www.asianinvestor.net/article.aspx?CIaNID= 75366, May 9, 2008.

15. Rick Desloge, "Venture Capital Squeezed as Credit, Economy Tighten," *St. Louis Business Journal,* October 3, 2008; retrieved from http://stlouis.bizjournals.com/stlouis/stories/2008/10/06/story13.html? b=1223265600^1710196, June 29, 2009.

16. Peter Rip, "EarlyStageVC 2.0," November 3, 2006; retrieved from http:// earlystagevc.typepad.com/earlystagevc/venture_capital_20/, June 28, 2009.

17. Charlie O'Donnell, "How to Get Started as a Venture Capital (VC) Analyst," blog post, June 6, 2007; retrieved from www.thisisgoingtobebig.com/2007/06/ how_to_get_star.html, June 29, 2009.

18. "Figure Out 'The New Economy'–Neil Shen Gives Talk to Cheung Kong 06MBA," *Cheung Kong MBA Newsletter,* no. 26, July 31, 2007; retrieved from www.ckgsb.edu.cn/web2005/files/MBA_newsletter_31_07_2007.pdf, June 29, 2009.

19. Jixun Foo, "Global View Insights and Interviews from Granite Global Ventures China Investment: Don't Throw Baby Out With the Baby Toys," n.d.; retrieved from www.ggvc.com/Global%20View_ChinaQuality_Final.pdf, July 5, 2009.

20. John Boudreau, "Start-Ups Pitch Their Ideas to VC Crowd," *San Jose Mercury News*, May 17, 2008; retrieved from www.tiesv.org/TGS/NM/newsview/view NewsPT?id_news=313, June 29, 2009.
21. Haley Wachdorf, "Flywheel Interns Man Both Sides of Venture Capital Table," *New Mexico Business Weekly*, July 14, 2006; retrieved from www.bizjournals.com/albuquerque/stories/2006/07/17/story8.html?from_rss=1, June 29, 2009.

7

The Partnership Becomes Wildly Successful

Stressed spelled backwards is desserts. Coincidence? I think not!
—Anonymous

The exit signals the end of the exhilarating entrepreneurial ride. You go public (IPO) or sell the venture to another firm (that is, trade sale)—those are the harvesting alternatives that normally receive the most attention by VCs. It is no surprise that typical VCs spend 75 percent of their time on harvesting, with a sharp focus on an IPO. To entrepreneurs, an IPO is a badge of honor. This chapter outlines the techniques that top VCs and entrepreneurs employ in a winning exit. Figure 7.1 summarizes what each side needs to do.

While the initial public offering may be the most glamorous and heralded type of exit for the venture capitalist and owners of the company, a fund's intended method for liquidating its holdings is predicated on achieving the maximum possible return. Other successful exits of venture investments occur through a merger or acquisition of the company by either the original founders or another company or a recapitalization. These strategies depend on exit climates including market conditions and industry trends.

Figure 7.1 Makings of a Successful Partnership

Bing Gordon of Kleiner Perkins Caufield & Byers shares this story: In 1991, Don Mattrick sold his Vancouver-based company, Distinctive Software, to Electronic Arts (Wikipedia pegs the deal at US$11 million). DS was the leading game developer in British Columbia, but Mattrick and his execs felt they could play a bigger role in the video game industry. They cold-called EA management with a proposal to be acquired, because Electronic Arts had a reputation for management and success, along with had a reputation for fairness with employees, and it was in the same time zone.

Mission accomplished. Within five years, DSI had morphed into Electronic Arts Canada; grown from 60 to 500 employees; grown revenues from US$10 million to US$500 million; invented such hit franchises as FIFA Football, Need for Speed, NBA Live, and Triple Play Baseball; and founder Don Mattrick was elevated to president of EA Studios, with co-founder Paul Lee elevated to COO. "That was a great ride," Mattrick recalls. Incidentally, Bing Gordon wrote the business plan that first attracted Kleiner Perkins to make its investment in Electronic Arts.

CASE STUDY: Mengniu Dairy

In early 2004, Gensheng Niu looks across the Inner Mongolian plains, with their lush greenery, as he contemplates the game-changing move that Mengniu is making.

Gensheng Niu began his career as a milk bottle washer for another dairy group in 1982, and rapidly ascended to general manager. But in 1999, he left over differences with his boss and founded Mengniu Dairy Industry.[1] In eight years, his company moved from the bottom of the dairy producer ranks in China to number one.

In July 2004, the US$227 million Mengniu Dairy listing was an exercise in simplicity and seamless execution. If anyone were looking for an IPO candidate where they could tick every box, this was it: both a defensive stock and a high-growth story, modest in size but large enough to be noteworthy. It is a consumer play with a high-profile brand. It has management that has been honed for several years pre-listing by the presence of big-name international investors.

It came as little surprise when joint-arrangers BNP Paribas, Peregrine, and Morgan Stanley—the same team that managed the virtually simultaneous and difficult China Shipping debut—priced the 350 million-share IPO at the top end of a revised range. A dream come true for Gensheng Niu and Mengniu.

CDH Ventures was one of the backers of Mengniu. Yan Huang, Partner of CDH, believes that its success is attributable to the quick decision process. He adds, ``A rapid response is not only required at the time of investment, but also post-investment. Top VCs react quickly to requests of their portfolio companies and adjustments to business model. It is important to have a local decision process. Most foreign VCs have local establishments in China and more decision processes are moving to China. For example, Sequoia Capital used to be based in Silicon Valley. Now they are in China.''

What Star VCs Do: Winning Techniques

Venture capitalists generally seek to exit the investment in a portfolio company within three to five years of the initial investment. The interval varies depending on the investment focus and strategy of the venture firm, but exit is always the plan. Executing the plan involves some specific techniques:

- Begin with the end in mind.
- Wait until the time is right.
- Remember that less really can be more.
- Take good care of the golden goose.

WINNING TECHNIQUE #1 Begin with the End in Mind

The top VCs interviewed for this book planned for the exit of their businesses the day they made the first investment. Was the original business plan valid? they asked, and What is the likelihood positive cash flow might be achieved with a last round of our capital to bring the company to an originally planned IPO exit strategy? Do the potential rewards justify the risks? VCs evaluate a business on its ability to return the investment on exit. If you don't have a viable plan for being sold, going public, or bringing in ample profits, then your business will be viewed as less desirable. Entrepreneurs who show the ability to exit well from day one are golden!

Exit Type: Initial Public Offering   A well-functioning IPO market is crucial is reducing the cost of capital to venture capital enterprises. With well-functioning liquidity markets, the firm has access to equity at low cost.[2]

In recent years technology, IPOs have been in the limelight. At public offering, the venture firm is considered an insider and will receive stock in the company, but the firm is regulated and restricted in how that stock can be sold or liquidated for a set period. Once the shares are freely tradable, usually after about two years, the venture fund will distribute this stock or cash to its limited partner investors, who may then manage the public stock as a regular stock holding; they may liquidate it upon receipt. Over the last 25 years, almost 3,000 companies financed by venture funds have gone public.

Going public poses certain challenges for the company, and the hurdles for going public have grown more difficult in recent years. A top venture capitalist that we interviewed declares, "Where companies with revenues of US$30 million to US$50 million would have been viable IPO candidates in other times, the range today is US$80 million to US$90 million, creating a much higher bar in terms of critical mass. Companies should not plan to go public unless they have the visibility longer term to achieve at least a half-billion-dollar market cap."[3]

Randy Komisar of Kleiner Perkins Caufield & Byers echoes this advice, "From the company perspective, we are much more focused on performance—financial performance, bottom-line performance— before going into the public market. We are much more focused on substantiated business models that need expansion capital rather than venture capital from the public market in order to demonstrate that there is a business. In short, we are focused on fundamentals when we think about exposing those companies to the public market."

In instances where the IPO window is closed, most venture capitalists take their losses and are inclined to avoid throwing good money after bad.

Exit Type: Mergers and Acquisitions   Mergers and acquisitions represent the most common type of successful exit for venture investments. In the case of a merger or acquisition, the venture firm will receive stock or cash from the acquiring company and the venture investor will distribute the proceeds from the sale to its limited partners.

The strength of the mergers and acquisitions (M&A) market can sometimes offset a weak IPO market, making a trade sale more attractive to generate returns for shareholders and founders. In 2006, 41 venture-backed companies raised US$2.24 billion (average US$54 million per company) via IPOs compared to the US$27.33 billion raised by 356 M&A transactions (average US$77 million per company).

Dixon Doll, who co-founded DCM, invested in San Diego-based IPivot, a developer of Internet infrastructure technologies for load-balancing traffic flow to optimize website performance. As IPivot began to build up its sales organization, Intel expressed an interest in buying the company, primarily because IPivot's technology was ahead of all others in the industry. Intel acquired IPivot for US$500 million in cash, which represented the largest private company acquisition that Intel had made at that time.

Bing Gordon of Kleiner Perkins Caufield & Byers cautions, "The most difficult emotion for an entrepreneur comes with lingering failure. Quick failure is easy for most entrepreneurs, because they can move on to the next thing; but slow is agonizing. I am awed by the deep reservoirs of emotional commitment and staying power of some of the best company builders. The next most difficult emotion for an entrepreneur comes with success, surprisingly. Fast growth brings confusion, chaos, and constant struggles to scale and control. Any start-up struggles to maintain confidence and level-headedness. Fast growth challenges this, because leaders have to make so many decisions on imperfect information."

It is best when entrepreneurs maintain long-term commitment to the company they have founded. Whether as chairman, CEO, chief product officer, or in some other role, the founder's continuity can and should be deeply satisfying and powerful. It is always painful when someone loses control of a creation. This can occur in many ways, including a trade sale exit.

Norman A. Fogelsong, general partner at Institutional Venture Partners (IVP) says,

> These days, almost every potential IPO is dual-tracked, meaning that M&A conversations are also entertained in parallel. The IPO filing usually brings any potential strategic M&A buyers to the table. Over the past few years, we have had three IPOs (Arcsight, Comscore, and Synchronoss) as well as four significant M&A transactions (Business.com/Donnelley for US$350 million, Quigo/AOL for US$340 million, Danger/Microsoft for US$500 million, and MySQL/Sun for US$1 billion). The current window for IPOs seems to be closed for a while, but it will open again, as it always does, within the next year or two. At the same time, M&A has always been the predominant exit vehicle for all venture-backed companies.

Some of the M&A transactions I just mentioned were more attractive than an IPO. For example, before Danger was sold to Microsoft, for example, the company was considering an IPO at around US$300 million. When Microsoft offered US$500 million, everyone felt that was quite compelling.

For Bob Ackerman, founder of Allegis Capital, focusing on M&A as the primary exit strategy achieves three things: It means you have to be capital efficient, you need to be disciplined on valuations, and you need a larger percentage of your portfolio contributing to the returns of the fund. VCs should also look for corporate investors who might later want to acquire the start-up. Mergers and acquisitions now make up 98 percent of Allegis' returns. Recent deals include the sale of dot-com start-up IronPort to Cisco, and last summer's US$105 million sale of webphone software developer Ribbit to BT, which Ackerman says generated a fivefold return for Allegis.

WINNING TECHNIQUE #2: Wait Until the Time Is Right

Venture capitalist firms, especially younger firms, are often tempted to take a firm public prematurely in order to obtain a reputation (a practice known as *grandstanding*). Based on work by Harvard Business School professor Paul Gompers, companies financed by inexperienced venture capital firms are younger and more underpriced when they go public compared to companies backed by experienced venture capital firms.[4] This has been further explored by Butler and Goktan, two researchers at University of Texas, who reaffirmed this and in addition found that inexperienced VC firms—those with the strongest incentives to grandstand—tend to match with young and small companies within close proximity.[5] Grandstanding is the VC form of what psychologists call "hyperbolic discounting": the preference for more immediate payoffs relative to later payoffs, the closer to the present both payoffs are. It is highly desirable for both VCs and entrepreneurs to keep their eyes firmly on the prize and launch an IPO from a position of strength.

WINNING TECHNIQUE #3: Remember That Less Really Can Be More

VCs are looking for the company that will turn into a big win, so they would rather focus their efforts on selected companies than spread their efforts. Follow-on investments make up the majority of VC money going into companies. Out of thousands of business plans top-quartile VCs attract each year, the VCs fund only a handful of companies. Then they focus their efforts on a relatively small proportion of that favored few. When Entrepreneur.com ranked VCs in 2007, it found that on average, the top VCs had around 20 deals for early-stage investments and around seven deals for later-stage investments.

Looking at a new company that might be promising, the idea is to get in fast but small. The first one in line always gets the best deal, and getting involved too late in the company's life may mean lesser equity. Central actors (deal champions) will be better off not only because the network structure allows them to receive a greater share of rewards than peripheral actors but also because they can be more selective in terms of the resources they share with others.[6]

The value is in the worth, not in the number—a concept that goes back to antiquity. According to Aesop, the animals once argued about who the best mother was, which they defined as having the most babies. The mouse was winning until the lioness snorted and said, "I have only one—but that one is a lion!" The same principle applies in venture capital. Bing Gordon explains that acquirers can be looking to get a foothold in a new space, do a rollup or consolidation, or acquire a missing piece in a bigger portfolio, but ultimately, their intent is to "get bigger, get smarter, and get impossibly great people." This is manifested in different ways in VC investments. Good funds know the right investment pace. For Tom Perkins, three good deals made back all the money he ever spent (and more): Genentech, Google, and Amazon. Once you have invested in a firm like Google, there is a self-reinforcing virtuous cycle.

WINNING TECHNIQUE #4: Take Good Care of the Golden Goose

Venture capitalists typically commit to investments on the premises of potential high returns and availability of quick exit options. This pursuit of immediate gains may shift their focus from that of value creation to value capture, stunting the growth of budding companies and reducing the potential profitability of blockbuster products.

Remember the story of "The Goose That Laid the Golden Eggs"? The farmer who found that a goose in his yard was producing eggs with shells of pure gold was rich with the first one, and he would eventually have been rich beyond his wildest dreams, but he wanted to get at all the gold right away. He killed the goose to look inside, winding up with a dead bird and no more gold. This tale repeats itself over and over in modern business. VCs take biotechnology companies they've funded into trade sales to big biotechnology or pharmaceutical firms. The VC realizes profit and relieves itself of its investment while Big Pharma replenishes its desiccated pipeline with an innovative product from cash-starved biotech. The problem arises when the product fails to meet ambitious sales targets or when the acquirer restructures company operations. At this juncture, companies often shut down the acquisition's R&D unit and discontinue the product. Despite their financial muscle, Big Pharma companies are quick to kill acquisition projects at the first signs of trouble, because they need to keep a close eye on their bottom line and divert resources to products that will contribute to painting a robust picture of company financials. Sometimes, promising products may be dropped or acquisitions axed before they reach their intended synergies, either from impatience or from getting caught in a general pruning of the company's product portfolio.

For example, on October 18, 2007, Pfizer terminated its powder insulin product Exubera after barely one year of sales. The dismal figure of US$12 million in revenue in the first nine months of 2007 was a far cry from analyst estimates of US$1 billion to US$4 billion of annual sales. Acquisitions were also subjected to restructuring in Big Pharma firms. Johnson & Johnson shut down the R&D unit in Alza in August 2007 after deciding to trim its global workforce by 3 percent to 4 percent. Biotech firms are often vulnerable to Big Pharma's strategic business decisions, and promising products acquired in their infant stages of development may be denied development opportunities and R&D funding. VCs can reduce the likelihood of killing the golden goose if their financing allows for maturity of product development before exiting ventures.[7]

What Entrepreneurs Should Do: Commandments to Follow

Even in the last phases, there are things you need to do:

- Capture the timing in a cyclic industry.
- Remember that patience is a virtue.
- Think like a sectoral industrialist.

- Choose the right bourse.
- Assemble a good team.
- Develop a game plan and stick to it.

COMMANDMENT #1: Capture the Timing in a Cyclic Industry

"You can't run against the wind. You have to have the market with you," says Stan Reiss, a general partner at Matrix Ventures. "Timing is everything," adds Raj Kapoor, managing director at Mayfield. The first time he tried to sell Snapfish it was the right market but the wrong timing, and his investors didn't make any money. "We stuck around, got the opportunity to sell again, and did very well. The timing was right."

Andrew Braccia, a partner at Accel Partners, makes the same point: "We're in a cyclical business, but the trends are undeniably strong. IPO markets in the United States are going to be troublesome in the next couple of years, but if you [build value] you'll reap those rewards whenever they come." In one example of his theory, his firm is an investor in Facebook, one of the most talked-about companies in Silicon Valley. He said that the social media company has a unique opportunity to build a business in the private markets right now. "It will have the luxury of being private for a little longer," he said.

Bing Gordon of Kleiner Perkins Caufield & Byers believes that there have been more acquisitions than IPOs recently for two reasons. One is that the cost of being a public company (in the United States, at least) has risen, as a result of the unintended consequences of new laws and regulations like Sarbanes-Oxley. The second is that the benefits of being a public company, such as access to liquidity, have been constrained by a less enthusiastic reception to new IPOs. This seems to be prevalent across both information technology and companies Kleiner Perkins supports in life sciences and green tech as well.

As the saying goes, there is no formula for deciding when to get married, when to sell your house, when to sell a stock, or when to throw away an old pair of shoes.

"In general, the right time to exit is when a company needs the liquidity for a specific purpose and has high levels of confidence in its continued performance for four to eight quarters," Gordon adds.

David Weiden of Khosla Ventures feels that the timing of exit can be a tough decision. Key factors:

- Is exit an option at all?
- What are the odds the company will be worth more later?
- How much fun is it to operate the business as an independent company?

Garett Wiley, an attorney and serial entrepreneur in Shanghai, China, explains,

> In a downturn as severe as the one we are going through, new investments are slowing down significantly. Although quality deals can still get funding, there is less competition for deals and existing VCs are cherry-picking. VCs are more concerned about recent investments, consumer and advertising, B2C businesses which are cash flow negative. LPs are defaulting on capital calls. VC as an asset class may be fundamentally changed as a result of this downfall. With the proliferation of new funds in the past few years, we may see a shakeout of new funds with unproven teams as the IPO market is closed. A transaction priced at US$50 million a month ago has been repriced to US$2 million, and the company is forced to take the deal as there are no other alternatives.
>
> Most investors view China as a place to increase attention. LPs sitting on liquidity are seeing China correction as a growth opportunity. With no growth in the Western world for 5–10 years conservatively, India and China are seen as major engines of growth. High-net-worth individuals are falling over themselves to give money to deals in China.

David Siminoff, a partner at Venrock, says that in historic times of great inflation and war, people "want to put cash under the mattress, but you can't because of inflation." So there's still demand for quality companies, he adds, and those will eventually become public. "It's hard to find quality companies. It's the marginal companies that went public [in the dot-com heyday] that got killed," says Siminoff, whose firm is invested in Tudou, a China-based version of YouTube. "I'm telling all my companies to stay the course."

He adds, "There's not that many great companies ready to be bought or consolidated."

One research study by Josh Lerner shows that seasoned VCs take firms public at market peaks, relying on private financing when valuations are lower. Top VC firms know that rushing companies to the IPO market may impose costs on themselves. This may come in the form of underpricing of the company and a lower percentage equity stake for VCs with a shorter duration of board representation.[8]

COMMANDMENT #2: Remember That Patience Is a Virtue

Danny Rimer, a partner at Index Ventures, says that even in a recession, he doesn't believe that the industry is operating without exit options. Although the public markets have closed down—there were no venture-backed IPOs in the second quarter of 2008—his firm has sold four companies since the beginning of the year, an improvement on its success rate last year. He adds that the conventional thinking that a venture firm must have an exit within seven to eight years isn't always the best idea. One of Index's companies, Betfair, a betting exchange, has turned into one of the firm's best investments, now worth many times what the company put into it in 1998. "The duration argument is not a good one. We're going to wait as long as it takes to get the best exit for it," he says.

CASE IN POINT: Facebook

Before 2004, social networking was largely an unknown concept. It was gaining popularity very slowly due to networks such as Orkut and hi5. Mark Zuckerberg founded Facebook when he was a college student, launching the company from his Harvard dorm room in February 2004. The key features of Facebook included a home page with news feed and a variety of applications to play around with.[9] Facebook was started with the intention of being a platform where new students and faculty at Harvard could get to know each other. This was soon expanded to other colleges in the United States, followed by colleges around the world, and now anyone over the age of 13. (It currently has more than 150 million active users, and more than 70 percent of them are outside the United States.) By May 2005, when it received funding from Accel Partners, it had expanded to over 800 colleges in the United States. Facebook continued to expand its network, opening up to international schools and high schools by the end of 2005, increasing its active users to 5.5 million before its next round of financing in venture capital from Greylock Partners and Meritech Capital Partners in April 2006. August 2006, two years after its initial launch, its revenue-generating activity got going with the banner advertisement partnership with Microsoft. In September 2006, it finally opened up the site to everyone.

Milestones

Its revenue-generating activities took a boost in 2007 with the expansion of the Microsoft partnership and the launch of Facebook Ads, which had more than 60 partners on board. Little can be said about its profits, losses, and cash flows, as it is a private company yet to IPO. However, Microsoft's 1.6 percent equity stake has been valued at US$246 million, giving Facebook an implied post-money value of US$15.375 billion (US$246 million divided by 0.016). However, other sales of Facebook shares imply a much lower total valuation. Albukerk, the founder and director of EB Exchange Funds, recently sold shares implying a valuation of US$5 billion, and some investment firms have bought Facebook shares at an implied valuation of US$3.75 billion.

Founder Zuckerberg admits to still figuring out what the optimum model is for Facebook. He mentioned in a 2007 interview that ``an IPO is not anytime soon. It's not the core focus of our company.'' Facebook is very much still in its expansion and high-growth stage. In November 2007, Asian investor Ka-Shing Li invested US$60 million in Facebook, with a right to acquire another US$60 million stake. This corresponds to the time when Facebook announced the launch of Facebook Ads and its partnership with over 60 major brand and Internet companies.

For Facebook, the company at the heart of the online social networking and advertising trends, the exit and legacy is an IPO (mint employees and investors as millionaires) and the entrepreneurial legacy of the founding team (relevance in history). Facebook will be running at a negative US$150 million cash flow for 2008, despite Zuckerberg's comments that ``something we've tried to do with Facebook ever since the early days is to run at break-even.''

The alternative: risk losing it all in competitive warfare where you're undermatched and overgunned; employees waiting year after year for an exit via IPO; founders who get replaced by hostile investors; the risks can go on and on.[10] Through Ads or Beacon, the current management of Facebook has yet to find that killer strategy to make them a successful—or at least profitable—company later on. Facebook should focus on finding a high-growth business with a decent margin—its version of AdWords or eBay auctions. Going public is not the end goal, but going public and continuing to grow in such a way that the company can achieve its grander ambitions makes it a useful goal to go on with.

COMMANDMENT #3: Think Like a Sectoral Industrialist

Truly world-class VCs, intentionally or unintentionally, are also industrialists who have built a vibrant industry, contributing to at least one core large player and a range of cottage industries. In 34 years, KPCB has made more than 475 investments, generating US$90 billion in revenue and creating 275,000 jobs. KPCB funded 167 companies that later went public, including Amazon, AOL, Genentech, Google, and Netscape. These companies in turn generated a their own supporting industries. Imagine the quality of the components of the NASDAQ 100 without the participation of venture-backed companies. Zac Boon of McLean Watson adds, "[Top VCs] do not dilute their effort by getting a thousand flowers to bloom. They pick three to five areas that they are proficient in and are experiencing high growth, and then put in a lot of money and monitor profusely."

The issues differ by industry, between mainstream tech and biotech, for example. For IT companies, the money manager has to know when to exit—exiting Google upon IPO vis-à-vis selling Google at US$200 per share makes a significant difference to realized profits. Damien Lim of Bioveda Ventures elaborates, "When I am asked whether I had recovered my money on an IT investment, the return on investment ranged from 0 to 3x depending on the point of exit." For biotech, milestone events increase the valuation—passing a clinical trial boosts the valuation of the company; failing one makes it tank. In biotech, it is harder to subscribe to the old venture cliché about failing often but fast, because the trials last so long and the sector tends to be capital-inefficient. Due to the long time horizon for biotech, publicly listed biotech companies may not even have a viable product yet. Thus, the exit strategy for IT companies and biotech companies hinges on different milestone events and progress on different time lines, and a shrewd investor would compare like-for-like.

COMMANDMENT #4: Choose the Right Bourse

You need potential investors who understand the nature of the industry you are presenting. For example, in a mining venture, the Canada, London, and Australia bourses are popular. The Singapore and Taiwan investors don't understand mines and perceive mining as a high-risk investment. Thus, your success depends on what assets are in the listing vehicle and whether investors appreciate them.

Certain jurisdictions matter. Chinese investors are more inward looking than outward looking due to the country's large and growing market. For Chinese companies, certain monetary restrictions make life difficult for those wishing to list in foreign bourses.

CASE IN POINT: SMR, Subsidiary of Basic Element

Strikeforce Mining and Resources Ltd. (SMR) is the metals and mining unit subsidiary of Basic Element, owned by Oleg Vladimirovich Deripaska, a Russian billionaire. Basic Element has 120 companies, and SMR, which produces about 6 percent of the world's supply of ferromolybdenum (used in stainless steel), is the first of seven units that Deripaska's Basic Element holding company plans to offer to the public, with more than 20 in the pipeline if the first float succeeds. SMR carries out a range of exploration and mining activities and also produces and sells copper and molybdenum concentrate.

Where to list? Deripaska chose Hong Kong as the venue for his first initial public offering. The decision reflects the higher valuations for metals companies available on Asian stock exchanges over rival European and North American bourses. "There is more liquidity in Hong Kong, and the multiple is higher," says SMR CEO Geoff Cowley. "Toronto is too far away. London is too big. We would be a small deal in London. If we are only raising US$350 million, we would not get in index and attract the likes of Goldman Sachs and Morgan Stanley. In addition, there are no Russian companies in HKSE. We would attract investors as we are backed by the richest Russian in the markets. Hong Kong also operates on the British system and is international."

COMMANDMENT #5: Assemble a Good Team

The most visible members of the IPO team are the CEO and the CFO. Usually, the CFO can coordinate the whole IPO process. However, companies often find it more effective to appoint an executive to act as full-time project manager.

Choose Advisers and Brokers Carefully Hire professional advisers (investment bankers and accounting firms) to see whether an IPO is feasible. Typically, the company must have some track record (minimum of two years) of earnings and have readily accessible and clean financial accounts. The choice of investment bank depends on how much money you are after and where you are going to raise it from. Look for experience in a similar industry and the knowledge of which investors would bite. The fees are about the same. The bigger investment houses have bigger reach.

Choose an underwriter with a good track record. The job of the underwriter is to make clear how to make money through this stock for investors. The underwriter wants the number of shares traded at IPO to be minimal to as this helps maintain a healthy price. On the other hand, the bigger the IPO, the bigger the underwriter's commission. Yan Huang, Partner at CDH Ventures, emphasizes this point: "For emerging geographies like China, where the investment structure is complex, entrepreneurs need good advice to navigate legal structure, especially when overseas listing is frowned upon by the Chinese government."

Consult Widely Speak to people who have experienced an IPO. Do lots of preliminary marketing and listen to what the market is telling you. However, pay attention to regulations. In the United States, for example, restrictions on what is called "jumping the gun" prevent the pre-marketing of IPOs before they are approved by the regulator. For Hong Kong, mainland Chinese investors can participate through the compulsory retail tranche that all HK IPOs must have, or they can participate through the institutional tranche. However, the latter requires they meet the legal definition of "sophisticated investors."

Manage Expectations A top-tier VC we interviewed for the book says, "VCs spend time saving companies. Each month, we do a call with LPs. They typically expect us to tell them good things. When the company is doing well, they will query why there is no exit. When the company is not doing well, they will be worried. For example, one of our portfolio companies was in the process of selecting an investment banker [for an IPO]. Even though the market was starting to come down, we educated investors who were most concerned and spent about four months helping the company get ready its prospectus, calls with investment bankers, attending strategy sessions, finally yielding an IPO. Then Bear Stearns collapsed. (It was a close shave.)''

COMMANDMENT #6: Develop a Game Plan and Stick to It

Once you decide to go public, you may need to spend more than half your time for the next six months, or longer, focusing on the IPO. How will the business cope in this period? After you put together an IPO team, the team should set a realistic timetable. Preparing for life as a listed entity takes time and adjustments. Set clear objectives and be clear on plans—and beware of the tendency to underestimate time and resources needed. In preparation for the IPO, the companies' financial statements are likely to be recast and the shares restructured. Prepare for more public scrutiny.

In response to a question on the process of preparing the IPO and setting up roadshows, a top-quartile venture capitalist in Asia who wished to remain unnamed explained, "You need to structure the listing vehicle. [Then you would] need to inject the assets that produce income. Hong Kong requires a three-year track record period. There are special provisions that are more lenient for mining companies, but this is rarely used. Then you call in the bankers and lawyers who do the due diligence and draft the prospectus. Then management prepares for the roadshow. The investment bankers will do pre-marketing to gauge valuations the investors are willing to pay. They will take this back to management. If management agree then roadshows will begin. Then you open the bookbuild and pray the deal is covered.''

Reflect on Your Status   In the game plan, ask yourself key questions:

- Are you experiencing favorable macro-conditions?
- Do you have a strong asset base?

- Do you have a strong team and development capability?
- Is the capital expenditures road map well-planned and is there efficient use of proceeds?
- What is your marketing capability, and do you have a list of blue-chip customers?

David Weiden of Khosla Ventures quotes the example of Tellme Networks. It was on its way toward building a company that could do a successful IPO, but Microsoft made a compelling offer both financially and in terms of increasing the likelihood of Tellme's vision being achieved, so the VC and the entrepreneurs agreed that a trade sale would be the best exit.

Pitfalls to Avoid

The end of the VC process is no less fraught with potential trouble than the other stages. It is necessary to watch out for the following pitfalls:

- Forgetting additional reporting requirements
- Believing larger is always better
- Neglecting a contingency plan

PITFALL #1: Forgetting Additional Reporting Requirements

In response to a question on the potential pitfalls of IPOs in Asia, a top-quartile venture capitalist explains, "The company will be a public company, with all the reporting requirements this entails. Existing shareholders will be diluted if the IPO involves the sale of primary stock [which is a matter for concern even though it is] usually a good idea as the company gets money for some R&D and capital expenditure." However, reporting requirements are not trivial. Common problem areas include:

- Vital intangible assets of the company, such as brand, not belonging to the listed company
- Tax evasion (particularly tricky and prevalent problem in Asia)
- Infringement of intellectual property rights
- Imperfection of asset rights, such as mining license
- Imperfection of insurance

- Hazards in operations
- Pension liabilities

PITFALL #2: Believing Larger Is Always Better

Small (investment) can be beautiful. Dana Settle, a partner with Greycroft Partners, says her firm invests in smaller companies that need less than US$1 million to get off the ground. For that reason, she hasn't seen the same exit issues that tend to plague a venture fund putting US$20 million into a start-up. With that kind of investment, a venture firm would need a sale of more than US$100 million to get a good return on the investment, she points out. Settle told us her firm had two great company acquisitions just in the six weeks before our interview. "There's a great opportunity for smaller funds—there are tons of companies that don't need a ton of capital," Settle says. She's particularly excited about one of her investments, K2 Network, which is a massively multiplayer online game company. VC firms like Greycroft Partners and others like Index Ventures and First Round Capital primarily rely on larger companies to buy smaller VC-funded companies, and if that market continues to dry up, then their business will be under pressure.

PITFALL #3: Neglecting a Contingency Plan

When Plan A doesn't work, you're in deep trouble if you don't have a Plan B in the drawer. Alternatives include raising funds through a private placement or reducing the burn rate by cutting costs. Industry Ventures, a secondary fund in San Francisco with US$400 million under management, has interests in 50 venture funds and 75 companies as a result of purchasing stakes in venture funds or directly buying out the shares of company founders, senior managers, or venture fund investments. Hans Swildens, its principal and founder, says that in the downturn, he's getting a lot more queries from shareholders who are thinking about selling their shares in venture-backed companies for cash. "They want to know what kind of price they can get," Swildens says. "There are more people selling too. It's what you would expect in this environment. If they can afford to wait a short time, they will. But they don't want to wait for years." The downside, of course, is that shareholders can't expect to get top dollar for the shares that they sell. Industry Ventures and its competitors are typically viewed as a liquidity source of last resort, and even then, it's not for everyone. Transactions range from US$1 million to US$50 million, so this type of company doesn't offer an exit for the smallest shareholders.

Nonetheless, the secondary market industry is thriving, with an estimated US$2.5 billion in transactions in 2007. Swildens sees a pipeline of more than US$1 billion in possible business at the moment, making it perhaps three times bigger than when Industry Ventures started eight years ago. That has drawn some competition. Other secondary funds include Goldman Sachs Vintage Fund, CS First Boston Strategic Partners, and Pantheon Ventures and Paul Capital Partners, both in San Francisco.[11]

Cutting your losses is sometimes necessary. "Losing money is part of this business and I hate it," says Sean Dalton, general partner at Highland Capital. The real challenge, he adds, is recognizing when it's over and cutting off funding. After seeing a venture he'd pulled out of go on to do very well, however, Dalton made a prediction that probably rang true for the other panelists: "I'm going to lose money again, I promise."

Endnotes

1. China Daily, "Niu Gensheng: Dairy Industry King," China Assistor, 9 November 2007; retrieved from http://news.chinaassistor.com/2007/1108/1194488441_5058.html, June 30, 2009.
2. Paul J. Halpern, *Financing Growth in Canada* (Calgary: University of Calgary Press, 1997).
3. "Transition: Global Venture Capital Insights Report 2006," Ernst & Young, 2006; retrieved from www.altassets.com/pdfs/EY--2006_Global%20_VC-Report --TRANSITION_(Final_84-p)(2).pdf, July 5, 2009.
4. The original work is Paul Gompers, "Grandstanding in the Venture Capital Industry," *Journal of Finance* 42 (1996): 133–256. For more recent research, see Melody Keung, "A New Empirical Study of Grandstanding in the Venture Capital Industry," Unpublished honors thesis, School of Economics, Washington University, St. Louis, January 30, 2003.
5. Alexander Butler and Sinan Goktan, "Does Distance Still Matter? Evidence from the Venture Capital Market," University of Texas at Dallas working paper, 2007.
6. Kaisa Snellman and Mikolaj Piskorski, "Network Structure of Exploitation: Venture Capital Syndicate Structure and Time to IPO," paper presented at the annual meeting of the American Sociological Association, Atlanta Hilton Hotel, Atlanta, Georgia, August 16, 2003; retrieved from www.allacademic.com/meta/p107469_index.html, June 30, 2009.

7. Prabhavathi Fernandes, "Biotechnology Financing, Not Acquisitions, for Filling the Pharma Pipeline—a Sustaining Strategy," *Expert Opinion on Drug Discovery* 2, no. 7 (2007): 917–921. George S. Mack, "Pfizer Dumps Exubera," *Nature Biotechnology* 25, no. 2 (2007): 1331. Stephanie Saul, "Johnson & Johnson Plans to Cut 4800 Jobs," *New York Times*, August 1, 2007; retrieved from www .nytimes.com/2007/08/01/business/01drug.html, June 30, 2009.

8. Paul Gompers and Josh Lerner, "The Venture Capital Revolution," *Journal of Economic Perspectives* 15, no. 2 (2001): 145–168.

9. Peter Kafka, "Zuckerberg: Facebook Will Have a Business Plan in Three Years," Silicon Alley Insider, October 9, 2008; retrieved from www.alleyinsider.com/2008/10/zuckerberg-facebook-will-have-a-business-plan-in-three-years, June 30, 2009. Michael Arrington, "Facebook Launches Facebook Platform—They Are the Anti-Myspace," TechCrunch, May 24, 2007; retrieved from www .techcrunch.com/2007/05/24/facebook-launches-facebook-platform-they-are-the-anti-myspace/, June 30, 2009.

10. John Furrier, "Facebook IPO—Microsoft IS Facebook's IPO—Not the NAS-DAQ," blog entry, May 19, 2008; retrieved from http://furrier.org/2008/05/19/facebook-ipo-microsoft-is-facebooks-ipo-not-the-nasdaq/, June 30, 2009.

11. Dean Takahashi, "The Dry IPO Market Is Creating Demand for Alternate Liquidity," Venture Beat, June 26, 2008; retrieved from http://venturebeat .com/2008/06/26/the-dry-ipo-market-is-creating-demand-for-alternate-liquidity/, June 30, 2009.

8

Conclusion

On Sand Hill Road, venture capitalists like to say:

Founders are like players
CEOs are like team captains
Early-stage VCs are like team coaches
Later-stage VCs are like team owners

Do it, run it, teach it, or own it; that's what venture capitalists believe. In writing *The Way of the VC: Having Top Venture Capitalists on Your Board,* I found much to learn in each of these core processes. The writing has been a long and arduous but ultimately rewarding journey. While the aim is to demystify the interaction with potential VCs for entrepreneurs, explaining the fundamental process and breaking down the venture capital framework into understandable winning techniques, the journey has also led to a collection of gems for people who would like to enter the exclusive circle of VCs. It is my hope that the book will deliver to readers all the reward my colleagues and I derived from writing it.

Another challenge in completing the book was grappling with the full-throttle pace of change in the venture capital industry. From the boom in 2007 to the recession in 2009, the operating environment changed between the interviews and the publication date. All the information had to be painstakingly updated and reviewed with each interviewee before the book went to press. Then, too, some of our group of high-powered VCs were promoted or switched venture firms between their interview and the publication date. Such is the whirlwind environment in the venture capital ecosystem.

Setting aside the ongoing comparison of venture capitalists to chefs, it seems useful to look at another analogy. When it comes to the relationship between the venture capitalist and the entrepreneur, it's a lot like tango dancing. Just like a pair of tango dancers, VCs and entrepreneurs must understand each other's roles, coordinate their moves, and work with the same expectations. Entrepreneurs need to ask themselves, "Do I want to dance? If so, how do I choose a partner? After I have found a partner, how can I dance in sync?" What makes it a bit of a stretch is that venture capital is a game of three—*it takes three to do this tango.* Despite the common belief in entrepreneurial circles, VCs are not generally investors in their own right; they are highly specialized financial intermediaries, investing funds committed by their investors (the limited partners) in risky projects and monitoring the fund recipients on their behalf. In this context, the managers, monitors, and investors (or, in VC terminology: the entrepreneurs, GPs, and LPs) are highly dependent upon each other. In this dance of imperfect information, subtle influence principles play an important role.

In this conclusion, I recap the key points covered in the book by reviewing the key winning techniques my colleagues and I uncovered in our interviews with the VCs, entrepreneurs, and LPs. The pages that follow present the main findings, but first, the quotes that made the strongest impression as I reviewed the material for this book:

> "When you see venture capital more than double from one year to the next, and IPO values double from one year to the next, that's the sign of a bubble in the making."
> —*Matthew M. Nordan, president of Lux, a New York research firm*

> "LP has to be entrepreneurial, GP has to entrepreneurial, the entrepreneur, of course, has to be entrepreneurial. A good VC has to be able to constantly think: "How can I help you?"
> —*Kelvin Chan, Senior Vice President Partners Group (Alternative Investments Asia-Pacific) Pte. Ltd.*

> "Buy low, sell high, and make sure other investors get to sell even higher."
> —*Bing Gordon, Partner at Kleiner Perkins Caufield & Byers*

"China VC is still in its early stage and will undergo a teething process. Some of the current practices will work but most won't."
—*Lin Hong Wong, former Managing Director of Business Development, Temasek Holdings*

"In the VC industry, there is free flow of talent, it is a people
business."
—*Soo Boon Koh, Founder & Managing Partner, iGlobe Partners*

"Failure to execute operationally is not the only source of risk;
every venture is also subject to volatility in the price and
availability of capital due to the volatility of the stock market.
After the collapse of the Internet bubble, many promising
companies foundered because their funding dried up."
—*William Janeway, Managing Director of Warburg Pincus*

1. The Call to Adventure

Winning Techniques

- Follow the romance, not the finance.
- Build a company around the entrepreneur.
- Source for deals in a densely innovative geography.

Commandments

- Weigh the costs and benefits of venture capital.
- Remember that the right sector attracts the dollars.
- Be disruptively innovative.
- Position yourself in an intersection of markets and technology.
- Employ weapons of influence.

Pitfalls

- Believing the herd is always right
- Overconfidence
- Concealing skeletons in the closet

2. Finding the Right Partner at the Right Time

Winning Techniques

- Gauge supply and demand.

- Catch a bubble at its formation and exit at the peak.
- Apply the funnel model.
- Monitor macro conditions, not short-term trends.
- Remember that star first-time funds can overcome newcomer bias.
- Pursue the 3M of venture capital (money, markets, and management).

Commandments

- Choose a diverse team (with diverse skillsets).
- Choose the partners with the right experience.

Pitfalls

- Forgetting that the devil is in the details, and the details are in the term sheet
- Getting blinded by the VC brand

3. Transitions in Partnership

Winning Techniques

- Be less confident in good times, more confident in bad times.
- Maximize chances in a lottery.
- Prioritize risk; invest cross-spectrum to reduce risks.
- Maximize exposure to successful entrepreneurs.
- Manage talent.
- Maintain strength in character.
- Network for success.

Commandments

- Focus on the fundamentals.
- Reduce technical and market uncertainty.
- Remember that money is blood.
- Separate price and value: price is what you pay, value is what you get.

Pitfalls

- Inability to confront difficult issues
- Distraction and overcommitment

- Lack of alignment among board members and investors
- Temptation to make excessive capital investments in the initial phases of a business
- Failure to focus on market and industry analysis

4. Growing Together

Winning Techniques

- Look for a self-reinforcing virtuous reputation.
- Count on experience, but only to a certain extent.
- Value-add with a balanced team.
- Be adept at assessing weight of factors.

Commandments

- Tailor your strategy to suit your background.
- Know the unique market gap in each market.
- Adjust for risk in immature and volatile markets.

Pitfalls

- Assuming an emergent market will behave like a settled one
- Ignoring unique characteristics in markets
- Believing people are the same everywhere
- Trusting the regulatory framework to work smoothly
- Doing what the Romans do

5. Smart Money

Winning Techniques

- If possible, win preemptive acceptance.
- Match the increasing sophistication of the new breed of entrepreneurs.
- Diversify risk and minimize mistakes.

Commandments

- Do not expect VCs to have all the answers.
- Look for the deal with the highest probability of closing.

- Find the entrepreneurial passion.
- Pay attention to VC brand name.
- Seek ruth.
- Follow personal chemistry.
- Do your due diligence on the VC.
- Find VCs who can add complementary value on your multi-faceted challenges.
- Remember that nothing replaces actual operating experience.
- Watch the track record of your board.

Pitfalls

- Bringing in outside investors despite a difference in interests
- Mismatching expectations between entrepreneur and VC
- Becoming meat in a sandwich
- Training your replacement

6. If You Need to Woo a Turkey Buzzard

Winning Techniques for VCs

- Deal with information asymmetry and the LP conundrum.
- Understand the hidden markers.
- Mind the Pareto principle.
- Welcome competition; it begets quality.
- Control the built-in moral hazard in the LP-VC relationship.
- Look for companies funded by more experienced VCs; they are more likely to go public.
- Stake claims in emerging markets.
- Understand the LP dilemma.
- Remember that excess capital is the enemy of returns.

Commandments for VCs and LPs

- Focus on the numbers.
- Go for growth cities.
- Look for LPs who value-add.
- Understand the thought process of LPs.
- Use track record as the litmus test.
- Exercise people judgment.

- Ensure an appropriate alignment between GP and LP.
- Promote capital efficiency.

Commandments for Would-Be VCs

- Have realistic expectations.
- Market the skills that matter.
- Display less mercenary spirit, more passion and selflessness.
- Get close to VCs.

Pitfalls

- Overconfidence
- Whimsical recruiting
- Status quo biases
- Proximity biases
- Ignoring preexisting personal relationships
- Misreading scientific and commercial factors

7. The Partnership Becomes Wildly Successful

Winning Techniques

- Begin with the end in mind.
- Wait until the time is right.
- Remember that less really can be more.
- Take good care of the golden goose.

Commandments

- Capture the timing in a cyclic industry.
- Remember that patience is a virtue.
- Think like a sectoral industrialist.
- Choose the right bourse.
- Assemble a good team.
- Develop a game plan and stick to it.

Pitfalls

- Forgetting additional reporting requirements
- Believing larger is always better
- Neglecting a contingency plan

Appendix

Here are introductions to some of the people who shared their insights for this book.

Robert Ackerman, Managing Director & Co-founder, Allegis Capital

Robert Ackerman directs Allegis Capital's Media Technology Ventures family of strategic corporate venture capital funds. The concept and structure behind Allegis Capital's unique model of active corporate partnering grew out of Ackerman's prior 15 years of experience as a successful founder and CEO of start-up technology companies and as a strategic mergers and acquisitions adviser to major corporations and the venture capital community. Prior to forming Allegis Capital, he managed the Ackerman Group, a strategic advisory firm focused on applying the complementary strengths of innovative start-up companies and established corporate market leaders for mutual competitive advantage. Previously, he was CEO of UniSoft Corporation, a leading UNIX systems house with operations in the United States, Europe, and Asia. He was also the founder and chairman of InfoGear Technology Corporation, the first Internet appliance company, acquired by CISCO in 2000. Ackerman has a B.S. degree in computer science and is a member of the boards of directors of IronPort Systems and RFco.

Noubar Afeyan, Managing Partner & CEO, Flagship Ventures

Noubar Afeyan co-founded Flagship Ventures in 2000. He is also a senior lecturer at MIT in both the Sloan School of Management and the Biological Engineering Department. Afeyan has authored numerous scientific publications and acquired several patents since earning his Ph.D. in biochemical engineering from MIT in 1987. A technologist, entrepreneur, and venture capitalist, Afeyan has co-founded and helped build 20 successful life science and technology ventures during the past two decades. He was founder and CEO of PerSeptive Biosystems (NASDAQ: PBIO), a leader in the bio-instrumentation field. After PerSeptive's acquisition by Applera Corporation (NYSE: ABI), he was senior vice president and chief business officer of Applera, where he initiated and oversaw the creation of Celera Genomics (NASDAQ: CRA). Afeyan was previously founding director and investor in several successful ventures including Chemgenics Pharmaceuticals, Color Kinetics, Antigenics, EXACT Sciences, and Adnexus Therapeutics, and currently serves on a number of public and private company boards. He is a director and part of the founding team for Flagship portfolio companies Affinnova, BG Medicine, Ensemble Discovery, Genstruct, Helicos BioSciences (NASDAQ: HLCS), and LS9. He is a member of the Board of Overseers of Boston University, the Board of Visitors of Boston University School of Medicine, and the Board of Overseers of the Boston Symphony Orchestra. He is also a member of several advisory boards including the Whitehead Institute at MIT, the Harvard-MIT Division of Health Sciences and Technology (HST), and the SKOLKOVO School of Management in Moscow. Afeyan is co-founder and board member of Armenia 2020, an international economic development project focusing on the former Soviet Republic of Armenia. He was honored in 2008 as one of the Ellis Island Medal of Honor recipients, recognizing his contributions to the local community as well as his extensive role in supporting long-range visions for the country of Armenia, its business environment and culture, and world-wide understanding and awareness of Armenian issues.

Toivo Annus, Co-founder, Ambient Sound Investments and Co-founder, Skype

Toivo Annus leads ASI's technology investments and is closely involved in managing several portfolio companies post-investment. Prior to co-founding ASI, Annus co-founded communication software company Skype, where he built and led a world-class engineering organization of 120 team members. He has extensive experience with emerging technologies and maintains a very broad as well as deep understanding of the tech sector. While his ability to work 24/7 is legendary, Annus knows how to enjoy life too, be it in the company of good friends, charging around in his ATV, or on the squash court. He holds a degree in economics from Tallinn University of Technology.

Sujit Banerjee, Partner, BlueRun Ventures

Sujit Banerjee joined BlueRun Ventures in February 2003 and is based in Menlo Park, California, where he focuses on semiconductor, material science, and energy companies. He is also active in exploring investment opportunities in India. Banerjee is on the boards of directors of CyOptics, Deeya Energy, MagSil, NexPlanar, Petra Solar, and SliceX. Prior to joining BlueRun Ventures, Banerjee was a principal with TL Ventures and before that worked as an investment banker at Merrill Lynch in the Global Technology Group. Past experience includes positions as manager in the PriceWaterhouse High Technology consulting practice and engineer with Synoptics Communications. Banerjee received his M.B.A. from the Wharton Business School, where he was chairman of the Wharton India Economic Forum, and holds a B.S. in electrical engineering from Rensselaer Polytechnic Institute with Eta Kappa Nu academic honors.

Orna Berry, Venture Partner, Gemini Israel Funds Ltd.

Dr Orna Berry is a venture partner at Gemini Israel Funds, a venture capital firm with more than US$700 million under management. Berry has spent over 25 years in science and technology industries as an academic researcher, entrepreneur, executive, and policymaker, as well as a venture capitalist. She is also the outgoing chairperson of the Israel Venture Association and recently became the chairperson of the Academic College of Tel Aviv Jaffa.

Israeli Venture Capital activity began in the early 1990s with the "Yozma Program" and has grown to become the major source of financing for start-up and early-stage technology companies. With more than US$13 billion in capital, Israeli VCs have played a major role in making the country an important global source of innovation. As a Venture Partner at Gemini, Berry applies her expertise to assist Gemini portfolio companies, including serving as Chairperson of

Prime Sense, a developer of gesture-based user interfaces for computer gaming, TV, and other applications (www.primesense.com).

In addition, Berry has served as the chief scientist and director of the Industrial R&D Administration of the Israeli government's Ministry of Industry, Trade & Labor. Prior to that, in 1993, she co-founded Ornet Data Communication Technologies Ltd., which was sold to Siemens in 1995. She has also worked as the chief scientist of Fibronics, as a senior research engineer at IBM and UNISYS, and as a consultant to Intel. She received her Ph.D. in computer science from the University of Southern California, and M.A. and B.A. degrees in statistics and mathematics from Tel Aviv and Haifa Universities.

Zacchaeus Boon, Partner, McLean Watson Venture Capital

Zacchaeus Boon has more than 15 years' experience in the software industry, along with extensive investment credentials. He was previously a network engineer working on military projects before joining Lotus Development as a software engineer. At Lotus, he worked on localization of software such as cc:Mail and Lotus Smartsuite for Asia Pacific markets such as PRC, Taiwan, Korea, and Japan. As an account manager for public sector in the Singapore office of Lotus, he was instrumental in winning strategic accounts like the Civil Service and Singapore Airlines. His last role in IBM/Lotus was director (alliances/small medium business) with Asia Pacific coverage. Prior to MW, Boon worked as an investment director with Singapore-based venture capital firm Venture TDF which backed some of the most successful technology companies in Asia including Alibaba and Sina. He was an active angel investor who seed-funded several successful start-ups including AceFusion acquired by Savi, which was subsequently acquired by Lockheed Martin (NYSE: LMT), and Hardware-Zone acquired by Singapore Press Holdings (SGX: SPH). Boon represents MW on the Board of Directors for Ntegrator International (listed on SGX) and Amplus Communication. He holds a bachelor's degree in computer science from University of Newcastle, Australia.

Kelvin Chan, Senior Vice President, Partners Group Asia Pacific Ltd.

Kelvin Chan heads up Partners Group's private equity fund and direct investments activities in the Asia-Pacific region. Partners

Group is an independent global alternative asset management firm headquartered in Baar, Switzerland, with offices in New York, London, and Singapore. Presently, assets under management exceed US$6 billion for private equity fund investments and US$1.5 billion for hedge fund investments. Chan is a member of the Primary Investment Committee within Partners Group, the Executive Committee of the Singapore Venture Capital and Private Equity Association, and the Singapore Institute of Directors. Prior to Partners Group, he was a senior vice president and member of the Investment Approval Committee while with TIF Ventures (a wholly owned subsidiary of EDB), which manages US$1.3 billion for private equity fund investments on behalf of the Singapore government. Chan has been involved in private equity fund and direct investing globally for more than 12 years, and in corporate and private banking in Asia-Pacific region for more than five years. He has also held various senior positions at EDB Investments, Credit Agricole, ING Bank, and Overseas Union Bank. Chan holds a B.Sc. degree with honors in biochemistry from National University of Singapore and has an M.B.A. in banking and finance from Nanyang Technological University.

K. Bobby Chao, Founding Managing Partner, DFJ DragonFund China

K. Bobby Chao works with technology-focused ventures in China and internationally. His skills and insight have been honed through outstanding operational experience in the semiconductor, hardware, and software industries, where he served as both an entrepreneur and a C-level officer. Chao was born in China and spent his professional career in the U.S. and Asia. He began his career as one of the original founders of Cadence Design Systems and was Cadence's vice president and GM of Asia, responsible for sales, marketing, and operations in Asia and Japan. After Cadence, he founded and served as chairman and CEO of OCRON, a pioneer in the optical character recognition and document management space, until its acquisition by Umax Group. During his tenure with Umax, Chao was responsible for corporate investment and marketing. He later incubated and served as chairman and CEO of VA Linux (LNUX). Subsequently, he was an early investor in and board member of AboveNet (ABVT), Oplink (OPLK), Omnivision (OVTI), and NetScreen (JNPR). Chao co-founded DragonVenture as Chairman in 1999, and since then, he has been a dedicated venture capital investor in Greater China. He is currently serving as the chairman and board director of several China and U.S.-based companies. He was the co-founder and chairman of DragonVenture in 1999 before the founding of DFJ DragonFund I. He holds M.S. degrees in physics and in aeronautical engineering from Georgia State University and Stanford University, respectively.

York Chen, President & Managing General Partner, iD TechVentures

York Chen has been one of the most active venture capitalists in China and termed by media as a "VC Evangelist" and "VC Scholar," unselfishly sharing his deep observation and advice on the China VC market to peer groups at home and abroad. His firm started its operation in early 2000 with offices in Shanghai, Taipei, and Beijing, managing more than US$400 million in LP funds. With eight partners, iDT VC is one of the few seasoned, localized, and stable VC teams in China; it has more than eight years' solid presence in local operations and a delivered track record (3 NASDAQ, 1 in Hong Kong, and more than 17 other IPOs and M&A deals), and it is recognized as one of the most reliable GP partners in China. Before 2000, Chen was a board member of Singapore-listed Acer Computer International Ltd. He initiated, managed, and oversaw more than 10 diversified national and JV operations spanning from Moscow to Auckland, from Seoul to Bangalore. Before 1991, Chen was involved in Acer's successful presence in Mexico and ex-Soviet Union markets. He was the first Chinese to deliver a public speech in the Kremlin, addressing some 2000 Russian political and industrial leaders in May 1991. Chen started his career in the public sector. He holds a B.S. from National Taiwan University, an M.B.A. from Fordham University, and an E.M.B.A. from Peking University.

Jeffrey Chi, Vice Chairman, Vickers Capital Group

Jeffrey Chi is a managing director of the General Partner and a member of the Investment Committee. Based in Shanghai, he oversees investments in China, and sits on the boards of Cambridge Real Estate (REIT IPO, July 2006), Mobinex, and California University of Technology. He is also responsible for the supervision of Saybot, iPartment, and United Eagle Airlines. Chi's experience covers a variety of industries including information technology, health care, and media. His operational background includes seven years on the management team of an engineering and construction group. As its managing director, he led the group into the Enterprise 50 in 1997, a ranking of the top 50 privately held enterprises in Singapore. Chi oversaw operations in Singapore, Malaysia, Taiwan, and Indonesia, established the group's construction business, and successfully combined it with the original engineering business, enabling the firm to become a provider of integrated solutions to its clients. In 1994–1995, he managed the firm's joint venture with a major Chinese construction group. After being appointed group managing director in 1996, he tripled the firm's revenues within three years. Chi is also active in promoting entrepreneurship. He frequently speaks at public events including ones hosted by INSEAD, Fudan University, and Zhejiang University. He is a co-founder of the MIT Enterprise Forum, Shanghai Chapter, a not-for-profit alumni organization promoting technology entrepreneurship. Chi is a CFA Charter holder and graduated from Cambridge University with first-class Honours in Engineering. He earned his Ph.D. from the Massachusetts Institute of Technology in organizational knowledge and information technology.

Dixon Doll, Co-founder & General Partner, Doll Capital Management

For more than 35 years, Dixon Doll has influenced and guided entrepreneurs, investors, and executives in the computer and communications industries. In recognition of his accomplishments in venture capital, Doll was named by *Forbes* magazine as one of the top 100 venture investors on its Midas List for four years in a row. In April 2005, he was elected to the board of directors of the National Venture Capital Association, where he subsequently served as chairman from 2008 through 2009 and as a member of the Executive Committee from 2007 through 2009. Doll has led DCM's investments in About.com (Acquired by The New York Times Co.), @Motion (Acquired by Openwave), Clearwire (NASDAQ: CLWR), Foundry Networks (NASDAQ: FDRY), Internap (NASDAQ: INAP), IPivot (Acquired by Intel) and Neutral Tandem (NASDAQ: TNDM), among others. In the mid-1980s, Doll co-founded the venture capital industry's first fund focused exclusively on telecommunications opportunities. Doll's funds launched such noteworthy companies as Alantec, Bridge Communication, Centillion Networks, Network Equipment

Technologies, Optilink, Picturetel, Polycom and UUNet. Prior to becoming a venture capitalist, Doll was the founder and CEO of an internationally recognized strategic consulting firm focused on telecommunications and computer networking. From 1972 to 1980, Doll served as a faculty member of the IBM Systems Research Institute in New York City. He authored the seminal text *Data Communications* (Wiley, 1978).

Timothy C. Draper, Founder & Managing Director, Draper Fisher Jurvetson

On behalf of Draper Fisher Jurvetson, Timothy C. Draper serves on the boards of Glam, Tagworld, SocialText, Kyte.tv, Chroma Graphics, Meebo, Increo, and Wigix. His original suggestion to use "viral marketing" in Web-based e-mail to geometrically spread an Internet product to its market was instrumental to the successes of Hotmail and YahooMail, and has been adopted as a standard marketing technique by hundreds of businesses. He launched the DFJ Global Network, an international network of early-stage venture capital funds with offices in more than 30 cities around the globe. He founded or co-founded DFJ ePlanet (global), Draper Fisher Jurvetson Gotham (NYC), Zone Ventures (LA), Epic Ventures (Salt Lake City), Draper Atlantic (Reston), Draper Triangle (Pittsburg), Timberline Ventures (Portland), Polaris Fund (Anchorage), DFJ Frontier (Sacramento and Santa Barbara), and DFJ DragonFund (Shanghai).

As an advocate for entrepreneurs and free markets, Draper is regularly featured as a keynote speaker in entrepreneurial conferences throughout the world, has been recognized as a leader in his field through numerous awards and honors, and has frequent TV, radio, and headline appearances. He was #7 on Forbes Midas List and #52 on the list of the most influential Harvard alumni. He was named Always-On #1 top venture capital deal maker for 2008. And DFJ was honored as #1 Dealmaking Venture Capital firm for 2008. Draper is also the course creator and chairman of BizWorld, a 501(c)(3) organization built around teaching entrepreneurship and business to children via simulations. He has served on the California State Board of Education. In November 2000, Draper launched a statewide cyber-initiative on school choice for the California general election. He is a member of Singapore's Economic Advisory Council and

Ukraine's Orange Circle. He is on the Board of U.C. Berkeley's Haas School of Business. He has a B.S. in electrical engineering from Stanford University and an M.B.A. from Harvard Business School.

Barry Drayson, Chief Executive Officer, NanoComposites Inc.

Barry Drayson joined NCI in September 2004 as a founding shareholder. His experience spans Europe, Asia, and North America, where he has been responsible for growing revenues and building key customer relationships. His career in the world's brokerage markets culminated with becoming president of MKI Securities Corp., followed by a decade at Reuters, where he became managing director of global sales and marketing. Drayson has 25 years' experience in the identification, analysis, negotiation, and management of strategic partnerships; the majority of which still exist today. Most recently, he has been involved in the early growth stages of four start-up companies. He received a B.S. in economics and international business from New York University and an M.B.A. in finance and international business from the New York University Graduate School of Business Administration.

Norman Fogelsong, General Partner, Institutional Venture Partners

Norman Fogelsong joined Institutional Venture Partners (IVP) in March 1989. With more than 30 years of high-technology venture capital and growth equity experience, he currently emphasizes investments in private later-stage companies and in select public market opportunities. Fogelsong has led investments in Cortina Systems, Danger (MSFT), Gaia Online, Integrated Circuit Works (CY), Lam Research (LRCX), Motion Computing, Platinum Software (EPIC), Polycom (PLCM), TelCom Semiconductor (TLCM), and Websense (WBSN), among many others. For Cortina Systems, he arranged a US$132 million investment syndicate, the largest private venture financing done that year. The proceeds were used to buy a US$100 million division that was being spun out of Intel. In addition, Fogelsong recently led IVP's investments in Gaia Online, the leading online hangout for teenagers on the Web. He began his career as a computer programmer and systems analyst at Hewlett-Packard. He then worked as a management consultant with McKinsey & Company, where he specialized in product and market strategy. Prior to joining

IVP, he was a general partner with Mayfield Fund. He has served the local community as treasurer of the Children's Health Council, secretary of the Churchill Club, and as a member of the Major Gifts Committees at Menlo School and Stanford University. Fogelsong earned a B.S. in management science and engineering from Stanford University (Phi Beta Kappa), an M.B.A. from Harvard Business School, and a J.D. from Harvard Law School.

Hian Goh and Maria Brown, Co-founders & Managing Directors, Asian Food Channel

The Asian Food Channel was co-founded by Singaporean Hian Goh and Briton Maria Brown, both of whom have extensive experience in business and media. Goh was a technology and media investment banker and Brown was a producer with the British Broadcasting Corporation. Both hold joint roles as managing directors of the company.

Bing Gordon, Partner, Kleiner Perkins Caufield & Byers

Bing Gordon was chief creative officer of Electronic Arts from 1998 to 2008, after heading EA marketing and product development off and on since EA's founding. He joined EA in 1982 and helped write the founding business plan that attracted KPCB as an initial investor. Gordon has driven EA's branding strategy with EA Sports and EA's pricing strategy for package goods and online games, and has contributed design and marketing on many EA franchises including John Madden Football, The Sims, Sim City, Need for Speed, Tiger Woods Golf, Club Pogo and Command and Conquer. He has been a director at Amazon since 2003, and was a founding director of Audible, Inc. He is also a trustee of the Urban School of San Francisco, and serves on the Yale President's Advisory Council. Gordon earned an M.B.A. degree from Stanford University, and a B.A. degree from Yale University.

Patricia Hedley, Senior Vice President, General Atlantic

Patricia Hedley joined General Atlantic in 1987 as an associate, became a principal in 1990, and worked as an investment professional until 1996. She focused on investment prospecting activities and worked closely with several portfolio companies assisting with their growth strategies including helping evaluate and pursue M&A opportunities and regional expansion. Currently, as a member of the firm's Operations Group, she assists global portfolio companies with a broad range of operational issues including human capital management (executive management and board search, equity programs, talent capture, and external provider relationship management) and marketing (branding, PR, and IR). In addition, she is responsible for General Atlantic's global marketing and communications activities. Hedley has worked in this role since January 2000. Prior to General Atlantic, Hedley worked as director of information technology for MediVision, a health care start-up funded by Bain Capital. Previously, she had been an associate consultant with Bain & Company. She holds an A.B. in computer science and government from Dartmouth College and an M.B.A. from Harvard Business School. She is on the board of Reach the World, a nonprofit connecting inner-city students with world travelers through technology.

Pierre Hennes, Co-founder & Partner, Upstream Ventures

Co-founder and Partner of Upstream Ventures, Pierre Hennes has more than six years' experience in VC and new venture creation across Asia, supported by eight years of international corporate and start-up experience. He has worked as an IT consultant to the financial services industry with Accenture in New York City, and as a private strategic consultant in Europe and the United States for companies across various sectors including Internet and new media, mobile communications, real estate, and the arts. Hennes also worked extensively throughout Russia with the Deloitte Touche ILA Group to stimulate regional economic growth and investment through the commercialization of local emergent technologies. Prior to Upstream Ventures, he held the position of Director of Marketing for a Brussels-based B2B e-procurement start-up. Hennes currently serves on the board of several Upstream Ventures portfolio companies and is a frequent guest speaker, lecturer, and business plan judge at industry events and universities such as INSEAD, SMU, NUS, and NTU. He earned a B.A. with Honors in international relations from Boston University, and an M.B.A.

from New York University's Stern School of Business. He also studied at the Hochschule St. Gallen in St. Gallen, Switzerland as part of NYU's International Management Program.

Soo Boon Koh, Founder & Managing Partner, iGlobe Partners (www.iGlobePartners.com)

Soo Boon Koh is an experienced venture capitalist, specializing in cross-border investing. She has been in the fund management business for over two decades.

In 1988, Koh started Vertex Management Inc. (Redwood City), the venture capital arm of Singapore Technologies, and went on to start its European office in 1996. During that period, she made numerous successful investments, resulting in several IPOs. Examples include Lattice Semiconductor, Creative Technologies, Premisys Communications, Proxim, Aurum Software, GRIC Communications, Activcard SA, SCM Microsystems, Brokat, Infosystems, Integra SA, and Genesys SA.

In December 1999, Koh founded iGlobe Partners (headquartered in Singapore) with offices in Silicon Valley, Shanghai, and Auckland. iGlobe Partners Fund, LP of US$72.5 million, was launched under the sponsorship of the Singapore EDB. This fund invests mainly in Silicon Valley companies and also European and Asian companies with cross-border operations. In June 2003, a NZ$31 million iGlobe Treasury Fund (headquartered in Auckland) was set up with the support of the New Zealand government. iGlobe Treasury invests in early-stage New Zealand companies with global ambitions. Koh is the managing partner of these two funds. She also serves on the boards of u-blox AG (SWX: UBXN) and several private companies.

Koh is an EXCO member of the Singapore Chinese Chamber of Commerce, and she is also Singapore adviser to SwissNex Singapore.

Josh Lerner, Jacob H. Schiff Professor of Investment Banking, Harvard Business School

Josh Lerner has a joint appointment in the Finance and Entrepreneurial Management Units at Harvard Business School. He graduated from Yale College with a special divisional major that combined physics with the history of technology. After working for several years on issues concerning technological innovation and public policy at the Brookings Institution for a public-private task force in Chicago, and on Capitol Hill, he obtained a Ph.D. from Harvard's Economics Department. Much of his research focuses on the structure and role of venture capital and private equity organizations. (This research is collected in two books, *The Venture Capital Cycle* and *The Money of Invention*.) He also examines technological innovation and how firms are responding to changing public policies. He founded, raised funding for, and organizes two groups at the National Bureau of Economic Research: Entrepreneurship and Innovation Policy and the Economy. He is a member of a number of other NBER groups and serves as coeditor of their publication, *Innovation Policy and the Economy*. His work has been published in a variety of top academic journals. In the 1993–94 academic year, he introduced an elective course for second-year MBAs on private equity finance. In recent years, "Venture Capital and Private Equity" has consistently been one of the largest elective courses at Harvard Business School. He also teaches a doctoral course on entrepreneurship and in the Owners-Presidents-Managers Program and organizes an annual executive course on private equity in Boston and Beijing. He recently led an international team of scholars in a study of the economic impact of private equity for the World Economic Forum.

Damien Lim, General Partner, BioVeda Capital

Damien Lim is co-founder and general partner of BioVeda Capital. He has more than 18 years of private equity and investment banking experience. He was previously director of investments with Prime-Partners, a boutique private equity firm. Prior to that, he was executive director of Vickers Ballas Asset Management and concurrently senior vice president of Vickers Ballas Holdings (now part of DBS Bank), where he was involved in private equity investments and strategic acquisitions. Prior to Vickers, he was associate director, corporate finance with Morgan Grenfell Asia (now part of Deutsche Bank), where he managed IPOs, debt and equity financing, and corporate advisory transactions. Lim started his career as a financial journalist with the *Straits Times*. He received his B.B.A. from the University of Houston.

Scott Maxwell, Senior Managing Director, OpenView Venture Partners

Prior to OpenView, Scott Maxwell was a managing director at Insight Venture Partners, having joined Insight in 2000 as the chief operating officer. At Insight, Scott led the effort to institutionalize the investment process, outbound program, value-add program, and finance, legal, and administration departments, and was the partner responsible for eight Insight investments. Maxwell was previously a partner at Putnam Investments, where he was managing director for corporate development. Before joining Putnam, Maxwell was a senior vice president at Lehman Brothers, where he was the chief financial officer of the Global Equity Division and a member of the Global Equities Executive Committee. Prior to Lehman, he was a management consultant at McKinsey & Company. Maxwell graduated from MIT with a Ph.D. in mechanical engineering (Sigma Xi) and an M.B.A. from the M.I.T. Sloan School of Management. He has B.S. and M.S. degrees in mechanical engineering from the University of California, Davis. Maxwell maintains a blog—"Now What?"—focused on the issues surrounding building information technology companies from the expansion stage.

Hodong (Ho) Nam, General Partner & Co-founder, Altos Ventures

Ho Nam is a general partner and co-founder of Altos Ventures, focusing on investments in the areas of software, services, and infrastructure technologies. He currently serves as a director of Accolo, Billeo, JS-Kit, Saynow, Telekenex, Trilibis Mobile, and White-Hat Security. Ho Nam led the firm's prior investments in Axis Systems (Cadence), Evolve Software (Oracle), Listen.com (Real Networks), Nishan Systems (McDATA), Pixo (Sun Microsystems), Provato (I-Many) and Soundpipe (Comdial). All were deals in which Altos was the lead investor in the seed or first round of funding.

Before joining Altos Ventures in 1996, Ho Nam worked at Silicon Graphics and Octel Communications (Lucent). He began his VC career at Trinity Ventures and began his professional career at Bain & Company, where he advised clients in the semiconductor industry on product and corporate strategy. He received an M.B.A. from Stanford University and a B.S. in engineering from Harvey Mudd College.

Yoram Oron, Founder & Managing Partner, Vertex Venture Capital

Yoram Oron has an impressive record as a founder and manager of several successful high-technology companies. He was previously president and CEO of Aryt Industries; co-founder, president, and CEO of Reshef Technologies; and co-founder and chairman of Telegate Ltd. Oron graduated with a B.Sc. in electrical engineering from the Technion–Israel Institute of Technology; he has an MBA from Tel Aviv University, Israel, and completed postgraduate studies at the Wharton School of the University of Pennsylvania.

Joe Rouse, Former General Partner, Pioneer Capital Partners

Joe Rouse has more than 15 years of technology and biotechnology business experience via executive management, consulting, and investment. Now an adviser to National University of Singapore's venture arm, he was a general partner with Pioneer Capital Partners of New Zealand as well as founding partner of MSBi Capital, a venture fund that invests in seed- and early-stage technology companies associated with three leading Canadian universities. He holds a bachelor's degree in biochemistry and physiology, and an M.B.A., both from Queen's University at Kingston, Ontario, Canada.

Kim Seng Tan, General Partner, 3V SourceOne Capital

Kim Seng Tan co-founded 3V Capital Pte. Ltd. in Singapore, which subsequently merged with SourceOne Venture Management to form 3V SourceOne Capital. He is an alumnus of the U.S. Venture Capital Institute. From 1995 to June 2000, he was the principal fund manager of UOB Venture Investment II Ltd., a S$105 million VC fund managed by UOB Venture Management Pte. Ltd. in Singapore, where he served as an executive director before he left the company. His past portfolio includes investments in information technology, electronics, life sciences, and traditional industries in the Asia-Pacific region, Greater China, and the United States. Prior to becoming a venture capitalist, Tan was an assistant vice president at United Overseas Bank in Singapore. He was involved in credit and marketing of corporate banking facilities for corporate clients in the electronics and information technology industries. In IT planning and development, he was involved in the management of a large-scale electronic banking network, a nationwide stored value smart-card project, and an EDI system. He was a member of Operation Committee of the Network for Electronic Transfer System, which owns and manages the EFTPOS network in Singapore. Tan was also chairman of the Retail Electronic Banking Committee of the Association of Banks in Singapore in 1991–1992. From 1988 to 1990, he headed the Product Integrity Section at Northern Telecom Asia and was responsible for the introduction of new telecommunications products (ISDN, digital communication systems and terminals, and so on) in South East Asia and Australia. He holds an M.S. degree in industrial engineering and a bachelor's degree in electrical engineering (Honors) from National University of Singapore.

Lip Bu Tan, Chairman & Founder, Walden International

Lip Bu Tan introduced and pioneered the U.S. venture capital concept in Asia in 1985. His firm currently manages more than US$2.8 billion, investing primarily in industries relating to semiconductor components, alternative energy, and digital media. He currently serves on the boards of Cadence Design Systems, Inc. (NYSE: CN), Creative Technology (NASDAQ: CREAM), Flextronics International (NASDAQ: FLEX), Mind Tree Consulting (BASE: MCL IN), SINA (NASDAQ: SINA), and Semiconductor Manufacturing International Corp. (NYSE: SIM; HKSE: 981). During his tenure at Walden, he has made investments in Advanced Micro-Fabrication Equipment Corporation, Ambarella, Inc., Beceem Communications, Inphi Corporation, Photop Technologies, Silicon Mitus, SolarEdge Technologies, Inc., Telegent Systems, TierLogic, Inc., and Tilera Corporation, Premisys Communication, S3, Centillium (NASDAQ: CTLM), Endwave (NASDAQ: ENWV), Integrated Silicon Solutions Inc. (NASDAQ: ISSI), Leadis (NASDAQ: LDIS), Network Peripheral, and Unisem (KLSE: UNI). Prior to Walden, Tan was vice president at Chappell & Co.; he also held management positions at EDS Nuclear and ECHO Energy. He received his B.S. from Nanyang University in Singapore, his M.B.A. from the University of San Francisco, and his M.S. (in nuclear engineering) from the Massachusetts Institute of Technology. Additionally, he serves on the Visiting Committee for the Department of Electrical Engineering & Computer Science at the Massachusetts Institute of Technology, as a trustee of Nanyang Technological University in Singapore, on the Regent College Board of Governors, and as trustee of the San Francisco Opera. Tan was ranked among the Top 10 Venture Capitalists in China by Zero2IPO and the Top 50 Venture Capitalists on the Forbes Midas List.

Andy Tang, Managing Director, DFJ DragonFund China

Andy Tang has more than 15 years of operating, R&D, investment banking, and investing experience in the IT industry. He is a founding managing director of DFJ DragonFund China, and has led and managed investments in Miartech, Mobim, Yeepay, Broadbus (MOT), Imago Scientific, Zettacom (IDTI), Packet Video, NuTool (ASMI), Santur, and Corrent. Most recently, he was a partner and member of the investment committee at Infineon Ventures.[1] Prior to that, he was an investment banker with Credit Suisse First Boston's technology group in Palo Alto. He worked on the Magma IPO (LAVA), as well as numerous M&A transactions. Before CSFB, Tang was a senior engineer and marketing manager at Intel Corporation. He was responsible for chip design as well as market enabling for the Pentium and Itanium processors. Tang holds an M.B.A. from the Wharton School, as well as M.S.E.E. and B.S.E.E. degrees from Massachusetts Institute of Technology and the University of Texas at Austin, respectively. Tang also holds one U.S. patent in silicon germanium thin-film transistor applications.

Eric Tao, Vice President, Keystone Ventures (former Kleiner Perkins Caufield & Byers)

Eric Tao is vice president of Keytone Ventures. Prior to Keytone, he was an associate at KPCB (Kleiner Perkins Caufield & Byers) China Fund. Before KPCB, he was one of the six global investment managers in QUALCOMM Ventures, the strategic investment arm of the telecommunications giant, covering venture investments in wireless space, including applications, software, content, handset, and wireless supply chain, infrastructure, and enabling technologies. Tao has two venture experiences before entering the venture capital field. He was co-founder of an e-commerce comparison shopping portal, responsible for fundraising and operations. He also had a start-up experience in a clean energy company, where he was responsible for fundraising and business development in China. Tao's investments are focused in wireless communications, semiconductors, and clean-tech. His investments include AMEC, GreatWall Software, BORQS, and LatticePower. Eric holds B.S. from Tsinghua University, and an M.S. and a Ph.D. from Stanford University, all in engineering. Tao holds three international patents and two U.S. patents.

Hans Tung, Partner, Qiming Venture Partners

Hans Tung joined Qiming in late 2007 as a partner in its second fund. He now sits on the board of eHi Car Rental, VANCL, Youxign, and Kaixin001, and 6DX. Prior to Qiming, Tung initiated Bessemer Venture Partners' China investment practice in 2005 and was promoted to vice president in 2007. Tung started his career as an investment banker at Merrill Lynch in New York and Hong Kong. He was a founding member of Crimson Asia Capital, helped to raise US$435 million, and was involved with two successful investments. He was also an entrepreneur and co-founder of two award-winning Internet start-ups: Asia2B in Hong Kong and Silicon Valley-head-quartered HelloAsia in Singapore.

David Weiden, General Partner, Khosla Ventures

David Weiden has been a partner at Khosla Ventures since 2006, focusing on Internet software, services, and communications. He has led investments including Aliph (a.k.a. Jawbone), Bitfone (HPQ), Frengo, iLike, RingCentral, Slide, and WideOrbit. Prior personal investments and advisory relationships include FON, Good Technology (MOT), Ingenio (T), loopt, LogMeIn, Opsware (HPQ), SmartPay, Spot Runner, and Tellme (MSFT). Before joining Khosla Ventures, Weiden worked at McCaw Cellular (now AT&T), Morgan Stanley, Netscape/AOL, and Tellme. He led AOL's Communications, Community & Instant Messaging product divisions as they surpassed 50 million users worldwide. He then joined Tellme Networks as senior vice president for marketing and business development. Using a quantitative framework called Rifle, his team helped grow the company's revenue beyond US$100 million in revenue and to profitability. He grew up in Seattle and graduated from Harvard magna cum laude with highest honors in the special major organizational behavior and economics, with additional coursework at MIT and NYU in engineering.

Lin Hong Wong, Managing Director, Wingz Capital Pte. Ltd.

Lin Hong Wong is the author of *Venture Capital Fund Management: A Comprehensive Approach to Investment Practices & the Entire Operations of a VC Firm*, published by Aspatore Books in November 2005. He has 10 years' experience as a senior partner in a leading Asian venture capital firm, two and a half years in the mentoring and incubation of start-ups, nine years as a CEO in high-tech manufacturing firms, and 11 years in the Singapore Economic Development Board, promoting the development of the electronics industry. He was managing director for business development in Temasek Capital (Pte.) Ltd. from October 2000 to March 2003. His responsibility was to set up Temasek's incubation program, which provided funding, support, and mentoring services to start-ups and early-stage companies. Prior to joining Temasek, Wong was executive vice president of Transpac Capital Pte. Ltd. from 1990 to 2000. Transpac was established in 1986 and grew to become one of the largest venture capital firms in South-East Asia, managing more than US$820 million of funds in 2000, which were invested in a broad range of companies in Asia and the United States. He has a bachelor's degree in electrical engineering and a diploma in business administration. He has served on the boards of listed companies (in the United States and Singapore), boards of private companies, boards of governors of educational institutes, and various government committees. He was awarded a Singapore Public Service Medal in 1992.

Ken Xu, General Partner, Gobi Partners Inc.

Born and raised in Shanghai, Xu joined Gobi Partners in 2003 and focuses on wireless and broadband applications, e-learning, and the digital TV sector within the digital media value chain. Xu has been a keynote speaker and panelist at various technology and VC forums including China VC Annual Forum and China DTV Forum. He also participates in various industry associations and is a regular columnist for several publications. He has experience in multiple industries including IT, financial services, real estate, and construction. Previously, he worked as an investment representative for Shanghai Golden Point Investment Corporation, where he was responsible for personal finance management and investment consulting services. He also completed internships at China Quest, a leading geographical information systems (GIS) company, and Shanghai Second Construction Corporation. Xu holds a B.S. in management engineering from Tongji University in Shanghai and an M.S. in economics and finance and a Certification in Economics from the University of York in the United Kingdom.

Endnote

1. The abbreviations in parentheses throughout these brief biographies refer to IPOs—important badges of honor for a venture capitalist.

Index